DESTRUCTION OF INNOCENCE

A True Story of Child Abduction

Rosalie Hollingsworth

iUniverse, Inc.
New York Bloomington

Destruction of Innocence
A True Story of Child Abduction

iUniverse books may be ordered through booksellers or by contacting:

iUniverse
1663 Liberty Drive
Bloomington, IN 47403
www.iuniverse.com
1-800-Authors (1-800-288-4677)

ISBN: 978-1-4401-2502-7 (pbk)
ISBN: 978-1-4401-2504-1 (cloth)
ISBN: 978-1-4401-2503-4 (ebk)

Printed in the United States of America

iUniverse rev. date: 7/16/2009

I dedicate this book to my daughters
Triana and Tisha
To my grandchildren
Eric, Anthony, Julyen, James and Ryan
May joy for living, happiness for what you have and Love of your
fellow man be your companion all through your life

Many thanks go out to the following individuals who encouraged and help me along the way in the completion of my book:

To my daughters, Triana and Tisha, one gaze, one smile, one hug from them reminds me every day why I could not give up the search. I love you both with all my heart.

To Don Lund, for his help in recovering my child after the first abduction

To my ex-husband Stan, for his support in the many years I searched for Triana.

To Joseph and Julie Said, for their assistance in the final retrieving of my child from Bolivia.

To Kitty for her accounts of what occurred while she was in South America.

To Louis Payne for his reading the manuscript and editing suggestions.

To Cal Paranteau, for his encouragement and assistance.

To my living sisters Betty Gardner and Shirley Minard.

To Janet Owens Greig, who taught me to laugh.

Special thanks go out to; Myriam Spreen, Kathy Vusovich, Toni Berardino Kallin, Danica Olivo, and Jim and Clare Weber. Thanks for your encouragement and friendship.

To my many friends, too many to thank individually, who constantly encouraged me to write my story.

In Memory of

Carol Marie White McGaughy
Mary Ellen Mayer
Jeanne Skinner Vogliotti
Nancy Robertson
Sally Jordan
LeRoy King

INTRODUCTION

Since 1932, when the Lindbergh baby was kidnapped, The National Missing Children's Locate Center, Inc. reported nationally over one million new cases of children missing each year. One child is reported missing every 40 seconds. Over the past year, more than seven million photo fliers of missing children were published and displayed throughout the United States and Canada. We know how common this is because we see their faces staring at us every day from advertisements on TV, on fliers in our mail and, more recently, we have the Amber Alert.

Of those millions of children, an appalling eighty percent are parental kidnapping victims. Angry, jealous, fearful and, in some cases, deranged parents defy the law, stealing their children and disappearing. In the wake of each kidnapping are untold stories of despair and agony. After one year, over fifty percent of these cases will remain forever unsolved.

This story is about my daughter, Triana, who was twice taken from me. In the first abduction, my estranged Italian husband took our one-year-old baby and fled to Italy. The government was unable to help or intervene.

Eight months after he disappeared with my daughter, Franco contacted me. I met him in Paris, with difficulty drugged him and brought my daughter back to the United States. Six years later, he kidnapped her again, disappearing with her into the remote jungles of South America.

The events in this story are a retelling of the actual events that took place in the United States, Italy, France and South America. Some of the conversations and scenes have been re-created from information supplied to me either by a participant in the abduction or by eyewitnesses to those conversations and events. The placement of the events may not be in the exact order in which they happened; however, they all transpired.

At times, I have had to intuit Franco's thoughts in an attempt to explain his behavior. However, I have written them drawing from the knowledge and experience of the years I spent with him--those years taught me well the way his mind worked. I have also interjected thought that most likely were similar to those thoughts of the individuals, considering the circumstances of the moment.

Some of the names have been changed.

CHAPTER ONE

June 26, 1973
En route to Argentina

The airliner raced over steep, rugged Central American Mountains still covered with ash from recent volcanic eruptions. For days, nature's havoc had painted the heavens with bright, hot ash. Millions of shining particles remained suspended in the atmosphere. The residue that nature had left behind mocked the radiant, western sunset. I tried to focus my attention on the alluring crimson drapery to the east, but no matter how hard I tried, this beauty could not erase my despair. My mind kept centering on the race to find my missing daughter, Triana. I wondered if this search would ever end. I had first lost her when she was one-year-old, and it took me eight months to find her. This time she had been missing for over two years. I would search for her, and would do so until I found her, if it took my entire life.

For a few brief moments, the soft voice coming down the narrow aisle replaced my thoughts of Triana and my desperate search for her. I looked up, trying to focus my eyes on the stewardess. The crowded cabin had already darkened as the sun hurried toward the west. It was difficult to make out the young woman's features.

"I'm sorry," I replied, "I didn't hear what you said."

"You looked as if you were about to drop off to sleep," the young woman said hesitantly. "I thought you might be more comfortable with a pillow and blanket."

Touched by her concern, I forced a smile but shook my head. "Thank you. No, I don't feel like sleeping. Maybe later."

Reality dimmed my smile. Even the power of the majestic sky had provided only a brief respite. My life had been a single grim reality. My child had been kidnapped. My daughter had been barely seven when her father, Franco, had abducted her this last time; now she was nine. No passing stranger could understand my pain and determination; only devoted parents in similar circumstances, out there wondering whether they would ever see their child again, alive and free from harm, could understand.

Some of my friends were unsympathetic about my drive to recover my child. "You don't know what you'll get back, or if she'll even want to come back. Her dad wouldn't harm her. Leave her with him, go on with your life," one friend encouraged.

What would I find when the plane touched down in Buenos Aires? I had no assurance that Franco, Kitty and the three children would still be in Argentina. Perhaps it was already too late. With his almost superhuman ability to elude me, Franco may already have fled to another country, even another continent.

If they were in Argentina, how could I find them when a powerful, international detective agency had never found even the slightest trace of them? I had a lot more at stake and a lot more fortitude. I would find my child. My child had breathed life into the dry corners of my heart. The love my parents had denied me, I had given without reserve to Triana, and this gave my life meaning, self-worth and purpose.

I wanted to comfort Triana, protect her, to wipe away her tears and hold her when nightmares haunted her dreams. I desperately longed to explain why we had been kept apart. Losing her had left me isolated and overwhelmed by loss. I could neither change my own childhood nor rewrite the past. The only thing I could do was save my daughter's life. But the months and years were slipping away. Time had become my enemy.

My only clues to Triana's whereabouts were the names of an obscure city and a distant Catholic church, which seemed pitifully meager information on which to base this search. For one terrible moment, I felt hopelessly inadequate for the job that lay ahead. What if I failed?

No, I told myself. I won't fail. I'm stronger than Franco, more determined. This world is not big enough for him to hide in. No matter how hard Franco tries to keep me from my daughter, I will find Triana and bring her home.

The young flight attendant provided a blanket and pillow for the passenger in front of me, and then glanced in my direction. An expression of alarm crossed her face as our eyes met. It was a moment before I realized that she saw the slick of tears across my cheeks.

"Are you all right?" she asked quickly. "Perhaps a glass of water or..."

I so desperately wanted company in my misery that, for a moment, I wanted to reveal everything to her, as if this stranger would have the time to listen to me and could somehow help me. Her words trailed off as I wiped away my tears and composed myself. "I'm fine, really," I said. Reassured, the young woman moved on to other passengers. I turned back to the window, staring down through the approaching darkness and the volcanic ash to the foreign land below.

When I had discovered that Triana might be in Argentina, I began to research South America, a continent that previously held little interest for me as a student. I learned that five hundred years ago Francisco Pizarro had destroyed over a million Incas with his small army of men. This army had come to plunder the untapped riches of the hemisphere, to wrench treasures from the virgin soil and the natives. The Spanish destroyed over half the populations of the Incas and the Aztecs through war and disease ruthlessly destroying entire cultures in their lust for riches, power and glory as they moved southward.

Argentina, a country about one-third the size of the United States, was a land of towering, snow-capped mountains and endless plains, of bustling modern cities coexisting with tiny rural villages. It was a country that had remained virtually unchanged since the conquistadores claimed much of North and South America for their Spanish king. I could not help but feel that no Spanish king or

3

general, no mercenary soldier had ever fought for anything more precious than I did now.

I fought to control my emotions and the lump that crept into my throat whenever I thought of Triana. In the twenty-five months and twenty seven days since Franco had kidnapped our child, Triana had never been out of my thoughts. Even as I slept, nightmares of Triana--dirty, homeless, and starving--haunted my sleep. Every glimpse of a child of Triana's age brought back feelings of helplessness and despair. What had happened to her? If I could only know that she was well and happy! *"Oh God, help me find my child; let me know that she is alive and safe,"* I prayed. I imagined the first heart-piercing moment when I would squeeze her tiny body in my arms, her face against my own, mingling our tears of happiness. Best of all would be the moment when I would take Triana's small hand and place it against my own abdomen to feel the new life growing there.

"I'm going to have a baby, darling," I would tell her, watching for her expression of delight. "Perhaps you'll have that sister you always wanted.

"Remember how you were always asking me for a little sister?" I could only hope that Triana would feel joy at the idea of a new sibling. A sudden chill passed through me as I remembered the bitter disappointment of each miscarriage. I wanted children so badly, but had lost each baby in the first trimester. Nine failed pregnancies. Franco had never been concerned. On the contrary, he seemed relieved. To him, it was another problem solved. To me each miscarriage had been the death of a life. Now I was scarcely three months pregnant, a dangerous time for me, especially since the recent illness I had suffered in Rome.

A letter from Kitty, Franco's new wife, addressed to Lea, her sister in Montana, contained the first real clue I had received since the day Franco and Kitty had abducted Triana and Kitty's two daughters, Amber and Emily. That letter propelled me from California to Rome. The return address read, *Convento Ara Coeli, Scala dell'Arco, Capitolina*, Rome, Italy, in care of Father Emmanuel Romanelli. The trip to Italy, difficult and disappointing as it had been, had provided this one tiny clue to Franco's whereabouts, which had put me aboard this plane. My husband, Stan, and close friends had advised against my going to Buenos Aires, fearing that the long, exhausting trip might be too much for me. "Wait until the baby is born," each had said. As if a few more months wouldn't make that much difference. Knowing where my child was, how could I wait? I knew that Franco would never stay in one place long enough for me to give birth to this baby.

I had carried Triana to term and I would give life to this baby, no matter what. Yes, I understood I would have to be careful. I thought of Stan, now in Montana for the summer, with his sons from his previous marriage. Was it only seven months ago that we had exchanged our vows? The baby I was now carrying signaled a new beginning for Stan and me, as well as for Triana. I clung to the belief that at last I would have my family together, a whole family, a loving family.

As a child, I had been a dreamer, the source of my survival in a house of constant turmoil and pain. Now, as an adult, I still held fast to some of those same dreams. Dreams of a happy home life, one of laughter and of love. But until Triana was brought home, the complete fulfillment of my dream would not be absolute. A single day's delay could mean never finding her.

I turned from the window again. The cabin lights had come on, and the flight attendants prepared to serve dinner. I stretched my legs, trying to work out the cramps that had developed from my fixed position in the small seat.

Suddenly, I felt prying eyes on me. I glanced around and found a middle-aged man watching me from his seat across the narrow aisle. A smug grin covered his face, which I did not understand until I realized I had exposed my thigh when my skirt had slipped up above my knees. He seemed to gloat over his stolen glimpse. I blushed, feeling vulnerable, and tugged at my skirt. I suddenly wished I had accepted the offer of the blanket.

I stiffened with a familiar fear as the man got up. He took a few unsteady steps towards me, and I slipped deeper into my seat. As he leaned over, I could smell the nauseating aroma of cigarette smoke, rum and a strong, vaguely feminine cologne. For a moment, I thought I would vomit.

"We both seem to be traveling alone, *Señora*," the man said. "Perhaps you'll join me in a drink before they serve dinner." This was not a question but a self-assured statement of fact, spoken in English with a heavy Spanish accent. On his large frame and over his potbelly hung expensive but outdated clothing, reminding me of a Spanish crook from an old swashbuckler movie. I guessed him to be either a businessman or a petty government official.

"Leave me alone, please," I said, trying to keep the rising anger from my voice. "I don't want a drink or any company." He draped one plump arm over the seat back and leaned closer, letting his eyes roam over my rigid body. I felt trapped and helpless under his penetrating eyes.

"You appear so lonely, *Señora,*" he went on, grinning at my obvious discomfort, "and so sad. A woman as beautiful as you should never be lonely or sad." He laughed, as if he had said something witty. I saw only a stalking animal ready to devour its prey. He fished into his pocket, producing a gold lighter to relight the cold ash of his cigarette. A sudden puff of strong smoke floated over my head. My stomach churned.

"Please leave me alone or I'll ring for the flight attendant," I warned him.

His smile was replaced by an expression of incredulity that I had no interest in him.

"As you wish," he replied coldly. He straightened up, muttered "fucking bitch," and moved toward the front of the plane.

Some of the Latin men I had met were as loving and sensitive as the man to whom I was now married. But this brassy, self-confident pig clearly felt entitled to whatever he wanted. I surmised that to him, women were mindless possessions, created to gratify and serve the emotional and sexual needs of a little boy shrouded in a man's body. Even though the year was 1973, and women were giving themselves to partners as heartily as at the height of the free love movement, I felt as though a time warp had sent me back to the Dark Ages, when women had no choices. What was I doing? I realized that I was putting myself in a situation where I would be alone among many men of this sort: swaggering, strutting males who would exploit me ruthlessly if I let down my guard. My confidence began to waver.

Hours ago, during the layover in Panama, from Los Angeles to Buenos Aires, I had felt a growing fear. It wasn't only the leering, cold-eyes of the officials who seem to devour me visually; it was also the presence everywhere you looked of the military, with their pistols and machine guns. The reality I faced was that I would have few rights in Central and South America. Unless I quickly learned to step around these men, to be elusive, to play their games, I could be in real danger. And whose side would these men take concerning Franco's kidnapping of Triana? In this society of patriarchal law and custom, I did not doubt that Franco would have the upper hand. Nevertheless, I hadn't come halfway around the world, over 12,000 miles, to be intimidated by men like this.

I rang for the flight attendant, declined dinner and requested a blanket. In a few moments, I was wrapped in soft wool, my eyes closed, my mind shutting out everything around me. However, I could not shut out the circumstances that had put me on this plane--I was surrounded by strangers, handicapped by a foreign language, en route to a place I had never seen, all in a desperate attempt to regain the daughter who had been stolen from me.

CHAPTER TWO

October 1959 to October 1964
Portland, Oregon, Rome, Italy,
Los Angeles, California

I met him at a restaurant where he worked as a waiter in Portland, Oregon. The handsome, slender man stood barely two inches taller than my five-feet-six. He exuded an air of pride and confidence that made my knees go weak. Franco Allatere was different from anyone I had ever met. With his olive complexion, liquid brown eyes, and wavy black hair, he reminded me of a young Rudolph Valentino. An impeccable dresser, he wore expensive, hand-tailored suits. He was a dreamer's answer to love and eternal happiness.

Franco delivered words of love and devotion so easily that he instantly swept me off my feet. "You are so beautiful. I love your body," he would say. "I've never met anyone like you before." There was none of the awkwardness I had known with other men. Franco was maddeningly self-assured, suave, conciliatory, and worshipping. He served the patrons with all the polish and sophistication of a crown prince. Franco always insisted that my friends and I sit at one of his tables, which I was more than happy to do.

On our first date, Franco treated me like a queen. He took me dining and dancing at the best restaurants in town. Before I knew what was happening, Franco made it clear that he was deeply and sincerely in love with me. I was inundated with gifts, beautiful flowers and expensive chocolates. But the best present of all was how he made me feel. I had become the most desirable woman in the world. Franco was the ultimate lover.

For a child whose early years were spent in shacks with outdoor plumbing, being pursued by someone as exciting and worldly as Franco overwhelmed me. My memories of picking my way through a chicken pen to my grandmother's privy in Oklahoma vanished.

Franco chose a glamorous setting to tell me about his background. He took me to a restaurant where the tables gracefully encircled a large dance floor. When it was show time, the dance floor magically parted and disappeared, revealing a huge swimming pool where, to my astonishment, a water ballet was enacted.

I already knew that Franco was an Italian citizen, but I was unprepared for the rest of his story. He had come to America as an adventure, he told me. He told me his great-grandfather had been an Austrian Count, a man of great wealth and position. Over the years, the great-grandfather had lost much of his wealth to gambling in Monaco and the pursuit of women. Franco's own father, who had died in the past year, had been a Doctor of Pharmacy. Of course, there was still money. Franco assured me there was both money and property. His mother Carmen, the Countess Allatere, now lived in Rome, awaiting her son's return to assume his duties as the Count Allatere. I hardly knew what to say when, six weeks after we met, he asked if I would marry him and share his exciting life. My fairy tale dreams were coming to life.

What I did not know, of course, was there wasn't a fairy tale life in my near future.

Had Franco chosen to tell me the truth about his family situation I would have married him anyway. I was mesmerized

Carmen's own parents had never married, but instead of complaining, Carmen's mother had raised her three daughters with devotion. Carmen's father, the Marquis, was already married to an invalid and divorce was out of the question. For the most part, he spent all his time with his new family, but he unfailingly met his responsibility to his invalid wife. Carmen and her sisters lacked nothing money could buy, and they were taught to respect God and the Church. Carmen, the most devoted of the three girls, would have entered the convent had she not met Vittorio at the University. She was instantly captivated by his charm. Carmen and Vittorio married and bought a pharmacy on the outskirts of Rome. After several unsuccessful pregnancies, Carmen finally gave birth to Franco.

From the moment he was born, she worshiped him. As a toddler, and later as a young boy, he learned to charm almost everyone who crossed his path. Those who resisted his spell were cast aside as unimportant. Carmen made Franco the center of her universe and he was equal to the part. When Franco was four, Carmen gave birth to another son, Mario, who succumbed to a weak heart within two months. Carmen blamed herself for the tragedy, insisting that she had bathed him in water that was too hot, and that the shock had killed him. She took refuge from her guilt by devoting even more of her attention to little Franco. He was the first youngster in the neighborhood to own a tricycle. His toys were the envy of his friends.

Early in his youth, Franco began to show a remarkable similarity to his father in his fascination with what lay beneath feminine attire. He spent many hours in the pharmacy pretending to play with the lower displays while in fact viewing the sights under ladies' dresses. Many a medicine display was toppled in his attempts to satisfy his curiosity about female anatomy. Carmen dismissed his behavior as that of a normal, playful boy.

World War II broke out in Europe and Franco's parents' sympathies lay with the Allies. As the Germans marched toward Rome, the boy saw his parents hide American soldiers in the basement while simultaneously wining and dining German soldiers upstairs as though they were long-lost friends. The combination of pretense and danger proved heady for the youngster; skilled deceit became part of his every day existence. Fooling people was easy and brought him immense pleasure, almost as much as exercising control over them. Deception and control were to influence his behavior for the rest of his life.

By the time Franco was twelve, the war was over and, like other youngsters, he played in the burned-out rubble of the city. A heavy, half-hinged door left swinging in a bombed-out building fell on his leg, breaking it in several places. Soon an infection set in, leaving him with a twelve-inch scar and one leg shorter than the other. It caused a permanent limp that would always require a built-up shoe.

Into his early teens, his education often included imitating his father's activities. Carmen and Vittorio took turns working in the pharmacy, and on the days that his father was at home, Franco made it his business to be home, too. On those occasions, Vittorio took his pleasure with the maids, and young Franco spied on them. Eventually, he acquired first-hand experience with the local girls.

Carmen had ignored her husband's promiscuity, after all, he was a man and they had their needs. After she discovered her son's escapades, she spent endless hours in church praying for his and Vittorio souls and that God would forgive them and guide them to better judgments in the future. She loved them both and would stick by them, no matter what they did.

Vittorio contracted syphilis as a young man, from one of the maids. He was cured, but when Franco was young, his father again contracted the disease. This time he ignored it for far too long, and once all hope was gone, he had to be taken away in a straitjacket, incurably demented.

Unfortunately, he managed to outlive his money, and Carmen was forced to sell the pharmacy. She secured a chief accountant's job with Twentieth Century Fox in Rome. She worked hard to support her son, as well as to pay her beloved husband's hospital expenses. Finally, screaming in mindless agony, Vittorio died. His sins and transgressions paid for in full.

Although Carmen had to work outside her home from morning until night, Franco's needs were never neglected. She cooked his meals, washed his clothes, made his bed, and drew his baths every night. At the same time, she managed to work ten to twelve hours a day. She believed that heaven had decreed that she provide for her son's needs and encouraged his aspirations, whatever they were.

After his second year of college, Carmen gathered enough courage to suggest that Franco look for work. He had studied many languages including English and she urged him to put those talents to profitable use. She reasoned that she had done everything humanly possible to provide stability for Franco. She has suppressed her own complaints, accepted without question everything that God had sent, endured the tragic death of her infant son and lost her beloved Vittorio. What more could a woman do? She was not to blame for Franco's lack of responsibility. He was young and men behaved as they did because they were men. It was as simple as that. And besides, Franco was a good boy.

Franco had grown into a handsome, charismatic young man, with black wavy hair and smoldering brown eyes. His slim, wiry physique made him appear taller than his five feet eight. Because of his carefully mastered poise and his stylish rhythmic walk, only his closest friends knew that he had a slight limp. With his charming, uninhibited personality, good looks, and uncanny ability to fool people, he decided to try his hand at acting. He took some training and, through his mother's connections at Twentieth Century, he appeared in bit parts in a few Italian and American films. Hollywood, he decided, was waiting for his talents. He applied for a visitor's visa, refusing to wait his turn to immigrate to the United States. Franco was in a hurry and he and his friends concluded that he could beat the system by becoming a famous actor or by marrying an American woman. With a kiss on his mother's forehead, he bid her goodbye, promising that he would send for her soon.

In Hollywood, life wasn't nearly as easy or as glamorous as Franco had imagined, and he quickly grew restless. The time and effort it took to become an actor was much too high a price to pay. After a few rejections, an impatient Franco threw in the towel.

Franco then turned to his second goal: becoming a permanent United States' resident. His visa would soon run out and he certainly didn't intend to return to Italy. The United States appealed to him, it was the land of tremendous opportunities, the envy of the rest of the world, and he intended to stay. Although he had rejected the thought of marrying any of the women he had met thus far, his search finally turned serious. By coincidence, he became acquainted with a man who was headed for Portland, Oregon, and Franco decided to tag along to this picturesque spot, where he found the solution to his residency problem: a vulnerable, and somewhat naive young woman named Rosalie White.

Nothing in my life had prepared me for a relationship with someone like Franco. His marriage proposal shocked me. Did he really want me to go to Rome as his wife? In all my life, I had never been more than a few hundred miles from home. Oklahoma, California and Oregon were the extent of my journeys. Europe was part of a map I had studied somewhere back in school.

I didn't dare ask if I would become a Countess. I was too overwhelmed, too awestruck, and too much in love to recognize Franco's faults. He was diabolically charming. I surrendered myself and deliberately ignored the telltale signs, which I later painfully realized were visible from the beginning: the towering jealousy, the contemptible deceit and the physical violence. I said yes. We crossed over the Columbia River from Portland, to Vancouver, Washington and were married by a Justice of the Peace on December 9, 1960.

It would be many years before I understood why Franco had insisted that we marry in the state of Washington. Some flimsy excuse he offered had circumvented the real reason. He had wished to avoid the mandatory blood test, fearing that he could have inherited his father's dreaded disease. The ink on our marriage license was still wet when my life changed dramatically.

A few days after the wedding, while Franco was at work, I accepted an invitation to watch television with an elderly husband and wife who lived next door. I had often visited this lonely couple and they had become my friends. To celebrate my marriage, they offered me an imitation onyx ring. I was touched by their thoughtfulness. That sweet little old lady had worn the ring for fifteen years. Poor as they were, they had gladly given me the wedding gift.

While I was gone, Franco had called. When no one answered, he rushed home. Franco burst in livid with rage, and saw the ring on my finger. He suggested angrily that the ring had been a gift from a secret lover. When I tried to tell him the truth, that it was a gift from the elderly couple next door, and that is was a mere dime store ring that they had offered to me as a wedding gift, Franco shouted that my story was a lie. No, he wouldn't lower himself to ask them, since they would probably lie for me. He ignored my tears and stalked out, slamming the door behind him. I spent the night in bewilderment.

When Franco returned the next day, he appeared completely rational and begged my forgiveness. All my instincts screamed that I had made a serious mistake in marrying this volatile Latin. I knew in my heart that I should end this marriage. But even the harsh lessons of my childhood, as powerful as they had been, could not overcome my need for this man's love and I succumbed to his earnest pleas for another chance. He swore that such a scene would never happen again, that he loved me and wanted only to make me happy. At first I remained unconvinced, but finally my pride stood in the way of better judgment. How would I explain such a dreadful mistake? My vow to avoid my parents' mistakes loomed before me accusingly. Had I, too, lost control of my values and my dreams? Maybe I could make it work after all. Perhaps I was just what he needed. I could soften his temperament, keep him happy and make our fairytale marriage work. I decided to stick it out.

Two weeks after our marriage Franco's visitor's visa was expiring. Our marriage seemed to be on a firmer footing. Now married to an American citizen, Franco had no fear of losing his freedom of movement in and out of the United States. He could apply for residence without going through the immigration quota system. It was time for him to visit his momma. I was delighted when, Franco suggested that the time was right for me to meet his mother in Rome.

For awhile, our marriage improved. Franco was more relaxed, and took great pleasure in showing me the magnificent city. He reveled in my childish delight at visiting the Coliseum, walking down the Spanish Steps, gazing upwards at Michelangelo's ceiling in the Sistine Chapel. I was granted the ultimate privilege of stroking the feet of the *Pietá*. For me, these places had been mere pictures in books. Now I was their witness, becoming a part of them. My dreams seem to be materializing, and I danced through the streets of Rome, escorted by my prince.

It made no difference when I finally discovered the truth about Franco's family property and money. In fact, both Franco and

Carmen went to work each day just to make ends meet. Franco worked for Alitalia Airlines while Nona held down her longtime position at Twentieth Century Fox.

I loved Carmen. I grew comfortable with her and began to call her Nona, the affectionate nickname that many of her Italian friends and relatives used. This tiny, Italian matron possessed a heart that belied her stature. She lavished adoration and obedience on her son. Franco was truly the center of her life. I understood. She had suffered the death of a second son. Now her husband was gone. For Carmen, Franco was all that remained. It would be years before I would understand that her devotion to Franco would become my most vicious adversary.

Her short, gray, wavy hair curled gently away from her naturally rosy cheeks and she wore no make-up. Hers was a gentle visage, darkened only in the increasingly frequent moments when Carmen faced Franco's volatile and irrational behavior. At such times, she retreated to her beloved rosary and I soon grew to recognize it as a permanent extension of the slender fingers that moved so energetically, so purposefully over the beads. She whispered the endless prayers in Italian. Although Carmen was highly intelligent and educated, her traditional belief in the subservient role of the female dominated her decision-making and her behavior. We were worlds apart in our culture, but under the same spell.

I was also submissive to Franco's demands in the early months. I was not to talk to any man when he was not present. I was allowed to go to the American Library, have tea with a friend he had introduced me to or to stay in the house. I was never to look out the window at another man and never to open the door to anyone. At the time, I accepted his rules without question. The memories of my experiences with Franco made me shudder inwardly. I had been a virtual prisoner during the three months that we lived in Rome.

April, 1961, found us back in the United States, landing in Los Angeles. It had taken four months to clear Franco's papers and to deal with his nagging medical problem: tubercular-like scars on his lungs, which had originally prevented his emigration to the United States. As soon as we arrived, we settled in an apartment under the

LAX flight pattern, conveniently near Franco's new job as an airline ticket agent. At first, I resumed my work as a beautician, but in the interests of increased stability, set hours and additional income, I soon switched to banking.

We moved to a slightly larger apartment in Florence, near Crenshaw, where Carmen joined us before the year was out. At first, the arrangement seemed to work. She never interfered in our decisions or invaded our personal time together. She stayed in the background and kept house for the working newlyweds. Carmen's submissiveness to Franco's every whim had influenced me in Rome, and as long as I followed her lead here in the U.S. there was peace. Vivid memories of the ugly quarrels between my own parents haunted me; I did everything possible to prevent scenes.

Shortly after Carmen joined us, Franco began to take on additional "jobs" at night. His absences increased, but I was only dimly aware that his income did not. Since he controlled our finances, I had no idea of what came in, much less what went out. I wanted to believe the best. I clung to my dream, convincing myself that all of his hard work and efforts would pay off.

More than anything else, I wanted a child. I soon convinced Franco it was time to have a family. But it was not immediately to be. For two years miscarriage followed miscarriage. My determination to be a mother persisted, however, and finally led to corrective surgery in May of 1962. The following fall Franco and I joyously celebrated my pregnancy. Our little apartment began to change. I borrowed a crib, reveled in purchasing baby clothes, and enjoyed a delightful shower given by close friends.

Seven months into my pregnancy, I was rushed to the hospital where our daughter, Danina, arrived prematurely. The birth went remarkably well. By the time the doctor arrived, Danina literally popped into his hands. An incubator stood near and the baby went from the doctor's hands to the plastic enclosure. I longed to hold her but could only admire her from a distance. I was elated with our beautiful dark-haired baby, and Franco was delighted with his "little one."

Premature or not, I willed her survival. I vowed that my strength and energy would become hers. I was a mother at last. The following morning the doctor released me from the hospital.

Reluctantly, I left little Danina behind in an incubator, where the doctors wanted her to stay until she gained enough weight and strength to come home. I visited her dozens of times a day, reveling in the warmth and love I felt toward this tiny human being. I longed to hold her close to me. My heart cried out just to touch her tiny hand. The nurses branded me a pest, but I didn't care. Three days after she was born, I headed for the department store to exchange blue nighties for pink ones. I juggled the packages under my arm as I called the doctor from a pay phone to check on her condition. He told me to hurry to the hospital. Panic flooded my heart.

I stood at the nursery window, clawing at the glass, helpless and tormented as I watched my beautiful baby struggle for her last breaths. Her tiny heart and lungs were too weak and underdeveloped to survive. Tears streamed down my face as I pounded on the glass and begged the nurse to let me in, to let me keep her from dying, to let me hold her just once. But Danina had already taken her last breath.

"Please, please, give me my baby," I cried out as I ran through a door marked "keep out."

The nurse picked up my dead baby from the plastic enclosure and started toward me.

An angry doctor brushed past me and pointed to the exit door. Abruptly he intercepted this exchange between two women who understood the desperation of the moment. He quickly retrieved my child from the nurse, robbing me of the chance to hold Danina in my arms. Two new mothers kept their distance as they watched with mixed emotions, engulfed in the scene that had just taken place. They shared my grief but they fought off their own fright. Reality had touched too close to home. As I collapsed sobbing against the nursery window, the new mothers slowly drifted off to the security of their rooms.

Instead of Danina, I was handed a death certificate dated June 14, 1963.

Within months I became pregnant again and this time was able to carry the baby to term. On April 7, 1964, just short of nine months after I became pregnant, Triana was born. She was a lovely baby, beautiful, plump and healthy. Such an endearing baby that I wanted to cry every time I looked at her tiny face and her large hazel eyes.

Her entrance into the world was not without its frustrations. My milk didn't satisfy her. We made many trips to the doctor, who advised supplementary bottles; he suggested we change her formula or feed her more frequently. Nothing, however, made her happy and contented at feeding time. I had expected to feel completely fulfilled with the experience of motherhood. Instead, I felt totally inadequate to supply my baby's needs.

As the days wore on, Triana's inability to take sufficient nourishment without constant gasping and crying added to the tension between Franco and me. Ultimately, Triana herself compensated. At three months, I gave up nursing and Triana became exclusively a bottle-fed baby. But she never truly ate well, since her natural compensation for her problem brought her limited pleasure during the eating and drinking process. It was not until many years later a surgeon diagnosed a complicated adenoidal problem that had gone undiscovered in her infancy. I realized that she had held her breath to keep from choking. Unable to breathe through her nose, she naturally substituted breathing through her mouth. Trying to breathe while nursing had only frustrated the hungry baby.

Franco insisted I return to work, as we needed both incomes to pay the bills. Reluctantly I obeyed, leaving Triana in Nona's care. I wanted desperately to be home with Triana, feeding her, bathing her, dressing her and holding her. I grew envious of Nona's time with my child, and I resented Franco for forcing my premature separation from Triana. I soon felt like a stranger in my own home.

Triana had become too much the exclusive property of Franco and Nona. My ideas and opinions about childrearing were ignored. They scoffed and ridiculed the baby books I read. Triana would be raised in the Italian tradition! Their way was best; a roadblock was flung in front of my every suggestion. No matter how hard I fought, how much I pleaded with Nona for support, the inflexible answer rang through the rooms: "Franco knows best." When Franco commanded, Nona obeyed, even when it meant denying her own instincts. I could see her troubled and conflicted heart, and I watched in bitter silence as she retreated to her rosary.

When I could take no more, I finally turned on Franco and Nona savagely. It was my home and my baby, I announced firmly. No longer would I give in to them and their Italian customs. I would make the decisions as to how Triana would be raised.

Franco and Nona sulked, fought, sulked again. The strong-mindedness I had displayed as a child surfaced; I would submit no longer. I did not intend to give up my daughter's care any longer. I knew my marriage hung by a slender thread but my priorities were clear, *Let Franco and his mother think or do what they wanted*, I thought. This episode with Franco was but a mere taste of what lay ahead. I never imagined the horror and terror for Triana and me that lay in wait, less than six months away.

CHAPTER THREE

October, 1964 to November 28, 1965
Westchester and Inglewood, California

Triana was nine months old when Franco and I separated. His raging temper and unwarranted, irrational jealousy, combined with his unfaithfulness, escalated the inevitable.

Over and over again I found evidence of his infidelities. Once I inquired about a tube of lipstick I found in our new car. Blithely he told me he had loaned our car to a co-worker for a date with his girlfriend. On another occasion, a friend had dropped me off at the airport to meet Franco just before he left work. When we arrived at our car, we found a banner draped across the windshield, grossly illustrated with obscene gestures and lewd protestations of love. Someone had obviously mistaken our car for someone else's, was Franco's explanation, and he laughed.

I swallowed every inconceivable story he fed me.

A few years later, I would discover the truth about his escapades. Instead of the "side jobs" to bring in extra money, he had actually spent the time gambling and chasing other women. Franco was a victim of the same compulsions that had sent his grandfather to the poorhouse and his father to a syphilitic early grave. However, the deciding factor that led to our separation was the constant battles over rearing Triana. I could no longer bear the turmoil.

Close to midnight one evening, I heard our car pull in the driveway. I rushed to place his dinner on the table by the time he walked in the door. "Have you got the baby's bottle ready for her feeding?" he asked, hearing Triana start to fuss.

"No, Franco, when I took her to the doctor today, he said to start breaking her from her midnight feeding. At nine months and her present weight, she should be sleeping through the night. I'll rub her back and give her a pacifier. She'll go right back to sleep."

"I don't care what the fucking doctor said. If she wants a bottle ten times a night, you give it to her, do you hear?"

Franco, Nona and I had argued about her midnight feedings many times. "Give her what she wants," they had said, regardless of the fact that, as a working mother, I needed a schedule where she slept through the night.

"I gave her cereal in her last bottle and at her final feeding I gave her more substantial food. That should keep her satisfied through the night."

"You are wrong," he yelled. "You know nothing about caring for a baby. You are an unfit mother." I knew I was an inexperienced mother, but unfit? Never.

I gathered my courage. "You have got to give this a chance, Franco. Let's see if she will go back to sleep."

Enraged at my defiance, he picked up the edge of the kitchen table and threw it against the wall, scattering food, china, and utensils all the way to the opposite wall of the living room. "You'll do as I say or I'll beat you black and blue, do you hear?" he yelled.

Several lights in the neighborhood clicked on. Nona appeared, cringing in the doorway of her room, rosary beads clutched tightly in her hands. She made the sign of the cross repeatedly. "Please, children! The baby, the neighbors," she pleaded.

"Mama, go back to bed. This is not your concern. I'll handle this. Roe is going to obey me or else I'll make her wish she had. I am the man in this house." Franco gave his mother a small shove and closed her bedroom door.

My mother had been the last person to beat me, and I had solemnly promised myself that no one else ever would. "Franco, you lay one hand on me and I will call the police," I warned him. "This is the final straw, I've had enough of this nonsense; we'll never agree. I'm leaving."

The next day while Franco was at work, I called in sick and found a cheap unfurnished apartment in Inglewood that I could occupy immediately.

Carmen objected, begging me to reconsider. We were worlds apart in our thinking and I could never convince Carmen of my unhappiness. To her, it was my duty to stay and deal with the circumstances no matter how bad they were. Finally, shaking her head she retired to her room and rosary for comfort. I packed our things and left. Two days later, Triana slept peacefully through the night.

Each day, I dropped Triana off with a babysitter and picked her up after work. It was a delight to be reunited each evening with my loving, playful baby. Free from the pressure of Franco's excesses, I began to settle into a life of independence, hard work and joyful motherhood.

Franco called me regularly, begging to reconcile: "I need you. Please, just give me one more chance. Let me back, if only for the sake of the baby. I promise I'll change."

At first, I used my better judgment and resisted, but finally, Franco's pleading for Triana hit too close to home. How could I put my daughter through the suffering I had experienced in my own childhood? I remembered how much I had cried at night, longing for my father. Franco had located the weak spot that ruled my life. I surrendered, against my better judgment.

In January, two months after I left, Franco moved in with me while his mother, pending a trip back to Italy, moved into an apartment with one of her friends.

At first, Franco kept his promise. For the first time in four years, I could breathe without the fear of being smothered or interrogated. But by the end of March, with our reconciliation barely two months old, Franco resumed his familiar possessive posture. His attitude and rage were so reminiscent of my mother's that sometimes I questioned my own sanity.

His night jobs continued. He was often gone overnight, stuck in Santa Barbara, stuck in San Diego, car trouble in Bakersfield, always trying to sell an insurance policy, to no avail, he would say. I suspected that if he did work a second job and made money, it was spent on other women, other pleasures.

One evening after work, Paula, a co-worker and close friend, asked me to accompany her to a restaurant and cocktail lounge frequented by the employees of the bank. She was going to meet a friend there, but she didn't want to walk in alone. "Just stay with me a few minutes," she begged.

"Gee, I don't know," I hesitated. "Let me call Franco and see if he wants to join us. If he doesn't, I'll let him know I'll be ten minutes late."

I called Franco, who immediately flew into a rage. "No! I will not join you and don't you dare go yourself!" he thundered. "My wife does not hang around in bars!" He hung up without waiting for a reply.

I was furious. *So much for newly established trust and equal partnership.* I thought. I had made a mistake and it was time to face reality. I could not accept a life as a mere possession for Franco to order around. I would never be able to become a whole person until I freed myself of him. I could not talk to him about our problems. Any discussion quickly became a one-way monologue, crowned by his yelling and throwing whatever was available until everyone within range fearfully obeyed and submitted. I made up my mind that I would never submit again.

Paula brought me out of my thoughts. "Come on, Rosalie. It will only be for a few minutes."

"Paula, I have a serious problem, and I need to go home and straighten it out with Franco."

"Please, just walk in with me and then you can leave. Judy might even be there by the time we arrive."

"Okay fine. I'll go with you for five minutes. And I mean five minutes. Then I need to get home."

I accompanied Paula to the lounge; we waited outside for a few minutes for Judy, then I walked Paula in. A few of our co-workers were there. We walked to their table and Paula joined them. I refused a drink, said hello and goodbye, and took my leave. Meanwhile, Franco had called the restaurant and learned from the hostess that Paula and I had arrived.

Fearing a scene, I decided to go home before picking up Triana from the sitter's. Franco was standing outside the apartment when I drove up.

"How dare you?" he shouted. "I told you not to go to that place! You cheat, you liar!"

The intensity of Franco's rage caught me totally by surprise. He swiftly dragged me out of the car by my hair, slapped me back and forth, ripping my dress, and pulled me brutally toward our apartment, cursing me with every foul name that he could lay his tongue to in two languages. I was guilty of the ultimate sin: I had disobeyed.

Franco dragged me into the house, berating me at every painful step. In the living room, he continued to slap me viciously and shove me all over the room. He knocked me down and fell on top of me. Tears of rage filling my eyes, I cast desperately about, looking for a weapon, anything to stop this maniac. I spotted one of Triana's toys, a xylophone pull toy made of solid wood and metal. I barely managed to grasp it with my fingertips. At that moment, Franco shifted his weight to obtain leverage for his next blow and I grabbed a firm hold onto the toy and struck at him with all the strength I could summons from my pinned position. The full force of my swing caught him on the leg, striking the bone with a sickening crunch. The unexpected and excruciating pain forced him to release me. He limped away in agony toward the bedroom.

I crawled to the couch and collapsed. He would never do that to me again. Never. I got to my feet with difficulty and leaning against the wall for support, I struggled around the corner to the bedroom.

"Franco, we're through! Pack your things and go. I don't ever want to see you again!"

Franco was astounded; this wasn't part of his plan.

"Listen to me! I want you out of here! Now!" My voice trembled with uncontrollable fury. I turned and staggered into the living room.

In a few moments, Franco limped in. Dully he muttered, "I apologize," as though that would simply end the matter.

I couldn't bear to look at him. I was ashamed of my participation in the violence; it brought back painful childhood memories. The agony of the beating and the anguish of the memories brought forth a flood of violent tears.

"Roe, I'm sorry for what I did. It's just that.."

"It doesn't matter anymore, Franco," I cried. "Nothing between us matters anymore. It just won't work. You'll have to leave." The sound of my own voice gave me courage.

"You'll never lay a hand on me again as long as I live, we are finished. I'm a human being, with my own rights, not some dumb animal that you can kick around any time things don't go your way. You can't treat people the way you do and expect them to keep coming back for more. It may work that way where you come from, but it certainly doesn't work here and certainly not with me."

"But where will I go? I have no money." He whined.

"I'm sorry you're broke, but that doesn't change anything."

"Please Roe, let me stay. At least until I get paid." Franco was using his little boy charm and sincerity to convince me.

I felt myself beginning to weaken. "When will that be?" I asked reluctantly. I had experienced Franco's tactics more than once, and I could scarcely believe what I was saying.

"In about two weeks, and maybe.."

"Fine," I interrupted, "you sleep in the other bedroom. I'll move the baby in with me. But on April first, I want you out of here completely. For good."

With that ultimatum, I summoned my pride from somewhere deep within and, with head held high, left the house to pick up Triana under the curious eyes of my neighbors.

For the next week, Franco and I occupied the same house. He tried to placate me with gifts. Once he came home with some expensive shoes I had admired. I refused them. "It's over!" I told him. "Nothing you can say or do will change that!"

I was wrong.

On April 1, six days before Triana's first birthday, Franco stood at the living room window watching the heavy rain that had pounded the roof all night. This was the day he was to move out. "No point in trying to work today," Franco smiled. "No one wants to talk cargo sales on a rainy day. So why don't I save you babysitting money and watch Triana for you?"

My first reaction was to say no, but he seemed so sincere that I succumbed to his simple logic. Besides, I needed to save money. And I knew that even with all his faults, Franco idolized Triana and would see that no harm ever came to her.

"If you stay home, how are you going to get your check?" I asked. "Please don't play any games, Franco. What I said goes. You're leaving today."

"Oh sure, I know that. I've already got a place. I'll be packed up by the time you get home. Don't worry."

"But what about your check?" Don't you need to get that today?"

"Yeah, but I can pick it up from the night clerk tonight after I leave."

As I had so many times in the past, I found his answers plausible under the circumstances. He just wanted this last day with Triana, I convinced myself. For Triana's sake perhaps it was best that we part on this understanding note rather than in anger.

"All right, Franco," I sighed, "but please do us both a favor. Let's part company tonight quickly and easily, without any hassles."

"You're right, Roe. Much as I hate to admit it, we're through. I know that now and I'll just have to live with it." He spoke sorrowfully.

I was caught off-guard by this rare spurt of contrition.

I made the call to the sitter, kissed Triana goodbye, and as I turned to leave, said, "Thank you, Franco. I'll see you tonight."

At about eleven a.m., I called home from the office to find out how Franco and the baby were doing. The line was busy.

When I called again at noon, the line remained busy. I wasn't particularly concerned because I knew Franco could not stand to be alone. He was probably calling everyone he knew. I just hoped he wasn't making long-distance calls.

Throughout the day, when time allowed, I continued to call. The line was always busy. My annoyance grew. I liked to check on Triana during the day. Still, if a problem arose, I believed that Franco would call me.

Finally, the day was over and I drove home. As I walked into the house, the first thing that I saw was the phone receiver off the hook. A sickening feeling began to build in my stomach. I walked quickly to my room, over to the crib.

It was empty.

All of Triana's clothes and toys were missing. On the bureau lay a note.

Dear Roe:
Having no other choice, I have taken my baby and gone to Italy. If you think to change your mind about us, I will send for you. I will write to you when we are settled.
Sincerely,
Franco

"No!" I cried out, "Oh God, no!" My whole body shook violently. I raced through the apartment, looking desperately everywhere for proof that they hadn't really gone, that this was just one of Franco's cruel jokes. I searched the bathroom, the closets and the cupboards. Fear and disbelief took over. "Help me!" I screamed to an empty echoing apartment, "Somebody, help me…."

I grabbed the phone. Unable to dial the numbers through heavy tears, I asked the operator to get the police for me. They listened to my story and told me that there was nothing they could do. Since there was no divorce nor custody agreement, the child was as much his as she was mine.

I asked the operator to dial my friend, Myriam. Myriam, alarmed for me, called another close friend, Mary, and they both rushed over to find me sobbing hysterically.

"Maybe he'll come back," Myriam offered hopefully. "He might just be trying to scare you into reconciling and he'll walk in here in a little while as though nothing has happened."

"No, no," I sobbed, holding up the letter, "don't you understand?

He left this note and he took everything. He'll never come back, I know he won't!"

Myriam and Mary checked the apartment and discovered that Franco had indeed cleaned the place out. He had taken everything that could be readily converted into cash: a clock radio, the TV, the vacuum cleaner, anything that could be pawned or sold. But the most importantly, Triana was missing. Nothing else mattered.

After several hours of calls to Franco's friends, we arrived at a dead-end. Myriam had to go home to tend to her own family. As she reluctantly left, she hugged me tightly. "Everything will be all right," she said softly. "That dirty bastard will get what he deserves. I'll call you later."

Mary turned to me. "Rosalie, there's no point in you staying here all alone in this empty place. Come on, I'll help you get a few things together, and you'll spend the night with me."

"What?" I muttered, uncomprehending as Mary began to pack for me.

"You'll come home with me.."

"No!" I panicked. "I don't want to leave! I want to stay here. He may call me."

"Please," Mary urged, "come on, it's for the best." Mary led me, numb and dazed, out of the deserted apartment. We had gone only a few blocks when I realized where I was.

"Mary, please take me back to my apartment, don't you understand, it's my only connection to Triana," I cried. "Oh, God, Mary, I can't leave my apartment, I might hear something tonight!" I moaned and cried hysterically.

"Now, Rosalie," Mary soothed, "you shouldn't be alone right now. I think you'd be much better off at my place." The car approached a stoplight. "I'll bring you back tomorrow morning."

"Mary!" I shouted. "What do you think I'm going to do? Kill myself?" I have to be home in case he calls me. Don't you understand?"

The car had rolled to a stop. I jumped out and began running back toward the empty apartment, dodging a truck that came within inches of hitting me.

Mary turned the car around. She coaxed me back inside and drove me back to my cold, empty apartment. She left me sitting hopelessly in front of the telephone.

At four-thirty a.m., still clutching the silent phone, I dozed lightly on the floor.

I had tried everyone I could think of. Carmen's Italian friend Loretta who lived nearby in Torrance could not supply me with Carmen's phone number or address. She had not heard from her since her departure two weeks earlier for Rome. Loretta promised to call me immediately if she received a letter.

"Will you talk to Lina for me if I can locate her phone number?" I asked Loretta. "I will be more than happy to pay the charges." Lina was Carmen's sister: Franco's aunt.

A call to Italy information yielded no number for Carmen.

A frantic week ensued. No one could help. Every phone call, every conversation was filled with hysteria. Soon the gnawing sense of permanent loss set in.

A second call to the police told me that they were helpless. Inasmuch as there wasn't even a legal separation, no laws had been broken. Ours was merely a domestic dispute. Under the law, a child belonged equally to both parents during their marriage. There was nothing they could do.

Calls to the passport agency and several airlines confirmed that Franco had included Triana on his passport and had indeed left the United States with her. My disjointed emotions swung wildly from an inability to cope with the simplest idea to a sharp plunge into a desire for revenge and hatred, only to retreat to feelings of failure, believing that I was beaten. Franco had hurt me in the only way he knew he could.

When I began to be more rational, a week after Franco took Triana, I visited Nona's friend Loretta again. She still had not heard from Carmen. Franco's friends just brushed me off; they didn't want to deal with the problem or me. His company stated that he had given his notice two weeks earlier and they did not know where he had gone.

I knew that if Franco had gone back to Italy; it was likely to his mother.

I wrote a letter to his aunt Lina, begging for information about Franco and Triana's location.

Lina answered back through an English-speaking friend. She did not know where Franco was. She was sorry. There was nothing she could tell me. I could only hope that eventually I would hear from Franco.

Six days after Franco's departure, somewhere in the world Triana celebrated her first birthday. I felt cheated and deeply sad. I had no idea how my child was spending this day. I wondered if she missed me, if she was being cared for properly. I was furious at the pain this monster had caused me. Misery tore at my heart. At the insistence of my friends, I spent the day at their home.

As days passed, my despondency turned to determination. The sorrow remained as I struggled through the endless days, throwing myself into my work at the bank as best I could.

Six weeks after Franco had kidnapped Triana, a finance company where he had obtained a loan showed up with a large truck, to take away everything that I owned. I sat in the middle of the floor of the empty living room and alternated between crying and laughing hysterically. One of the kind-hearted movers overlooked some pots and pans and dishes, purposely pretending that he hadn't seen them, helping me to save some small part of my possessions. As they were leaving, one of the workers turned and said sympathetically, "Don't worry, lady. Everything will be all right." I reacted with a fresh peal of nervous laughter turning quickly to hot tears.

Franco left me with many bills. Bills I had known nothing about, bills I had not agreed to, but bills I was now responsible for paying. I simply didn't make enough money to pay for his extravagant tastes. I took my problem to the bank president who advised me to wash my hands of the heavy debt and, reluctantly, I filed for bankruptcy, a decision that took a great toll on my pride.

Three months after Franco left, I received a letter from Italy. There was no return address and the postmark was illegible. The note read:

Dear Roe,

"Triana is doing fine here with me and Nona. She grows everyday plumper and cuter. I have enclosed a picture for you, should you forget what our baby looks like. I will write to you periodically to let you know how she is.

Franco

The picture set off a whole new wave of despair and agony. I felt defeated as I stared at the photo of my child. Triana stood in front of a church, her two plump hands clasped together. She seemed oblivious to the pigeons bobbing and feeding around her. She stared straight at the camera, short, dark hair framing her beautiful baby face. Was she looking for something? Was she looking for me? Those beautiful, baby eyes pierced the paper. "Where are you, mommy?" I imagined her thinking.

She had been close to walking when Franco had taken her. Now she stood sturdily on her tiny feet, but I noticed immediately that one little foot was slightly turned inward. Was Franco putting her brace on every night to correct the minor problem the doctors had discovered? They had prescribed a corrective brace and special shoes. Had he paid any attention at all? Had he remembered? The doctor had assured me that the problem would be corrected by the time she was three if she religiously wore the brace. Franco had taken the brace with him and I could only hope he was using it.

I filed for divorce. Somehow, someway, I would recover my child.

CHAPTER FOUR

November 28, 1965 to December 16, 1965
Inglewood, California
Paris, France

The months passed. And then it happened: the phone rang sharply. I rushed to pick it up and I gasped when I heard his familiar accent.

"Hi, Roe, I'm in Milan," Franco said, as though he had talked to me every day since he took our child. "Well, how are you?" he asked brightly.

"Triana! What about Triana?" I screamed.

"Oh, she's just fine, such a cute bambina." There was a mocking tone to his voice. "Nona is taking very good care of her."

I bit down on my lip sharply to stifle the sobs. I could not speak.

Franco broke the silence. "Look, I've thought about this thing a lot, and I'm sorry about what I had to do.." Had to do! The words echoed in my head.

"I really miss you," he said softly, "and I want you back again... so much."

I held the phone, saying nothing, not trusting my voice. The image of my baby filled my mind.

"Say, look, Roe, if you come to Italy, we can get back together again and you will be with Triana again." He paused. "We would have to live in Italy. I've got a good job here in Milan. I'm a station

32

manager for an airline," he told me proudly. "It would be a good life for us. What do you say?"

"I want Triana back. I want her back more than anything in the world. But...about us...living in Italy." I was fighting for time, time to think, time to plan. "Franco, give me a few days to think this thing through. I'm too confused to give you any answer. Give me your number and I'll call you back day after tomorrow."

"Roe, oh, no, I'll call you back in a few days. You let me know then what you have decided."

"Please, call me back. By then I'll know what arrangements I can make at this end and what I'm going to do."

He agreed. "Okay, I'll call you in a few days. Please, Roe, make the right decision... for all of us. We can have a good life here, I promise you. You'll have Triana back and we'll all be together again. By the way, aren't you going to wish me happy birthday?"

It took all my strength to keep from screaming. I bit my tongue and simply said, "Happy Birthday, Franco."

"Thank you, Roe," he said, and hung up. All I could hear was the dial tone. Immediately I dialed the operator, but the international operator could not trace the call.

For the next couple of days, my mind worked at dazzling speed. In no way did I want Franco back in my life. But I had to make him think that I was willing to try again or he would disappear and this time he might never resurface. My only chance at getting Triana back was to stage an exceptional deception--one that could deceive the master deceiver.

On November 30, Franco's call came as promised.

"Have you decided yet?" His voice now sounded more demanding than the initial, conciliatory call. "Please, Roe, I want you here! Won't you come?"

I was ready, and answered him very carefully. "It will take me a couple of weeks to wind up my affairs here, but I will come, I plan on leaving around December fifteenth."

"Around... just what does that word mean, Roe? Are you coming or not?" His voice revealed the customary do-it-my-way attitude.

"Please, Franco," I said, attempting to reassure him, "you have to understand. I need to give at least two weeks' notice. It's not fair to Union Bank to quit without notice and besides they will dock my pay."

Convincing Franco to believe the initial stages of my plan was crucial to finding out whether I could deceive him. Besides, I needed more time.

After a moment's silence, Franco relented. "Okay, I'll send you a ticket and call you in a week."

I smiled. Good. He'd bought the first story. All I had to do was continue to guess how Franco would think under a similar circumstance. I had been sure that a delay related to money would strike a responsive chord, and I had been correct.

During the following week, I began to gather mounds of old clothing from friends and co-workers. I would need to look like I was moving to Italy, bringing all my clothes, clothing I would leave behind. I packed whatever I could get in several suitcases so Franco would conclude that I had, indeed, come to stay. Two of my friends from the bank, Mary Ellen and Toni, assisted me in planning my trip. We spent hours going over details and what-ifs. Their support and guidance were my strength.

We decided that I had to get Franco out of his native Italy and onto some neutral ground where I could have some degree of equal footing. My new boyfriend, Don, cashed in some of his bank stock and loaned me the money for the return trip.

By the time the ticket from Franco arrived in the mail, I was ready. When he called at the end of the week, I adopted my most compliant tone of voice.

"Franco, could we possibly meet in Paris?"

"Paris?" he questioned, obviously taken aback.

"Yes, I have a long layover and the planes change there. I've never seen Paris. It would be so exciting. I need to get to know you again, and the baby. You know, it's been a long time since we've been together. Please, Franco, just the three of us."

"Well, I don't know.. I don't really want to bring the baby." His voice trailed off slightly, giving me a chance to interject.

"Oh, why not? Please bring Triana. It's been so long since I've seen her," I tried to sound enthusiastic. "It will give us an opportunity to be together as a family and for me to get to know her again. She's forgotten who I am. She won't be any trouble. It will only be for a few days. Then we'll go home to Milan. It'll be great!"

"Well, okay.. but I don't know about the baby. I'll see." He spoke with some bluster, but I knew he would not deny my request for a romantic setting for our reunion.

As I hung up the phone, my mind screamed with the first joy I had known in months. It worked! It really worked! I can do it. I'll get her back!

The office buzzed with excitement. More boxes of old clothes were brought to the bank. My suitcases overflowed. There was so much that the excess had to be given to Goodwill. Mr. Seman, my boss, took the whole busy, breathless intrigue in stride.

Meanwhile I went to my attorney, who had filed my divorce papers, and asked him for guidance on how I could prepare legal-appearing credentials. The next day I sat at a typewriter in my attorney's office and typed documents stating that I had custody of Triana. The only thing that was missing was the court stamp, which I could not obtain since the law stipulated that the litigant must have possession of the child at the time of the custody filing.

At Toni and Mary Ellen's suggestion I was to carry these documents, together with money for my return flight, in a secret compartment in my purse, which we created by slitting the plastic lining around the frame. Behind the lining I hid the documents and the key items to the most dangerous part of my plan. I had obtained some very strong sleeping tablets and liquid compounds from the doctor who had delivered Triana. These were to be the instruments of my escape from Franco. With all the documents in place, I carefully glued the lining back.

The day of my departure finally arrived.

On the way to the airport I stopped to purchase a gift for Triana, hoping it would help break down the barriers that might now exist between us. My choice was a small, cuddly bear with eager, friendly button eyes. I clutched and cuddled that fuzzy bear all the way across the ocean as if it was my daughter, herself.

The big jet touched down and taxied into its appointed spot at the Orly Airport terminal building. I held my breath as I disembarked. Had Franco brought Triana?

There he was, smiling broadly, the charming husband and doting father, and in his arms the child I had thought I would never see again. Now twenty months old, my beautiful baby was so much bigger than I had expected that I gasped. She was dressed in diapers covered with pink panties and a short pink top with tiny flowers. Franco held up Triana's plump, little arm and waved it at me as I ran toward my baby.

"Oh Triana, my darling, I've missed you so much," I cried.

Triana squirmed in my arms and whimpered. Though I knew, with a terrible pang in my heart, that she didn't remember me, I held her in my arms and, for the moment, that was all that counted.

She turned to her dad and stretched out her arms, wanting to go to him. I handed her back to Franco, choking back tears, and presented the soft, little stuffed bear to her.

"This is your mother Triana," Franco said to her over and over again until I wanted him to simply shut up. But the child clung tightly to her father. Although I had tried to prepare myself for this rejection, it broke my heart more than I could have expected. It would take time to rebuild our relationship.

We took a taxi from the airport, and on the way to the hotel, Franco stopped at the Italian Embassy. After speaking for a few moments to the driver in French, Franco turned to me. "You wait here, I'll be right back," he said.

He left the baby and me alone in the cab.

As I held my precious daughter on my lap, feeling her softness and smelling her sweetness, I fought the conflicted feelings that the situation presented. I had not been prepared for the suddenness of the opportunity that now presented itself. I was tempted to tell the cab driver to leave instantly, but the language was a problem. I was afraid he would not understand me. Besides, what if this was one of Franco's games, merely meant to test me? What if Franco had given the driver instructions just in case I tried to get away? Perhaps Franco was watching me from the safety of the building. My instincts told me to be patient. I elected not to make a fatal mistake that could cost me my child yet again.

Presently, Franco returned. I could barely control the pounding of my heart. Our destination was a tiny, tidy little hotel on a busy street corner. It had one elevator off a very small lobby and, I noticed carefully, no staircase, or at least none that I could see. All guest traffic passed within ten or twelve feet of the desk. There was no rear entrance that could be used to escape.

Once in our room, I tried to play with Triana, but she would have none of me. She gave me inquisitive looks as if to ask what role I played in her life. Every once in a while I'd catch what seemed to be faint recognition, but the expression faded as rapidly as it surfaced. Even though I knew the rejection was normal, I felt letdown and depressed.

Weighing heavily on my mind was the knowledge that night was coming on and Triana would soon be asleep. Eventually I would have to go to bed myself, next to Franco. Fear, dread and loathing filled me to the core, and I had to concentrate heavily on Triana to avoid revealing my emotions to Franco. I washed Triana's clothes, spent a long hour bathing her, and lingered over putting her to bed. The child accepted this attention only as long as her father was nearby. I was reluctant to let go of these moments. It was the first time that Triana had let me come close to her.

"Franco, where is Triana's brace?" I asked.

"I threw that thing away. It was too uncomfortable for her and she didn't like it."

"You what? Do you realize that without that brace, she will either need an operation or will always have a problem with her foot turning in?"

"I tell you, it was too difficult for her to turn over in her bed with that thing on. She's fine without it. Drop the subject, do you hear?"

The typical Franco had emerged. However, I was not going to press the issue. I gently tucked Triana into bed and kissed her good night. Her eyes closed in seconds. Franco gently placed his arm around my shoulders. His touch revolted me. *Give me strength to endure what I must, if I must*, I told myself.

"I feel exhausted after that long trip, and the change of time," I told Franco easily. "I'm going to relax, soak in a hot tub and just go to bed."

Franco reached for me, pulling me to him. I could feel his erection through his trousers. I pushed him away and headed for the bathroom and locked the door. I leaned against the door. How was I going to survive the night?

I ran the bath water, undressed and crawled into the tub, wondering just how long I could stay in the water. I could not allow him to make love to me. Perhaps I could stay in there all night and tell him I fell asleep. No, he'd pound on the door if I stayed much longer. Maybe I would have to confront him with the truth: I despised him for all the pain he'd put me through. No, that wouldn't do. He'd probably knock me over the head and run off with Triana. I considered the possibility that he might try to kill me. I decided I would tell him a version of the truth.

After an hour and a half in the tub, I finally toweled dry and dressed in my most unattractive, long sleeved nightgown. I brushed my teeth, cleaned my face, and picked at a small pimple that had crept onto my chin. When I could find nothing else to do, I emerged from the bathroom.

Franco lay in wait for me in the double bed. Whatever happened from here on would be because I accepted the necessity of it, and while I felt only loathing and disgust for Franco, I knew that I had the strength to play out the scene without permitting it to touch me.

"Please, Franco, not just yet.. not like this.." I said pleadingly.

Franco hissed, "There's somebody else, isn't there? How many? When?" His rage escalated and his voice rose. "If you think that I brought you here just to be turned away, you've got another thing coming."

"Franco, that's just not true. There you go again, with your jealousy. It's the very thing that caused all our problems in the first place." I decided to reason with him. "Franco, I'm still married to you. I'm your wife and that means something to me. I saw other men while we were apart, but not like that, ever, not as long as I was still married."

Franco pulled me towards him.

"I do understand, Roe. It was the same for me.. believe me. The women at work, always throwing themselves at me, but I couldn't care less. After you, there could never be anyone else for me. All this time, I couldn't think of anything else but being with you again."

He spoke with all the sincerity and fervor that had so charmed me when we had first met. It was all I could do to keep from lashing out at him. Exhilarated by my success and certain that he suspected nothing, I gently turned from Franco's grasp.

"I'm glad you understand, Franco, it will give us the right attitude to rebuild our life together. But now," I smiled, "you'll have to give me time."

"Time for what, for God's sake? You've had almost all night!"

"No, no. I don't mean that. It's just that you hurt me very much by taking Triana and it's going to take me awhile to get over it. Please, Franco, try to understand." I was thinking wildly now, saying anything just to keep his hands from mauling me. To my surprise, he responded with unusual tenderness and paused in his fondling.

"I do understand, Roe. I want you to want this as much as I do."

In the next instant, the tenderness vanished as quickly as it had come, and the old anger surfaced.

"But what am I supposed to do? Wait ten years until you decide the time is right? I'm not going to live like that and you know it!" A tremor went though his body.

Once again, I teetered between success and failure, running the risk of physical harm. My time and my options were running out.

"Franco, just be patient with me for a little while. Things will be the way they were before. You'll see. You are a very understanding man and I know you realize what I am telling you will come about. I need time," I said as convincingly as I could.

Franco was taken back. For a moment, he seemed to want to understand. Characteristically, though, he didn't give up. For the rest of the night, he never ceased to snuggle provocatively against me. When the sun came up, both Franco and I rose exhausted.

The next morning, I decided to approach Franco with a change of plan. "Franco, I think that we should move to another hotel. This one is too noisy. None of us had a good night's sleep, including Triana. The noise from the street really bothered her. She tossed and turned all night."

"I sure didn't sleep, but it wasn't because of the noise," he grumbled.

"Seriously, Franco," I reasoned, "it's not only the noise, but there isn't even a fire escape, just that rickety old elevator. What if there was a fire? We'd be trapped in here."

"It's not likely that we will have a fire, but if you think the baby will sleep better.. all right, all right." He acquiesced grudgingly, more from a desire to put me in a romantic frame of mind than to agree with me.

We checked out, and took a taxi to the elegant Hotel DeGaulle. The new location suited my purposes perfectly. The hotel was a huge brick building with a large lobby and numerous exits. Confidently I anticipated carrying out my plan when the time arrived.

"Oh, Franco," I cooed happily, "this is perfect! Thank you so much. I know it was an inconvenience."

Overjoyed with my enthusiasm and unaware of its true source, he took my hands in his. "We are going to be so happy! Would you like a grand tour of Paris, the City of Romance?" His effusiveness was accompanied with a low bow and a grand sweep of his arm. In a flash, all that I saw was love and kindness. This was the side of Franco to which I was so vulnerable. If only he wasn't so unpredictable, so emotional, so jealous. I jerked myself back to reality.

"That would be heavenly, Franco! Could we?" I pretended to sparkle with anticipation.

"I'll arrange the whole thing for tomorrow," he promised.

"Great!" I replied. "Can we take a walk with the baby now? Maybe I could pick up a book to read while Triana is taking her nap." Carefully I began to scramble for time.

"Okay, sure," he said.

I suggested that Franco make the tour arrangements for the next day while I took Triana into the restaurant for lunch. It was critical to my success that Triana get used to being alone with me. She consistently looked to her daddy when we were all together, but gradually she was beginning to accept me. I wanted to continue to reinforce the relationship before making my escape.

In the restaurant, I ordered mindlessly: some pasta, a little cheese, and some fruit. Triana was hungry and as soon as the waiter brought the food, she began to eat. She smiled at me and offered me a slice of orange. "Bite?" she asked charmingly.

I leaned over and hugged her gently, accepting the fruit from my baby's hand. This child touched my very soul. The tears I could not control rose again.

Should I make a move now? I decided to risk speaking to the waiter. I spoke to him quietly. "Please, I need help. I am trying to get away from my husband. "He smiled and walked away. He had not understood a word I had said. A woman sitting nearby stared at me. Did she read the panic in my face? With sickening certainty, I realized that I was a stranger in a foreign land, and I had no friends here. Whatever I had to do, I would have to accomplish it alone. I calmed myself and began to think through the steps rationally.

Triana was still on Franco's passport. I had been unable to discover where Franco was keeping the passport although I believed he carried it with him. Somehow, I had to get it.

By the time lunch was over, Triana was ready for a nap.

I returned to the room and tenderly tucked her into the crib under Franco's watchful and approving eyes. He basked in the tranquility of the little domestic scene. Everything was going as he had hoped. I was certainly the perfect mother, but I hadn't performed my wifely duties. I was sure he felt confident that with the change of hotel, the quiet afternoon, and his own behavior the previous night, he had created the proper atmosphere.

As the day wore on, the tension grew. I realized that I would not be able to put off Franco's sexual advances much longer. I was running out of excuses and time. I had to wait for the right moment to make my escape, but every hour seemed an eternity. My escape with Triana had to succeed in France. Once in Italy, on Franco's native turf, it would be impossible. I remembered our first trip to Italy, how shocked I had been that Franco's friends watched me constantly, reporting my slightest movements and activities to him.

I would have to act soon. My first chance was undoubtedly going to be my only one.

December 17 1965

After dinner, I received some unexpected help. When we returned to our room, I bathed Triana and dressed her in her nightgown. Franco paced the floor, waiting impatiently for the cocktails he had ordered. I wondered if he sensed what I planned.

"While you're getting the baby ready for bed, I'll call and order room service tomorrow morning before we go on the tour." Franco dialed room service. "Hello, this is Monsieur Allatere in suite 872. I wish to place a breakfast order."

"I'm sorry, Monsieur, but we are no longer serving breakfast at this late hour," the room service clerk said. "Perhaps, something from our dinner selections." I could hear the loud voice from where I stood.

"No, no, no. I don't want anything now," Franco replied impatiently. "Tomorrow morning, I want breakfast in our room tomorrow, do you understand?" Franco's voice rose slightly.

"Of course, *Monsieur*, in the morning," replied the clerk in a wounded tone. "Your order, *s'il vous plait?*"

Over his shoulder Franco inquired, "What would you like, honey?"

"Oh, I don't care. Whatever Triana will have, I'll just share hers," I replied.

"Please, Roe, make up your mind. I'm having enough trouble with this idiot in room service," he replied testily.

Franco was in regular form again. Perhaps this could be to my advantage. It was hard to make love when you argued.

"I said I don't care, Franco," I snapped.

Franco's temper flared and he proceeded to take out his frustration on the clerk. "Do you think that you could possibly handle getting three *petites dejeuners* up here in the morning before eight o'clock?" he snarled.

"But of course!" The clerk's voice was icy. "Does *Monsieur* prefer *café au lait*, American coffee, or tea?"

"American..no, *café au lait*..no. Wait."

I ignored his conversation as I was tucking Triana into bed. The bliss of her smile touched me deeply as I gave her a small tickle on her toe. She gave me a shy laugh and turned to settle down.

"Uh, Roe, what kind of coffee?"

I continued to ignore him for a full minute. "I said I don't care, Franco."

Franco yelled into the receiver, "I don't care what you bring, just have it on time!" He slammed the phone down before the startled clerk had a chance to reply. "Stupid! Stupid! Stupid! How the hell did he get a job?" he complained.

Suddenly the phone rang again. Room service.

"*Monsieur* Allatere?" a new voice began. "This is the night kitchen manager and I just received your breakfast order for tomorrow morning. You have ordered American coffee, *café au lait*, and tea. Uh, how many are being served, *Monsieur*? How many cups will you need?"

Franco exploded. "I can't believe that you can't get a simple order straight down there. Why would I want all three? I told the clerk, bring anything, I don't care!"

There was a slight pause at the other end of the line. Obviously, the manager was not used to being talked to in this fashion.

"All we wished to know is the number of servings so that the waiter will not have to return to the kitchen for more cups. We wouldn't want anything to delay *Monsieur's* morning meal," the manager finished sarcastically.

Franco seethed. He saw himself as a guest, a man of substance, stature, and title. He snapped his reply into the receiver. "Two cups, thank you, and milk for my daughter." He hung up the phone before the manager could reply.

Triana stirred in her crib and gave her father a puzzled look. I grabbed my chance.

"Now see what's happened? She was just getting to sleep and now you woke up Triana. Let's just forget the silly breakfast!"

This was too much for Franco. He followed me into the sitting room, clearly intending to defend his position and let me know that he was not going to stand for any more of my distant attitude, when the phone rang again. Franco dashed toward the bedroom, hitting his leg on the side of the bed, and limped his way to the phone. He scooped up the receiver. I picked up the extension in the sitting room.

"Hello!" he cried, rubbing his bruised leg.

"Uh, *Monsieur,* I'm sorry to disturb you again, but you rang off before I could confirm the time of your order for the morning. It is eight o'clock. Right?"

Through the distance between the door and the frame I could see Franco's face turn red, then white. I could almost feel the fire from his body through the phone.

"You idiot! You woke up my sleeping daughter. I'm going to report you to the hotel manager, whom I know quite well!" He was screaming into the phone now. His hands were shaking and his whole body trembled.

Events were working in my favor. As Franco sat on the edge of the bed, the phone rang sharply yet again. Franco tore the receiver from its carriage with such violence that the phone fell to the floor.

"NOW, LISTEN, YOU STUPID!" he screamed.

"*Monsieur?*" A puzzled woman's voice was on the other end of the line. "This is Madame Fouchet, from *Champ de Elysees* Tours, your guide for tomorrow?" Her voice contained a question, as though she wasn't sure that she had reached the right party.

"Well, what do you want? Is the tour cancelled, I suppose? Nothing else seems to go right in this miserable place!"

"Oh, quite the contrary, *Monsieur,* we are looking forward to seeing you and your party in the morning. It is our custom to confirm our appointments. I hope that I haven't disturbed you."

"Of course, you've disturbed me! My daughter is sleeping! Yes, we are going on the tour tomorrow at 9:00 a.m. Now, if you please, do NOT call me again. If you have anything to say to me, leave word with the concierge!"

This time Franco threw the entire phone against the wall with such violence that I thought sure that the cord would rip from its connection. "Idiots! IDIOTS!" he screamed, his anger cresting in ever-higher waves.

I grew frightened, as I always had at these outbursts. But overriding my dread was the realization that, without much effort on my part, Franco was in the state of mind that I needed. My doctor's words came rushing back to me: "Even if you give him all six sleeping pills or all the liquid, it shouldn't really hurt him. It will just put him to sleep for a long time." Now it was time to choose. *Which would it be, the pills or the contents of the vial?* I knew I wouldn't have a second chance if I chose incorrectly. "The pills," I decided, "it has to be the pills." I went into the bathroom and returned with the pills and a glass of water.

"Franco," I said soothingly, "I know you're terribly upset. I am, too, and I've got a terrible headache from all this. I'm going to take one of these headache pills. Why don't you take some, too? It'll help relax us both, and then maybe later we can talk... about us," I coaxed him. Franco stopped shaking and looked up at me questioningly. As my words sank in, he recovered slightly.

"I'm all right, Roe. What I need I'm not going to get from any pills," he stated flatly. His eyes began to undress me.

"Oh, Franco, I can't think about anything but my headache right now. I'm in agony! Please, let's rest for a while. You take these and lie down; I'll be here in a while, as soon as my head feels better and I calm down a little," I reassured him.

"Great! Then we can just sleep all night, like before--right?"

It was now or never. I had to convince Franco to follow my lead.

"No, it'll be different tonight. You'll see." My voice dropped almost to a whisper. "Maybe you could wake me up.. like you used to. Remember?"

With that, I took the final step. I placed a pill under my tongue, planning to spit it out as soon as I got the chance. But when I swallowed the water, the pill slipped down my throat. *My God*, I screamed inside my head, *what have I done?*

A smile crept over Franco's face. He reached for the pills, grabbed the glass of water, and swallowed two pills in one gulp. Walking back into the bathroom I collapsed on the toilet, every nerve in my body seemed to explode with a mixture of fear and success. As soon as I recovered, I stuck my finger down my throat; it was too late, only the water regurgitated. I looked at my watch and wondered how long it would take Franco to feel the effect of the pills. Coffee, I thought! Could I resist the effects with coffee? No, coffee would require ordering from the kitchen; I couldn't risk using the phone.

I had been transferring the donated clothing into Franco's case and putting Triana's things into the one case I would need. This served two purposes: mingling our things made Franco believe I was there to stay; and placing the essentials for Triana and for me in one suitcase would make it easier to move rapidly.

As I lay in the tub, I questioned my ability to pull this off and remain alive. When I emerged from the bathroom, I saw Franco in bed, eyes closed. I walked into the sitting room and curled up in a chair, and waited. I tried to read, but within moments, the lines blurred. The pill was taking effect. What could I do? I heard the sound of Franco's heavy breathing and hoarse snoring. He was deeply asleep.

I tried to focus. It was too soon to make a move as Franco might waken. If I could only close my eyes for a few seconds until he was safely in a deep sleep. Slowly and quietly I rose from the chair and walked into the bedroom. Thankfully, the bed was king-sized and I could gently lower myself onto the edge farthest from Franco's sleeping form.

As soon as my head touched the pillow, my eyes closed. I struggled uselessly and fell asleep.

Suddenly my internal clock snapped me awake. My eyes shot open. The clock read 1:30 a.m. This was it. My heart pounded wildly. Franco still slept deeply as I crept around the room, packing the baby's remaining things. I then walked over to Franco's nightstand.

His lighter and cigarettes were the only things on top of the stand. I picked up a pack of cigarettes, lit one, and dropped the lighter on the stand as loudly as I could. I hated the taste of cigarettes, but, if Franco woke, I had an excuse for being where I was.

Franco turned over. I put out the cigarette and my entire body shook as I ran to the bathroom and threw up from nerves. When I returned to the bedroom, Franco was still sleeping soundly. I reached into the nightstand drawer and there it was--Franco's American passport, the one on which he had included Triana. I took a long look at his passport, if only I had thought to obtain a separate passport for Triana or include her on mine, I would not be in this situation. I slipped the passport into the pocket of my coat that hung just inside the closet door. I hoped this wouldn't create a problem. I had learned before I had left the States that if two people were on one passport, they should always travel together. I would have to think of some plausible explanation if I was questioned.

I looked over at little Triana, who was sleeping peacefully. What if she cried out when I picked her up? I was a bundle of nerves. To test Franco's depth of slumber again, I walked into the bathroom and slammed the door. He never stirred. If that didn't wake him, maybe I could escape. But I realized that a baby's cry was a stronger force for any parent.

I would have to take that chance.

Too nervous to dress, I threw the double-breasted winter coat over my knee-length nightgown, buttoning the coat carefully so that my nightclothes would not show. I then took my suitcase and set it outside the door. One of the bellhops passed by, and gave me a strange look. I returned to pick up my sleeping baby. I held my breath as Triana opened her beautiful hazel eyes and looked at me, a faint smile of recognition appearing on her sleepy face. My heart swelled with pride and gratitude and began to pound.

Carrying Triana tenderly, I left the room, closing the door softly behind me.

As I walked toward the elevator, a look of contempt appeared on the face of the bellboy who had seen me place the suitcase in the hall. In the elevator, he substituted any offer of assistance with a look of disapproval as I struggled with Triana and the suitcase. He was a proud Parisian and I was an American and obviously up to no good. Reaching the ground floor, I gave the bellboy a defiant glance, and headed for the check out counter.

"Are you leaving, Madame?" the clerk asked, in heavily accented English. A young, slender man of swarthy complexion, he seemed annoyed that some American woman was disturbing him at two a.m.

"Yes, I am, would you please call me a taxi?"

"Madame, do you wish to leave with your baby in the middle of the night in this weather? It is raining too hard to take the child out." He hesitated a moment, staring closely at me. "Madame, where is your husband? Is he not leaving with you?"

Although I had never seen him before, he had done his homework. He knew who I was and with whom I was traveling. Half-crazy with panic, I threw away my sense of caution and blurted out. "You don't understand; I'm taking my child back to the United States. My husband stole her from me and took her to Italy. I'm simply going home with my child." I spoke with courageous but dangerous finality.

The man behind the desk would have none of it. "We shall have to contact your husband to straighten this out," he insisted coldly.

"Please, please, monsieur," I begged. "Please don't do that! He'll create a terrible scene."

The clerk was not impressed. "Is your husband in your room?" he inquired. "Shall I ring?" He moved toward the phone.

Fear gripped my entire body. "Please wait, you don't understand. He'll kill me if you call him." I struggled desperately to think clearly. "What kind of publicity will this be for your hotel? You are making a terrible mistake. I assure you I have papers that give me the right to take my child back to the United States. They're right here in my purse."

Suddenly the desk reeled before me. I clutched at it to keep from fainting. I had left my purse in the sitting room of the suite! How could I have been so stupid? How could I go back into that room? If I did go back, surely someone would accompany me, possibly the unfriendly bell captain. What was to stop him from waking Franco and telling him what was going on? What if it was the manager and he couldn't wake him and thought that I had poisoned him?

Summoning up from some unknown place a light laugh and a casual toss of my head, I found my voice. "Well, I was so anxious to get away from him that I forgot my purse. It's still in the room. I'm going to have to go back and get it."

My steady and controlled manner suddenly changed the clerk's attitude. He hesitated a moment, studying me. His voice became more conciliatory. Perhaps he had heard about Franco from the kitchen help. "But what if your husband wakes up, Madame?"

"That's just a chance we'll have to take," I responded. "I need my identification and papers."

I needed to capitalize on the man's slight weakness, to include him as a co-conspirator. I was so terrified that I thought that I was going to be sick.

"Well, Madame," the clerk murmured thoughtfully, "I think that I'm beginning to understand your problem. However, we still cannot let you leave the hotel tonight. We will put you up in another room. You can discuss the whole matter with the day manager in the morning. He will make... how you say in English?" he faltered.

"Decision," I provided the missing word.

"Either he'll let you go or he will call the police." The man smiled. "You will see in the morning."

I was shown to a room on the fifth floor. It was across the courtyard and three stories down from where Franco slept. My room, directly across from the floor kitchen, was small, dark, and musty; it reminded me of a dungeon. A crib was provided for Triana. A bell captain fetched the cook from the small kitchen to watch Triana as he escorted me back to Franco's suite. All the way up in the elevator, I held my breath, not knowing what I would find. More than any other time in my life, I realized how much I truly feared this man. I had never doubted that he was capable of killing me in a mad rage, but so far I had done nothing to justify such an action. I was now tempting fate.

As we reached the door, the bell captain began to fumble with the key. I took my shoes off and slowly tiptoed into the sitting room, perspiring profusely. Cautiously I picked up my purse, and backed ever so carefully out the door. I glanced toward the bedroom, expecting to see Franco charging toward me. Suddenly he rolled over and reached for my side of the bed, his hand searching for me.

He's awake! I thought in a panic. My knees buckled. But whatever had disturbed him rose only from the depths of his subconscious. His heavy, even breathing resumed.

Quietly I left the suite, pulling the door shut but avoiding the click of the latch. Safely outside, I leaned against the wall, fighting fainting.

I jumped as I felt a hand on my shoulder. The bell captain stared at me, ready to catch me if I fell, but his expression was more dutiful than concerned. Back in my newly assigned room, I thanked the cook and tipped him. He bowed his thanks and I closed the door after him and bolted it securely.

I was a prisoner, but that room was a grateful sanctuary. They would have to break down the door before I would let Franco in.

My beautiful child slept peacefully in the hotel crib, unaware of any inconvenience. Unable to sleep, I collapsed in the nearby chair and assessed the events of the past half hour. Curiously, my mind flashed back to the day that Franco had taken Triana. He had left me a note. "Well," I said to myself, "why not? I'll leave him a note he'll never forget."

I wrote it and knocked on the door of the floor kitchen, asking the cook to look after Triana for just a few more moments. He agreed, and up the three flights of stairs I ran. I had decided not to use the elevator. I'd had enough frowns of disapproval from the young bellboy who was running it. I tiptoed to the door, slipped the note under it, and dashed at full speed back to my own room.

The note read, "Franco, having no other choice, I am taking my daughter and returning to the United States–Roe."

A mockery of the note he had left for me. I felt no remorse for my words, only anger for the months he had stolen from me.

At 7:30 the following morning, a sympathetic day-manager reviewed my papers. He decided to let me leave the hotel with Triana.

He even escorted me out through the service elevator to a waiting cab. As I was preparing to get into the cab, I inquired about Franco

"Has he come down from his room?"

"No, we have not seen him so far this morning. You had better get going, Madame. Good luck!"

He smiled at me as he closed the cab door and waved the driver on.

I was afraid to go directly to Orly Airport because it was the first place Franco would look for us. I instructed the cab driver to take me to the train station, where I boarded the next train for Calais, destination London. I found myself continually looking over my shoulder, afraid that somehow, some way, I would find Franco pursuing me.

The train made very few stops. Food was served aboard. Triana ate like a trouper, happily clutching at my fingers and playing with my hair. We played games and together watched the passing scenery from the train windows. Surprisingly, Triana did not ask for her father; it was though we had never been parted. I held my child close, pressing my face against her soft, smooth skin, and thanked God for being reunited with this beautiful, loving child.

The trip seemed all too long. I wished desperately for a bed. I was happy but very sleepy and emotionally drained. When we reached Calais, I carried a sleeping Triana aboard a ferry for the ride across the English Channel to Dover. Once the crossing began, the authorities processed the passengers for arrival in England. I held my breath as I approached the customs officers; my fears were unfounded, however, as I passed through English customs with no problem.

In Dover, I boarded another train, arriving at London's Victoria Station around four o'clock in the afternoon. Exhausted, I took a cab from the station to the Cumberland Hotel, in Marble Arch. After checking into the hotel, I bathed Triana and myself. I dressed, changed Triana and took her down to the dining room for an early dinner.

With Triana tucked in for the night, I sat on the edge of the bed looking at my sleeping child. I breathed a sigh of relief at the 500 miles I had put between Franco and myself. I reflected back to my friend Don, who had loaned me the money for the return trip. What a kind and loving gift he had given me.

After breakfast the next morning, I took Triana to the airline ticket office a small distance from the hotel. There I purchased our tickets for a flight that left that day at one-twenty p.m. from Heathrow Airport to New York. Back in the hotel room, I packed the few things we had used, fed Triana an early lunch and then headed for the airport.

Arriving at the airport, yet another unpleasant surprise awaited me.

The ticket agent pointed out that my passport was over four years old and had expired, and had expired even before I had departed from the United States. It had simply never occurred to me to check its date before I left home. The airline, Air France, responsible for making sure all passengers had a valid passport before boarding their aircraft, had not checked the date.

"But why didn't they tell me at the ticket office downtown? They looked at my passport," I cried hysterically. The thought of another delay was almost more than I could face. Large tears formed in my eyes. "I must leave Europe immediately, or.."

"Now calm down, ma'am, please," the clerk said kindly. "According to the law, you are not supposed to leave a country with an expired passport. We will need to make a report. The airline you left on should have checked. They are responsible for the error and will be subject to a heavy fine for their mistake."

The agent was patient and soft spoken, but he was determined to follow official policy.

"But what am I going to do now?" I asked. "The flight leaves in thirty minutes!"

"I'm very sorry, but there is no way to get you on that flight. You'll have to have your passport straightened out. I'll be glad to see if we can get you on a later flight." He glanced at Triana. "We have an excellent nursery here at the airport. You can leave your baby here while you make the trip back to London. It'll be much faster to get everything done if you aren't trying to haul a sleepy baby around."

"You don't understand. I just got her back from my husband. What if someone takes her?"

Why was I telling him all this? My voice rose in panic. The agent's eyes searched my face. Somehow he believed and trusted me.

"I'll tell you what," he said, "We'll have one of our agents stay with her until you get back. I assure you, she will be just fine. You will be able to take care of your passport and if it goes quickly, I'll see if we can get you on board the five-forty-five," the agent said soothingly.

The agent moved down the counter to speak to a pretty, young female agent. They exchanged a few words, and she looked up at me, smiling her agreement. Together we walked to the nursery where Triana was put into a crib and fell asleep in seconds.

"You won't leave her. You promise?"

The woman nodded her head and patted my shoulder.

At the United States Embassy, as I stood in front of the clerk, I lost control and sobbed out the whole story. Sympathetically the clerk directed me to a nearby photographer. Waiting for the developing of the pictures, I called the airport to see how Triana was. She was fine, the agent reported, adding that he had booked me on the 5:45 flight.

At the embassy, I was presented with a new passport in no more time than it took to seal the picture onto its proper page. I thanked them all and, as I rushed out the door, I glanced back and saw the clerk shaking his head in puzzled amazement.

At the airport, I hurried to the nursery to find the woman agent sitting by a sleeping Triana. I couldn't have been more relieved. We boarded the plane and began the flight across the Atlantic. For the first time in days, I felt truly free.

When I landed in New York, I passed through customs and the passport check without question. Relieved, I phoned my friend Don. When there was no answer, I phoned my attorney Ron, asking him to contact Don to pick Triana and me up at the Los Angeles airport.

"Of course," he said "and, Rosalie, congratulations. I knew you could do it."

"Thanks, Ron," I answered softly. "I'm so glad it's over. See you soon."

Over? My unconscious worry rose up in me. Would it ever be totally over? What was Franco thinking, and what steps would he take now?

"Triana." I whispered, "You're back with your mother now and we're going home; he'll never separate us again." I smiled.

CHAPTER FIVE

December 1965
Los Angeles, California

As soon as possible, I updated my divorce papers and asked for full and exclusive custody of Triana. With unreasoning illogic, the court denied my request. Franco was granted the usual "reasonable rights of visitation." When my final divorce was granted on February 11, 1966, I wrote to the U.S. Passport Office enclosing copies of my divorce and custody papers along with an explanation of what had happened. I requested that only I be granted a passport for Triana and that I would appear in person with proper identification to claim her new passport. I enclosed Franco's passport, asking that Triana be removed from it, and that a new one be issued for him.

My twinkling hazel-eyed toddler fascinated and bewildered me. Each day she changed. The enchanting sunbeam blossomed into a spirited young child. My eyes misted when I thought of the months of her life I had missed. Yet life was also better than I had dared hope.

After work, I picked up Triana from the babysitter and we returned home each night to our Inglewood apartment. We were a contented and happy twosome.

As time passed and my involvement with Triana grew stronger, my relationship with Don began to deteriorate. I was too wound up in Triana and not available for the many activities we had shared before her return. The gift he had given me, my child, was the thing that now separated us. We remained friends.

June 1966
Santa Monica, California

Six months after getting Triana back, I was sitting at work at my desk in the Union Bank. I looked up and hoped I was hallucinating, as Franco was headed straight for my desk.

I sat, petrified and immobile. How had he found me? What could he possibly want? Had he found Triana as well?

Before he spoke, he stood in front of my desk silently for a full minute. What seemed like hours were only minutes as he studied my expression. The entire bank seemed focused on me. They all knew of Franco and had been involved in the scheme. I felt like I was going to faint as I the color drained from my face.

"Roe," he began, "please talk to me, just for a few minutes. Will you?" His face was drawn and taut.

I rose slowly, steadying myself by holding firmly to my desk. "I'll see if Mr. Seman will let me take a break," I replied stiffly. Witnessing the scene from his desk behind me, Mr. Seman nodded his assent before I even asked.

In the Bat Rack restaurant next door to the bank, Franco and I sat across from each other in a booth. Surprisingly he began by apologizing, trying to explain why he had taken Triana to Italy, begging my forgiveness.

"Roe, please try to understand. I was out of my mind then. You didn't want me anymore. I was all alone. And I wouldn't get to see my baby. Now I'm so sorry, and all I want to do is to see Triana again."

"I'm sorry, Franco, but the answer is no," I said coldly.

As tears rolled down his face, Franco sat silent.

"You can't be trusted," I continued. "There is absolutely no way I ever want you to know where I live, much less to see Triana! You wouldn't be in this situation in the first place if you hadn't stolen her!"

"Please! Roe," he said through his tears, "you've got to let me see her. I promise I will never, never take her again. I swear on my mother, Roe."

After twenty minutes of his pleading and crying, I began to weaken, feeling the old sorrow and compassion for this beaten man whom I had once thought I loved. The years of separation from my own father haunted me. Did I have the right to keep Franco from seeing Triana? Would she someday resent the lack of a relationship with her father, as I had? Would she blame me?

"All right, Franco," I replied slowly. "Though it troubles me, Triana should know you. You are her father. But you will not be allowed to take her out of my sight, and you will see her only on weekends."

"Oh, Roe, thank you so much," he cried gratefully.

For the next six months, Triana and I met with Franco away from my house. Then, without warning, he disappeared for several months. Many years later, I learned he had married an older woman named Cara, who owned a motel in Arizona. The marriage was a short-lived affair--the lady's attorneys advised Franco to cancel his schemes to gain their client's money. The marriage was annulled.

When Franco reappeared, he asked to continue our meetings. We met for another four months in restaurants, parks and hotel lobbies. At one of our meetings Franco informed me he was living with a woman named Kitty and that he was sending for his mother. He asked if he could come to our house and see where his baby was living. Some months later, after Franco's constant begging and promising to never take our child away from me again, I consented for him to come to our house for a visit. After all, he had been behaving himself, he was in a relationship and his mother was now living with him.

One sunny day he asked if he could take Triana out for an ice cream. I had regained a modicum of trust in him; he had earned that much.

An hour passed. They didn't return. When I picked up the phone and called the police, I was shaking.

"But, Officer, he said he'd be gone only half an hour. That was what he promised."

"I'm sorry, ma'am. There's nothing that we can do."

Three hours later, Franco returned with Triana. Furious, I ran outside and met him in the driveway of the apartment building. He said he was sorry. He promised that he would never scare me that way again.

Many years later, I learned that Franco returned Triana only at the insistence of Kitty, his new girlfriend, and his mother. He had planned on stealing her that very day.

To Franco, a promise was a convenient tool to be used and discarded. I was to learn that the hard way, repeatedly, as my life changed and I moved into a new time of loving a new man.

October 1969
Santa Monica, California

Stan was a handsome, fair-haired, slender, thirty-four-year-old businessman with a square jaw and an endearing boyish, winning smile. Over the next eighteen months our friendship flourished and the feelings we felt for each other blossomed into love.

Stan and I had met in October, 1969. He had previously worked for Benmar, a marine radar company in Orange County, which he left to start Innovative Systems with two friends. Innovative Systems - located in Brentwood – was a customer at the Santa Monica branch of Union Bank, where I worked. The investment company the partners founded offered considerable expansion potential, and he entered the project with enthusiasm and diligence, only to suffer a serious blow when the economy suddenly slumped.

Stan had a fascinating, brilliant mind; he knew more about the world than I could ever imagine existed, he was quick-witted and a constant source of entertainment and fun. After we spent four evenings together, I knew he was the man I wanted to spend the rest of my life with.

The economy continued to falter and Innovative Systems finally closed its doors. Our relationship was beginning on rocky economical grounds, but we were happy in all other ways.

Stan and his partners returned to Orange County, settling in

Newport Beach, hoping to join the growth in this prosperous area. Commuting to see each other was difficult, so we decided that if our relationship were to continue, I would have to relocate.

In Costa Mesa, in a two-block area of four-plex apartments, I found a darling two-bedroom apartment near a school for Triana, who was starting the first grade. There was a lovely quiet park behind our apartment for her to play in and lots of children in the neighborhood.

Franco, Kitty, and Nona soon followed, moving into the same two-block area, less than a three-minute walk from ours. I had no objections. I felt it was important that Triana have the influence of both parents. It seemed the perfect situation - Nona watched Triana after school each day and I would pick her up after work. Triana had the best of both parents and her grandmother, who adored her.

April 20, 1971
Costa Mesa, CA

On my thirty-third birthday, Franco stopped by to see Triana and me.

He held something in his hands as he teased Triana with a small package. It was a gift, he said, from him and Triana. The gift, a jade pendant on a gold chain was much too expensive for a child to have chosen. Out of the corner of my eye, I could see Triana's twinkling hazel eyes smiling with anticipation. Barely seven, she was beautiful with her long dark hair, her olive complexion, and her beaming eyes. She joyfully bounced around me as I admired her gift. I accepted the present, registered the appropriate appreciation, and kissed Triana warmly before she bounded into her bedroom to play.

As soon as she left, Franco spoke.

"Please, Roe," he pleaded, his handsome features twisted into an expression of desperation, "you've just got to come back to me. We'll be a family again, you and me and Triana. Please, it's so important to all of us!" He seemed on the brink of tears.

As so many times in the past, at first I was touched by his intensity. But I had fallen into his emotional traps too many times. By now I was sure that I knew the signs. Every time Franco had a fight with a girlfriend, his first impulse was to drag me back into his bed. But this time his tone was different, more fervent, more intense, and almost desperate.

I backed away from my ex-husband, wondering what this strange and troubled man wanted from me after such a tumultuous marriage and six years apart. "No, Franco," I told him, "it just wouldn't work. I don't feel any love for you, and I wouldn't even consider subjecting myself or Triana to a home that's not filled with love. I won't expose her to living through the turmoil that I had to contend with as a child."

Franco grew agitated. "But Roe, please. I'm different now. I know that you should have more freedom and I can live with that now. I need you, and Triana needs a home with a mother and a father."

"Franco, listen to me very carefully," I said, struggling to find my composure. "We live close enough so that we can share in raising Triana. I haven't done anything to make her love you less, no matter how I feel about you. We get along better now than when we were married. You know that. Besides, you've been with Kitty for several years. Don't you feel any obligation to her? Does she suspect you don't love her and are just stringing her along, hoping that I will come back to you?"

"Don't worry, Roe," he waved aside my words, "I'll take care of her."

"How, Franco? By just dumping her as if she were one of your one-night stands? You don't deserve Kitty's love and devotion." I paused to get my courage together. "Franco, face it. Our life together is over. Accept it and let's stay friends for Triana's sake. Besides, you know how I feel about Stan. I love him very much." My voice trailed off to a whisper.

Franco scoffed, "Oh, come on, Roe, he'll probably go back to his wife after he has his fling! There's no future with him for you!"

"I don't know where my relationship with Stan is going, Franco," I conceded, "but I do know that right now, Stan and I love each other and I intend to give us every chance to build a permanent life together."

"Your decision breaks my heart, Roe, someday you'll be sorry," he said dejectedly. "I know you'll look back someday and wish you had chosen differently."

Many years later, I learned that Kitty and Franco had been married for several months when he begged me to return to him.

Then came Memorial Day weekend, Saturday, May 29, 1971, a little more than a month after that fateful conversation.

Memorial Day Weekend, 1971
Costa Mesa, CA

Franco had Triana for the weekend. He told me that he was taking her with Kitty and her two daughters on a fishing trip. He promised they would return Monday evening, Memorial Day. By Tuesday morning, when they had not returned, I called Triana's school to see if Franco or Kitty had driven her directly to school. The attendance clerk reported Triana absent.

Foolishly, I ran outside, looking wildly up and down the street, expecting Franco and Kitty to drive up at any moment, blurting out apologies and rational explanations for their delay. But no car drove up the street. No Franco, dripping apologies. No Kitty murmuring support. No Triana. I called Franco's apartment, no answer. When I arrived at their apartment, no one answered the door, no Carmen. A neighbor informed me that Carmen had gone to Italy to visit her sister.

The police listened to me, displayed perfunctory sympathy, and wrote down what I said.

Desperate now, I telephoned Franco's employer. I was told he had taken his vacation and would return in two weeks. Did they know where he had gone? Only that he had gone on a fishing trip with his family.

Four long days passed and then a call from a policeman came with the news that Franco's car had been located at Los Angeles International Airport. I accompanied the police to the airport, where we searched Franco's abandoned automobile, but it yielded no clue to his destination or present whereabouts. I wondered if he might have parked it there to throw me off the track. Perhaps he was still in Southern California.

Frantically, I dialed every international airline that flew out of Los Angeles. As far as they were concerned, I was working for the Costa Mesa Police. My first calls yielded nothing. Then, miraculously, I found the airline.

"Yes, we have a record of the people you're inquiring about: a party of five, two adults and three children," an airline clerk told me. "They left LAX on Braniff Flight 921 at 6:35 p.m. on Saturday, May 29."

I held my breath. "Where to?"

"The destination was Argentina, Buenos Aires, ma'am," the clerk went on. "We don't show any further destination on our records." There was a short pause before the man's voice spoke again. "There is one more thing, ma'am. The man paid for the tickets with a check that bounced. He owes us more than fourteen hundred dollars. If you know where he is, we'd like to talk to him ourselves, and collect the money."

"How could you let him board the plane without a passport for one of the children?" I asked angrily. "The mother has her passport in a safe deposit box just to prevent him from doing just such a thing."

"Well, ma'am, he couldn't get her on the plane without a passport. I don't know what to tell to you."

As I hung up, I realized that my worst fears had come true. Franco clearly did not intend to ever return to the U.S. As an airline employee, he would never have jeopardized his job by passing a bad check to another airline. That meant only one thing: He was burning his bridges behind him. Kitty had probably insisted that they take her two girls, who had been living with their father. They had escaped to a foreign land and they had taken Triana with them.

It was too terrifying for me to imagine that Franco had repeated this act. He had sworn on his mother, the one person who had loved and stood by him no matter what he did. The one person who had devoted her life to his needs and wants. Did she mean nothing to him?

Once again, Franco had stolen my beautiful Triana. What a naïve, trusting fool I had been to believe in him again. Tears overwhelmed me. My knees grew so weak that I collapsed in bitter, angry sobs. How could he do this to me, to Triana?

The authorities abandoned me. The interest and the urgency they would have felt if a stranger, instead, had kidnapped Triana, did not materialize. After all, they kept repeating, Franco was the girl's real father. Did I have reason to believe he would harm her? When I said no, they told me flatly there was simply nothing that they could do. He was most likely out of the country. It was merely a case of child stealing and since he probably was outside of the United States they could do nothing, their hands were tied.

For days, I succumbed to hysteria. I sat on her empty bed, fondled her favorite doll, touched her clothes, and inhaled her familiar scent. For the second time, I lived days and nights not knowing where she was, whether she was safe, whether she cried all the time, as I did, whether there was anyone to brush her long, brown hair with tender care as I had every night.

Then slowly, as the initial shock began to wear off, the same determination that had developed when Franco took Triana the first time came over me. This time it grew stronger and more intense. First, I felt anger: Franco had hurt me, yes, but if he thought he has outsmarted me, I said to myself, he doesn't know me. I would find my child and bring her home. Then I was consumed by a mother's rage: I would find Triana if it took the rest of my life. Nothing would stand in my way--not Franco's wiles, not official indifference, not poverty or loneliness or guilt. Nothing! I stood in her room on a moonless midnight and I took a solemn vow to get my child back.

From my steadier frame of mind, a plan evolved. I had to find out as much about Franco's life as I could. He, Kitty and Carmen had lived so close to my apartment that it surprised me how little I knew about their daily lives. I had rarely been to their house--only to deliver Triana or pick her up from a visit.

I decided to break into Franco's apartment and collect all the information I could find. Stan refused to help me. He stated adamantly that the police should handle everything. Even though he did not agree with what Franco had done, he believed that breaking the law by unlawfully entering Franco's apartment would prevent the police from helping me retrieve Triana. I realized that my actions were against the law, but my motives outweighed any thoughts of punishment. Who was going to complain? Certainly not Franco. The police had washed their hands of the case, and the FBI had just listened politely. I had no one to help me--I would have to do whatever it took to find my child. I was on my own.

My friend Kathy agreed to accompany me to Franco's apartment. Our hearts pounded so loudly we were certain we'd wake the neighbors. We found an unlocked window, entered, and searched for clues to Franco's whereabouts. They seemed to be disappointingly few: a letter from Kitty's sister, postmarked Stanford, Montana and another from her grandmother in Venice, California. There were also a few letters from Lina, Carmen's sister in Rome. We left as quickly as we could, our nerves ready to explode with fear, but we were determined to return the following night. The next night we were more thorough and picked up Franco's mail and any and all scraps of paper that might be of help. Among the interesting clues to his state of mind were Franco's bank statements. Meticulously, I read every line and scrutinized every item. The number of bad check notices from his bank revealed a spending spree. Had he intended to take the goods and sell them, I wondered, or had he already pawned the merchandise for cash? Kathy and I made one last trip to Franco's abandoned apartment, frantic to find anything we might have overlooked. This time we piled everything into a large paper bag, reasoning that it would be easier and safer to sift through the papers later at home. Nothing escaped our notice this time, especially the old telephone bills. Long distance calls could be traced and they might shed some light on Franco's plans. When we finished our search, we bolted the door from the inside, climbed out the window and taped a handwritten notice to the front door that asked anyone seeing Franco or having any knowledge of him to contact me.

One of the letters in his mail was from the dealer who sold Franco the car. I telephoned the company to let them know where the car was. The man told me they had been planning to repossess it, and thanked me for telling him where it could be found.

One of the numbers gleaned from the phone bill was that of Kitty's ex-husband. I called him, but other than having both lost our children to Franco, he and I had nothing in common. He seemed to have no feeling of loss or desperation. His children had simply gone with their mother, and he believed they were safe. Of course, he would like to have them back, he said. If I found out anything, he wanted me to please let him know. Other than that, to him the case was closed. The other numbers on the phone bill gave no immediate clues.

Three weeks after that fatal weekend, a letter arrived. My fingers trembled as I tore open the envelope postmarked Sao Paulo, Brazil. There was a letter from Franco, saying they would return to the U.S. at the end of the summer but only if I dropped any charges I had filed against him. He had ways, he assured me, of finding out what I was doing. Also enclosed was a letter from Triana. So few words, twenty-two in all, but they were the most beautiful and most painful words I had ever read because they were scrawled in the childish handwriting of my missing daughter.

Dear Mom,

Here it is very nice and warm. I like to stay with Micio (Kitty), Dadito and my sisters. Love, Triana

As I read it, the tears, no matter how hard I fought to stifle them, flowed uncontrollably. I knew the little note had undoubtedly been dictated, but the printing was unmistakably Triana's. Was it true that Triana was in Brazil? Or was Franco just trying to confuse me? Whatever the answer, those words were the first solid evidence of my daughter's possible location that I possessed.

Carefully, I taped the note to my mirror. It was the first thing I saw every morning and the last thing I read every night. As I read the note, I repeated to myself, "I survived his first kidnapping and recovered my child. I survived the horrendous abuse of my childhood and have become stronger. I will survive Franco's torturous stealing of our child and I will get her back. I will have the strength and fortitude to pull through the days, months and years that lie ahead."

CHAPTER SIX

1937 to 1964
California, Oklahoma, Oregon

For their entire marriage, my parents, Oscar and Bernice White, engaged in one long, never ending battle. They battled each other about their constant flirting with others, about money, and over my mother's constant dissatisfaction with where they lived; she was always looking for something different in a house. With each move, the boxes were barely unpacked before Mom began to complain about the new location.

As with my mother, my father had many faults, none of which I ever recognized. Dad had natural musical talent and played several string instruments by ear. He had a wonderful sense of humor and a loving smile. I loved him dearly.

I was the second of four girls born into this dirt-poor family. Oscar with his third grade education barely made enough money to put food on the table and clothing on his family. Our staple meal was beans and potatoes, with very little meat.

Oscar had desperately wanted a son, but there were only girls: Betty, the oldest, Shirley, Carol and myself in the middle. My father's greatest disappointment was when he found out that my mother had induced an abortion during one of their most trying periods. He never forgave her when she told him that the aborted child had been a boy.

I was a "daddy's girl" and my preference for my father filled my mother with anger frustration, and resentment. She turned her wrath on my uncomprehending mind and body. Once after a night of vicious fighting between the two, I wanted to have breakfast with dad; my mother pushed me down a flight of stairs trying to force me back to bed. The more she treated me harshly and punished me, the more I turned to my father for the love I craved, and the more my mother's anger grew.

Our mother's father sometimes lived with us. Our parents would occasionally have him sit with us when they went out. When I was five, an uglier force invaded my life. I felt bewilderment as his enormous hands lifted my little body to the small table. Tears flooded my eyes as I begged with him to stop. My pleas fell on deaf ears; my grandfather paid no attention to my cries that he was hurting me. The piercing pain as he penetrated my tiny body was an agony that would remain with me all my life. I wasn't the only victim.

"Shortly before our parents separated I tried to tell our mother of the molestation. "You're a hateful little girl with a terrible imagination," my mother shrieked when I told her that our grandfather had sexually molested me. "But Mom, it's true, he hurt all of us that way. Just ask Betty and Shirley, you'll see!"

"You don't know what you're talking about! I don't believe you for a moment! My dad would not do such a thing to my children, you've twisted your sisters' minds along with your own; you're a little liar! If I ever find out that you told Oscar, you'll regret your lies, believe me." So, afraid of our mother's anger, we never spoke of the abuse to our dad.

By the time I was six, my mother and I were enemies.

I was five-and-a-half-years-old when the inevitable divorce between my parents happened. The years of constant fighting, constant moving and constant infidelity had left the entire family emotionally drained. I was deeply affected by my dad's departure. My father had always shown me the kind and loving side of his nature, a stark contrast to my mother.

After dad moved out, our mother relied more and more on her father, no matter how much Betty, Shirley or I complained about his sexual abuse of us, our mother continued sending us to visit our granddad or let him care for us when she went out. Initially, as a baby, only Carol escaped our grandfather. Abandoned by our mother, we did all we could to avoid Grandfather Van Dyke as our babysitter. We protested wildly when we were told to visit the deranged old man. There were times when we had no choice.

When we did have a choice, we refused to go without one another and tried to avoid being separated or left alone with him. When we were together he tried to isolate one of us by sending the rest off to the store for ice cream, we understood what that meant. We learned early the importance of sticking together around our grandfather. One day, as he tried to pull me onto his lap again, drawing from defiance and inner forcefulness I didn't know I had, I stood my ground. I was five years old when he first raped me. I was close to seven before I was emotionally strong enough to stand up to him.

"I won't let you hurt me again," I said. He grumbled and cursed, but left me alone, to my surprise. Sad to say, my sisters Betty and Shirley, and later Carol, as well, remained his prey.

Dad's exodus did little to abate my mother's harsh feelings for me, and she continued to abuse me both physically and mentally. The harsher she treated me the more I clung to the moments of love shown to me by my father.

Once, after I squirmed in church to keep from wetting my pants, Mother dragged me home, threw me across a bed, and beat me into unconsciousness. Only my older sister's intervention rescued me from her insane rage.

The love and yearning for my father increased with each abuse. This devotion and need for my father's love would influence my decisions in years to come, when better judgments should have prevailed regarding my own daughter.

Within months of Dad's leaving, Mother found a job as a nurses' aide. Betty, Shirley, and I were shuffled to an endless succession of temporary homes with relatives, friends and occasionally mere acquaintances. Only Carol, the youngest and Mother's favorite, escaped this process of being farmed out. Granddad Van Dyke became her babysitter and she became his victim. Mother made very little money and our wandering, irresponsible father provided little or no support. One of our foster parents, a friend of my mother's who had once made her living as a prostitute and madam, constantly urged our mother to let her adopt Betty and me. Fortunately, the offer was refused.

By the time, I was seven and a half, and Shirley close to being six, our mother was living with her new boyfriend, Harry, in a small trailer that he used to follow the crops. Harry had a very strong dislike for children, this included Shirley and myself. Since Harry and Mother were constantly on the move, schooling for us was too bothersome and we were always in hiding from the truant officer. Betty was living with Lola, another of Mother's friends. Harry gave our mother an ultimatum: it was he or Shirley and I. Harry would tolerate Carol for the time being. Mother put Shirley and me on a train, and asked a stranger who was traveling part way in our direction if she would keep an eye on us. Frightened, we traveled over 1600 miles to Ada, Oklahoma, to Dad's mother.

Eventually, Dad remarried a woman with two children of her own. Dad, fetched Shirley and me from Oklahoma, and we moved to Ashland, Oregon. Jewell, Dad's new wife, was like a breath of fresh air. She was completely unlike my mother. Instead of living with a wild-tempered, constantly nagging, self-centered and compassionless woman, I found myself in the arms of a simple, unselfish, energetic friend. I never heard her complain about her responsibilities and the burdens of being a mother or a homemaker. Life was hard materially, but Jewell gave me the love and understanding I had never received from my own mother.

This was the happiest time in my childhood. I was free to experience the fun of just being a child. For the first time in my life, fear was no longer a daily companion, and I was able to experience the innocence of childhood. I felt a sense of adventure, security and self-respect. I was finally aware that love between a parent and a child was not unnatural.

Jewell, in her kind way, helped me to understand love. And as I entered puberty and started to develop, Jewell gently explained to me what was happening to my body. I vowed that in the future my own children would never know the trauma of the desperately unhappy childhood I had experienced.

After three years in Oregon, Dad moved us to Winters, California where he had a job in a logging mill in the mountains near town. But soon, my handsome father took up with the landlady and disappeared with her and her four-year-old daughter, deserting his family once again. As Jewell cried, so did I. I was once again devastated by my dad's departure. I knew only the pain that tugged at my heart. I was too young and self-absorbed to understand Jewell's own pain and dilemma.

Jewell was left to fend for herself, with only twenty dollars to her name, four children, and an unborn son fighting for life in her womb. Jewell's brother rescued our fatherless, penniless band and moved us to Napa, California, where we shared a tiny one-bedroom apartment with him, his wife and their two children. Jewell worked until the birth of Freddie, my new half brother. With no income and one very crowded apartment, Jewell contacted our mother. Shirley and I had no choice but to return to her.

Obedient, but miserable, we rejoined our mother and our sisters in Stockton, California. Mother had remarried, and our stepfather, Art, managed a sugar beet farm on the islands outside of town. Art was a good man and a very hard worker. Life was surprisingly good, for the short time we were on the farm. My sisters and I were all together for the first time in six years. Mother seemed to be preoccupied and was away from the house most of the time. We four girls found all sorts of ways to get reacquainted and entertain ourselves.

Art's job ended two years later and we moved into town and our lives changed for the worse. Art attempted to make a life for us, but my mother's domination exploited his natural weakness. Her temper flared constantly at the slightest provocation.

My sisters and I roamed the neighborhood, trying to stay away from the house as much as possible. We came home when our mother was away or it was getting dark. We visited friends, and played up and down the levies.

At fifteen, Betty married her boyfriend. At sixteen, still a child herself, she gave birth to her first daughter, Diana. I was happy to see my sister escape, but even at fourteen, I recognized that the life Betty had chosen could not be my salvation. Jewell had planted a seed that grew in my mind; we each had a choice. I could be the master of my future, no matter who held the strings, currently. I grew even more determined that my life would not repeat my parents' painful, loveless existence. I would make things different. I would never inflict the ugliness upon my own children that had been my fate.

My mother once again discovered God. Her church became her refuge from her guilt for not being a better mother. She forced the church on us with a vengeance. If we did not attend, our life was hell. I constantly rebelled. I could see absolutely no connection between what I believed to be God and my mother's constant rage. In my opinion, if God did exist, he certainly was not in the same room with my mother. No matter how violent she grew, I stood my ground and refused to attend her church with the rest of the family. The war that had existed between mother and toddler became a war between a mother and a rebellious teenager.

One Sunday, after a painful beating from my mother, I was sufficiently desperate to approach my detestable grandfather. I had avoided my grandfather who had recently moved to a shack behind where we lived. I asked him to take me to the police station. I would rather be in jail than live one minute longer in that house. When I refused to return to my mother's house, the police were at a loss to know what to do with me.

Finally, I was placed in a juvenile facility designed for seriously delinquent children. The first thing the authorities insisted upon was a thorough examination. I was terrified that the nurse would discover that I was no longer a virgin. If my mother hadn't believed me, why would these strangers believe the circumstances under which I had lost my virginity? Even though I had not yet begun my menstrual periods, I lied and told the nurse my period had just begun and I avoided the examination.

Even though I was placed in a section that housed children who were temporarily homeless or the subjects of custody battles, we all were detained behind locked doors in cells. I comforted myself that at least my mother couldn't get to me through those bars. When we were permitted to go out into the play yard we could see and hear the imprisoned delinquents who were separated from our section by strong, double fencing with some kind of sharp wire at the top. As I watched them, I vowed never to get into serious trouble. Nothing could be worse than to live confined in such a facility for no telling how long. I wondered what kind of life they had had and what they had done to be incarcerated.

I spent the longest and loneliest weeks of my life in that facility. In the coldness of the locked cell, I kept telling myself that at least I was safe from my mother.

A few months after Shirley and I left Napa, my dad, returned to Jewell and moved the family to North Bend, Oregon. I prayed that he would send me the money to join them. When I was called to the warden's office and told that my father had sent my bus fare, I wept with joy.

As soon as I began high school in North Bend, I found a position as a live-in babysitter and housekeeper for a local couple. It was a bittersweet moment when I realized that I no longer had to depend upon anyone but myself.

From that time on, I was on my own. I felt that I had full control of my life. Control of my dreams and of my future.

The years passed quickly. About to graduate from high school, I was advised by my guidance councilor to consider the offer of a scholarship to a beauty school in Coos Bay; I accepted. It would provide me with a way to support myself in a short period. When I completed my training, I was accepted for a full-time position in a beauty salon in Beaverton, Oregon, a suburb of Portland. The move was a lonely experience for me. I could no longer see my friends who had become my support group and surrogate family.

In Beaverton, I rented a makeshift apartment that had been created by sectioning off a corner of a basement. I had lived in much worse and this would have to do until I could save enough money to get a decent apartment.

I set about adjusting to the complexities of total independence. I made friends easily and proved to be popular with my co-workers.

Still, fear held me back from the kind of relationships many of my women friends were making with men. I wondered if I would ever fully recover from the scars of my grandfather's violation.

I avoided any relationship that might lead too far. I was frightened to take steps in the direction of intimacy. Consequently, the men I dated were the ones you could usually trust. If they tried to push a little too far, our relationship ended.

Until Franco.

CHAPTER SEVEN

June 3, 1971
En route to Salta, Argentina

The snow-capped peaks of South America, some of them the tallest in the world, rise above broad plains, looming over tropical jungles and the majestic southeastern valleys below. It is said that nowhere on this continent does contrast dazzle and shock the observer more than in Argentina. Her modern cities rival any of the world's leading metropolitan centers, yet her dirt-caked villages remain as they were before the Spanish conquistadores. This land of paradoxes has endured many hardships and known many leaders through *coup d'etat*, war and death.

Early June marks the beginning of the crackling, cold winter in Argentina. It's a winter that sucks everything desert-dry before freezing it into a glassy tapestry.

On this bitter June night, five travelers sat shivering on the wooden benches that served as coach fare accommodation on a train of Butch Cassidy vintage. The train puffed and strained to reach thirty miles per hour top speed through the desolate wasteland toward northwestern Argentina.

Seven-year-old Triana pulled the blanket tightly around herself as she lay on the hard, jolting bench. She tilted her head with curiosity at the strange people, who spoke quickly in a language she couldn't understand. Her father, who she had often heard talking in his native tongue with his mother was now speaking in a different language that she had sometimes heard in her preschool in California.

When they boarded the airplane in California, her dad had told her they were going fishing. It had been several days now and she wondered when that would happen. Three days earlier, at a hotel in the city where they had landed, she and Kitty's two daughters, Amber, who was seven, and Emily, ten, had cried when her dad told them that they could take only one small toy apiece. Most of their clothes and the rest of their treasures and belongings would have to be left behind. This included two large trunks full of household items.

All that seemed like an eternity ago, but for the moment, Triana was peaceful. Every now and then, her mind drifted back to the scene at the Buenos Aires airport. Why had her father yelled at her and given her such a hard spanking for losing her passport? She had never even seen a passport nor did she know what one was, all she knew was that her dad had made such a fuss at the airport. The uniformed men questioned him about the passport and the large trunks he had brought on such a short fishing trip. Her dad had gritted his teeth during the delay of having to check with the American government. The family was ordered to stay in a hotel until Franco's story could be verified.

The group had arrived early Sunday morning and it would be Tuesday before the authorities could finish their investigation and give them permission to leave. Franco had been told not to leave the city until his story and the existence of the passport could be confirmed. The hotel manager was to keep the other passports until he heard from the authorities that it was all right to release them. Monday was Memorial Day, a holiday in the United States. Franco knew he needed to move quickly. He made an instant decision to leave Buenos Aires. Certainly, he had no intention of telling Triana and the authorities the truth, which was that her passport was in the possession of her mother, from whom he had kidnapped Triana for a second time.

The next morning, carrying the fishing poles to authenticate his story, Franco left the hotel with Triana, Kitty, Emily and Amber. He announced to the hotel manager that they were going fishing and he left most of their belongings behind to strengthen the story.

Franco and Kitty hurried the children to the train station. Franco's command of the language and his Latin features helped them to easily blend with the rest of the passengers. If a question had arisen about Kitty's blonde-haired daughters, Franco planned to say that he was a widower who had recently married the lady with the two beautiful *niñas*. Triana, with her olive complexion, looked sufficiently native to arouse no curiosity. Franco had been playing a little game with her to keep her quiet when other people were within earshot. No one must realize that Triana did not speak Spanish.

Franco and his "troupe" rode the train for several days. Fatigue and hunger plagued the fugitives.

Kitty's body ached from hours of sleeping in a sitting position and she longed for her bed in Costa Mesa, or any bed for that matter. Looking out the window at the pitch-black night, Kitty thought to herself, *What am I doing here? How did I get myself involved in Franco's determined scheme to take Triana from her mother?* She loved him, but sometimes he was difficult to understand. Kitty remembered three weeks earlier, when Franco had returned from a trip to the northeast with some of his Italian friends and he told her he had witnessed a mob hit. He also said he accepted a large sum of money to perform a hit that he couldn't go through with. Their departure from Los Angeles was necessary to save his life. Kitty had seen the money but hadn't wanted to accept his explanation and now the money seemed to have vanished. Franco hadn't given her an explanation as to where it went; instead, he became angry and stormed out of the house.

Kitty's mind wandered back to the first day of the trip, when Franco had taken their fully packed trunks to the airport early in the morning; to ensure that the trunks were in Argentina by the time they arrived. But when they arrived at the Los Angeles airport with their suitcases and flight bags, their difficulties began immediately. Franco discovered he had left the tickets at their apartment. His rage was maniacal, but he made it to the apartment and back in time to execute the next deception; boarding the airplane without Triana's passport.

They waited for the final boarding call then rushed to the ticket counter at the last minute. The agent hurried them onto to the plane without thoroughly checking the passports. The plan had worked.

Franco's inventiveness fascinated and overwhelmed Kitty. *Maybe I should have protested.* But then she remembered how often she tried to avoid one of Franco's raging temper tantrums.

She glanced over at her two sleeping daughters, Amber and Emily. They were content and they were with her, and that always seem to make them happy. Kitty looked over at Triana sleeping next to Franco. She wondered what the child would say when she found out she was never going home. No doubt, Franco would invent some convincing tale.

June 2, 1971
Costa Mesa, California

As I sat at my small kitchen table, I visualized Carmen waiting apprehensively for the overseas operator to put through the person-to-person call from the States. She would frown and clutch her rosary. She was visiting her sister in Rome. Franco had sent her back to Italy two months ago, after he had unsuccessfully asked me to put our marriage back together. Carmen had always longed for her beloved country, her friends and her sister.

"Why am I worried?" she was probably muttering to herself now. "Don't borrow trouble. It could be good news. After all, if something had happened to Franco or Triana, Kitty would have called," she would say to herself.

There was some static on the line before the operator said, "Go ahead, please."

"Nona, Nona, are you there?"

Carmen immediately recognized my tearful voice. "Yes, Rosalie, I'm here," she answered.

She could not successfully hide the alarm she felt. I knew from her tone of voice that she resented any involvement in a dispute between me and her son.

"Nona, is Franco there in Italy with you? Do you know where he

77

is? He said he was going on a fishing trip with Triana, Kitty and her two girls. I found out he flew to South America with everyone."

Carmen sighed. "He most likely will return in a few days, and all will be well, Rosalie. Men do strange things sometimes, that, as women, we just don't understand." She said this, I believe, more to herself than to me. "We shouldn't try, Rosalie, we shouldn't try. It's always the same."

"But, Nona, it's not the same. He's done it again; he's taken my baby and vanished. I don't know what to do!"

"My beloved Vittorio," Nona rattled on. "It was the same with him. He had weaknesses. He gambled and had an eye for other women. I knew that these other females meant nothing to him; men are just made differently from women. And, eventually, Vittorio would tire of the affairs and be my beloved Vittorio once again. It is a woman's place to wait for her husband and stand beside him, no matter what. If you had realized that, my dear," Carmen said, "you would have Franco at your side instead of his taking Triana. It's not his fault he loves his daughter too much to take a trip and leave her behind."

"Nona, how can you say these things? How can you justify what Franco has done, not only to me, but also to Triana? I am her mother. She needs me, Carmen, as much as I need her!"

As Carmen listened to me weeping over the phone I was sure she remembered all these things. But she insisted that, despite his faults, Franco had been a good boy and now he was a good man.

"Please, Nona," I was crying, "you're a mother. You must know what I'm going through. Please, please tell me where they are."

"My dear, of course, I understand your feelings," the older woman said with sincerity. "But I do not know. You must believe me. My son has told me nothing of his plans. He has not contacted me. This is the first I am hearing of this. I'm sure there is some mistake. He will bring Triana back to you soon." She paused. "Rosalie, please," she said softly.

"All right, Nona." My voice trembled. It was impossible to tell if she was telling the truth. If there was one thing the two of us shared, it was an unshakable devotion to our children.

"Nona," I pleaded, "I need you to help me find my child. If you hear from Franco, will you let me know? Please, will you do that?"

Carmen hesitated. "Yes," she finally agreed. "But, Rosalie, you must understand, I sympathize with your grief, but Franco is my son."

Carmen hung up. Her son would call her. That I knew. He would always return to Mama when he needed help. When that happened, Carmen would be confronted with a difficult decision in her troubled life. Carmen knew as well as I what that decision would be. I was sure once she had hung up the phone, that she dropped to her knees, rosary beads in her hands, to begin her routine talk with God about the burdens that had been heaped upon her.

June 4, 1971
Salta, Argentina

Salta, Argentina was a medium-sized northwestern city established in the 17th century as a military outpost; it now supported the majority of its 370,000 populace through agricultural products, minerals and livestock. Various species of tropical plants adorned the cobblestone and dirt streets lined with white adobe shops, hotels and houses. The town was large enough to hide in and possibly find work.

When the train pulled into the city, Franco herded his fugitives toward a little park in the center of the city. Kitty and the girls welcomed his decision. The three days on the train had been exhausting, and it was good to be on solid ground again. They all sat down on a bench.

"Wow! You mean we don't have to go back to the Wicked Witch of the West?" Emily cried. She was referring to her stepmother, with whom she and Amber had been living.

Kitty shook her head. She knew that her daughters disliked their new stepmother.

Emily grabbed her little sister's hands and spun her around in a circle. "Whoopee!" the child cried. Amber giggled and nodded in agreement.

Abruptly, Franco jumped up and shouted, "Emily, you shut your mouth! Don't talk that way about your stepmother. You're stupid and you don't know anything."

The little girl froze, but glared defiantly at Franco. "We don't like her. She's not a nice person."

Franco whirled. "Yeah? Well, you do what you're told or else!" he snarled. "Kitty, why don't you teach that brat some manners? I don't know why I let you talk me into bringing them."

Accustomed to his outbursts, Kitty did not respond. "Girls," she said to her daughters, "see that fountain over there? Go over there and play, but I want you back in ten minutes. Understand?" Emily took Amber's hand, and the two marched defiantly off.

Obviously upset, Franco paced about. He knew the power of his charm, and expected that those he loved would follow his lead. His charismatic looks and manner and his total self-confidence had made him believe in his own invincibility. He felt he was equal to any challenge before him.

At the far end of the bench, little Triana was sobbing. For the first time she realized that she would never see her mother again.

Franco sat down next to his daughter and took her in his arms. "Triana, my *Penguina*." Franco called her softly by one of the affectionate names he had used from the time she was a baby. She was his little *penguin*. "There's nothing to cry about," he consoled. "I want you to be happy. We're all going to be happy here together. Please don't do this to me, *bambina*," he cajoled. "If you don't stop crying, you will ruin the trip for everyone."

The confused little girl could no longer control her grief and she broke into loud wailing. Instantly her father's concern turned to self-righteous anger. "Now see what you've done! You're upsetting me!" he shouted.

Triana did not understand what she had done to upset her father so. What she did know was that she felt strangely guilty, as though everyone's quarreling and problems were somehow her fault.

"Triana," Franco went on, "look, baby, I had to leave, or some bad guys would have harmed me and probably you, too."

"Why were those guys going to hurt you, Daddy?" Triana asked.

"Well, they wanted me to kill someone and I just couldn't do such a bad thing to this man." Franco hung his head down. "It's very important we never let anyone know where we are, the bad men could find out through anyone we contact."

Her mother's face rose in Triana's memory. "But Mommy, what about Mommy?" she implored.

Franco's eyes narrowed, but he managed to retain the semblance of sincerity, "You have to trust me." He answered her gently. "There are very good reasons for not contacting her, there are things about your mother that you have no way of knowing. But I know, and I'm doing this for you too. Isn't that right Kitty?" he added.

An incredulous Kitty stared at Franco, but his stern glare brought her up sharply. She managed a half-hearted approval. "Your dad loves you, Triana. You know that, don't you?"

"See?" Franco said heartily. "I'll explain it all to you later." He beckoned Kitty to him and put his other arm around her. "We're all going to be happy here. We're a family."

As far as Franco was concerned, the matter was settled. Triana would forget her mother. Franco had willed it and so it would be.

June 6, 1971
Costa Mesa, California

A tall thin man, in his mid forties, stood in the middle of the living room in my apartment. He and his wife had tracked Franco to my door. The man shook his head in disgust.

"I guess we've been conned, "Mr. Heiser muttered. "Our Italian vacation is off."

"He seemed like such a nice young man," Mrs. Heiser added. "My husband met his uncle who owned the charter airline that we were to fly to Italy on. Do you know what's happened to our tickets? Or how we can contact the uncle?"

Unfortunately, they were demanding an explanation that I couldn't give them.

I explained as gently as possible that Franco's only uncle died last year and when he was alive, he was never involved in the airline business. "I can't imagine who could have posed as his uncle. One of his Italian friends must have helped Franco in his scheme."

I felt sorry for the Heisers. Franco had been typically convincing. He had woven a clever story that his "uncle" was in a position to give Franco's friends tremendous discounts on overseas flights. Because the man had met Franco through the air cargo services where they both worked, he never suspected that Franco might deceive him. He was delighted with Franco's offer and did not hesitate to give him a check for four hundred and fifty dollars, made out to Franco personally. Franco had convinced them that as a relative only he was allowed to buy the discount tickets. He promised to deliver the tickets as soon as he received them. The names could be changed before departure. It all sounded plausible to the trusting couple.

When Franco failed to contact them, and when there was no answer to repeated phone calls, the couple decided to drive out to Costa Mesa to investigate. They found my note pinned on Franco's door.

"I'm sorry, but I think that you are just another in a long line of people this man has taken advantage of," Stan offered. He had insisted on being with me whenever I saw any victims of Franco's scams. He wanted to be sure people did not think I had been involved in any of Franco's fraudulence.

"No kidding!" the man exploded. "It's still hard for me to believe that all the things he told me were lies. I guess I am too gullible," he added sourly.

"Please believe me. He is capable of anything. He has fled to South America with my daughter as well as your money," I sighed. "They left two weeks ago. Would you consider filing charges against him? It may help in bringing him to justice and recovering my child, it might help us both."

"Sure, sure," the man responded dejectedly.

But the poor fellow was so embarrassed at being swindled out of several hundred hard-earned dollars that he never followed through with any legal action.

I continued to collect Franco's mail. Bad checks and unpaid

bills were perpetual. Every time I received a past due statement or a returned check notice, I called the creditor and notified them of Franco's departure. Talking to others who had been victimized by Franco made me feel less alone. I followed up every lead. The search kept me busy and my mind on other things. I tried not to think of my loss.

White Front Department store's collector was stern. "We're going to file a lawsuit, you know."

"Believe me, I hope you do. The bigger the case, the more help I will receive from the authorities. Can you tell me what he bought at your store? It might be important in locating him."

"Yeah, well, there was a television set, clothing, fishing equipment, and other items that came to over six hundred dollars."

"I wish I could give you more encouragement, but I can't. He's long gone, and it may be for good."

"You can't encourage me, huh," the collector said sarcastically, implying that I knew more than I was willing to tell him. I accepted his cynicism as an occupational trait. Bill collectors are not supposed to be trusting.

I had received some very strange calls from men who sounded Italian, but would not give their name or tell me why they were looking for Franco. They stated that they were friends of his and that it was important for them to contact him. His secret life was finally beginning to surface. I hoped that his bad checks, fraudulent activities, and unpaid debts might provoke some creditors to go beyond legal formalities in order to collect what was due them. I suspected that there might be people willing to take the law into their own hands, and if that were true, I realized why Franco had felt it imperative to leave the country. He had put himself in a position of danger and needed to run. Stealing Triana served a double purpose; he could punish me for rejecting him again and regain the control that had been denied him in Paris five years earlier, and, at the same time avoid some very questionable friends.

CHAPTER EIGHT

June 4, 1971
Salta, Argentina

Franco became wary of Salta's safety as a hideout and decided to move. Kitty objected, as she was relieved to be off the terrible train and yearned for a place to find her bearings. Desperately she wanted her life to return to some form of normality. But, as usual, Franco won. He snuck them out of the hotel without paying and packed them all aboard another cattle car. The strange party spent three more miserable days traveling on buses, boats and dusty suffocating trains. As they arrived at each new town, Franco always found something that displeased him. On they would go. Finally, exhausted and out of money, they returned to Salta.

Like most of Argentina, Salta was composed of equal portions of sublime beauty and abject destitution. In one direction, the sight of the magnificent Andes rising from the plains could take one's breath away. But much of life here was lived without the comforts that people in the larger cities took for granted. Most, but not all, had electricity, running water, adequate food and decent shelter. However, some of the houses were mere shacks. The residents accepted the reality of their lives and went about the business of living, working and procreating.

A melting pot of nationalities, Salta's population was composed of native Indians, their mixed-blood progeny, Germans, Arabs and various other immigrants all living side-by-side. Everyday, people ventured from their ethnic enclaves long enough to complete shopping or pressing business. Then, as quickly as possible, they rushed back to the security of their own kind. That was the only rushing that went on in Salta.

The day they returned to Salta, Franco gave Kitty an order: "You take the kids to that park you liked so much. I'll look around and find us a good place to spend the night."

Kitty welcomed the suggestion. The girls needed to run and play in the fresh, clean air, to forget that they were fugitives. Kitty longed to forget. When they had left the States, she had weighed 180 pounds. Now she wondered if she would ever experience the luxury of a full stomach again. The ten days since they left Los Angeles seemed like an eternity.

Kitty sat on a bench, watching the girls roll around on the grass like puppies. Her daughters had always enjoyed Triana when they had been together in Costa Mesa. Kitty understood this was one of the reasons that Franco had agreed to bring Emily and Amber along on his "adventure." Franco, the charmer, had made it sound so appealing, but now Kitty realized how foolish the whole scheme was. Here they were, caught in this outpost of civilization with no money and no place to stay, and, she realized painfully, no place to which they could return.

"Well, what's past is past," she told herself. Amber's shrill voice snapped Kitty back to the present.

"Mommy, look, I picked you a flower!"

Tagging behind, her shoulders stooped, Triana added, "I got you one, too, Kitty." Triana had not been herself since Franco made up the story about Rosalie and told her she was not going home.

"Children must play, right, Mom?" laughed Emily in her best grown-up voice.

It was beginning to get dark. Where was Franco? The old anxieties returned. As she hugged all three of them, Kitty hoped that things would take a turn for the better.

Not long after, Franco strode through the twilight, smiling broadly.

"I found us a place to stay," he announced happily. "Meals and all. What did I tell you? It's going to work out just fine."

The *pensione*, or boardinghouse, was a filthy, roach-infested dump with foul odors that saturated the bare, clay walls. Inside, the cracked and stained partitions of their nine-by-seven-foot room rose only partway to the ceiling, so that they could clearly hear any activity in the adjoining areas. The girls began to inspect everything with interest, but Kitty thought that never in her poorest moments had she been subjected to such squalor. She suspected that the place was a whorehouse.

With characteristic charm, Franco smiled. "Well, we can't expect the Waldorf Astoria in Salta, now can we?"

But Kitty was not consoled. "Franco, do you expect the girls to sleep in this place? The bathroom is four-doors down the hall. What if the kids have to go to the bathroom in the middle of the night? They'll get sick!"

Franco yanked her a few steps into the room before releasing his grip on the arms of the now terrified and speechless woman. He pointed to a small hole in the corner of the crusted floor. "See that?" he snapped. "That's the bathroom. Who cares where the hole goes?"

His harsh treatment and the shock of her surroundings defeated Kitty. She rubbed her throbbing arms and abjectly prepared the hovel for the night. Amber and Emily settled down immediately; however, Triana's continual sobbing disturbed the other occupants.

"Keep that brat quiet," a rough Spanish voice came from the next cubicle.

Before Kitty knew it, Franco and the infuriated adjoining occupant were in a heated quarrel. Before the argument ended, all the residents of the *pensione* were involved.

"Give her a break, for heaven's sake, her mother just died." Franco screamed to the irritated group, in their language.

"Just keep her silent so we can sleep," came a voice several cubicles away.

Franco sat on the bed trying to calm Triana. "Baby, you have to be quiet or they will kick us out of here. Please, you don't want the rest of us to suffer because of you, do you? Now stop crying and go to sleep."

As hard as she tried, Triana couldn't stop crying. She buried her head in the covers to muffle the sound and cried herself to sleep.

Most disturbing to Kitty was the crude sounds of lovemaking in the adjacent rooms that resounded vividly through their own tiny cubicle. Kitty prayed that the children did not comprehend their meaning.

The following day while Franco began to organize a strategy to find some money, Kitty attempted to entertain the children. When the partying and lovemaking in the adjacent rooms resumed, she herded the children outside. "The youngsters need fresh air and exercise, this Godforsaken dump is going to make them sick," she snapped, leaving Franco alone in the gloom and filth.

"Aw, they're not going to get sick," he yelled after them, "and, I don't like you showing your faces around here so much anyway. And have sense enough to bring the girls back in time for dinner."

Rice and more rice, plus strange-looking concoctions of unfamiliar texture were served morning noon and night. Kitty and Franco avoided considering the source of the meat. It was the only menu, however, and promptness at mealtime was required or you didn't eat.

When he thought about Triana, he smiled. She didn't seem to mind the awful food. She would look down at her plate, look up at him, and silently dig in. What a wonderful little kid! She still cried at night for her mother, so it was time to tell her something final. It was time for Triana to stop crying and forget about Rosalie and the past.

At the little park, Kitty leaned back on the bench, stretched her legs, and watched the children play. Small shops and restaurants surrounded the square. Between the noise and Franco's nightly sexual demands she was exhausted, now and then she nodded off. Franco had secured a cot for the girls so the children no longer occupied their bed. Their intercourse was of little pleasure for her, the lack of privacy was a constant distress and she struggled against the abhorrent room and the filth. She relished the few hours alone, away from the foul stench of the boardinghouse, away from Franco and his erratic moods, away from the burdensome reality of that to which she had become party.

Life at the *pensione* was hard work. Every day Kitty scrubbed what few clothes they had in an old laundry tub on the tawdry patio. If they had to live with flies, crawling insects, and dirt, at least their clothes would be clean. Clean was not a word that the other residents of the boardinghouse understood. The bathroom was the vilest of places. She would not allow the girls to use the slimy, rusty, fungus-infested bathtub and so had them sponge-bathe standing up.

She looked up to see four laughing girls and a little boy running toward her. Carrying a scrawny kitten in her arms, Amber was the first to stop giggling long enough to speak. "Mom," she pointed to a dark-haired little girl, "this is Veronica." Amber pronounced the name with a slight accent.

"Well, hello, Veronica. Is that your kitten Amber's holding?"

This brought a new fit of giggles from the girls.

"She doesn't speak English," Triana explained, "but she taught us a word."

"*Gatito*," Amber piped up, "that's the word."

"It's the kitten's name!" Triana chimed in. "*Gata*-something. Gosh, I forgot already!" she said with a giggle.

"It's Spanish. A friend of mine in school in Los Angeles told me that," added Emily.

Triana now held the kitten. She sat in the grass, petting the small furry ball and talking softly to it as it purred its thanks.

Kitty waved a greeting as she saw Franco walking toward them. He did not bother returning the greeting as he walked swiftly toward the group.

"Everybody back to the hotel!" Franco commanded. "It's almost time to eat. Right now!" Triana placed the kitten in her friend's arms and ran over to her father, who scooped her up and hugged her.

"Who are they?" Franco asked about the strange children.

"They live here," Kitty said pleasantly. "The girl's name is Veronica and I didn't catch the boy's name. The girls made friends with them."

Franco began an animated conversation with the little child in Spanish. After a few minutes, she waved and ran off, kitten in her arms, with her little brother close behind.

Franco's smile vanished. "She lives right around here," he said. "I want to meet their parents as soon as I can. We need to make some friends. You never know when they'll come in handy. Right, Kitty?"

Obediently, Kitty nodded her head, wondering what would happen next on this bizarre journey.

That night in the tiny cubicle in the *pensione*, Triana sat quietly on the dirty, sagging bed, staring at her father, wondering what he wanted to talk to her about. Through the walls of the flimsy partition came the discordant sounds of an un-tuned guitar accompanied by raucous voices and boisterous laughter. From the opposite wall came the familiar sounds of lusty sex that Franco and Kitty had become accustomed to. The acrid smell of sweaty bodies drifted into the room. The cacophony even upset Franco.

"Why don't you god-damned people shut up in there?" Franco cursed at them in English.

"They don't speak English," Emily offered guilelessly. "Maybe you should tell them in Spanish."

"Nobody's asking you!" Franco snarled. "Get outside on the patio and don't make any trouble, do you hear me? You, too, Amber."

As the two girls left, Franco turned to Triana, putting his arms around her, determined to continue his conversation. "I know you don't understand how it is to be a dope addict, Penguina. But that's what your mother has become. That's why we can't go back there and why she can't come to us. Remember those pills that she always had in her bedroom and the ones she gave you? Well, that was dope. Oh, it was a terrible, terrible thing, Triana. You can't be around someone like that, even if she is your mother. She is sick, very sick and would make you sick, too. Isn't that right, Kitty?"

Kitty hesitated but Franco glared at her until she spoke. "Triana, honey," Kitty began slowly, "dope addiction, what your father is talking about, is a very bad sickness." She faltered, but Franco glared at her again and she could not take back the lie she had begun.

Triana thought of her mother. She remembered the bottles of pills her mother and she had used daily. "Vitamins," is what her mother had said they were. The vitamins were in the shape of animals that she could chew. How could these things her dad was saying be true? How could she tell her dad she didn't believe her mother would ever try to harm her? She listened to him and tried to understand.

"Will she die?" Triana asked plaintively, tears brimming in her wide innocent eyes. Franco nodded solemnly. "Yes, she may be dead already," he said.

Looking away, Kitty shuddered at the thought of her ex-husband in Los Angeles saying such things to Emily and Amber.

Triana covered her face with her hands. She tried to shut out what her father had just told her.

"If she's still alive, can't I see her before she dies?" she sobbed softly.

"Oh, *Penguina*," Franco fumed, "don't do this to me. You've got to accept what Daddy tells you." He was beginning to cry now himself. "You can't see her. It's impossible. As Kitty told you, she's very, very sick." He held her and they cried together.

Triana wondered if somehow she was to blame for her mother's addiction, whatever that was. Had she somehow caused her mother to take too many pills?

Kitty watched in amazement. She had seen Franco use his acting talent, but he didn't seem to be acting now. If he was indeed acting he was doing a very good job, he actually seemed upset, Kitty thought. *Perhaps he just can't stand to see Triana unhappy.*

On the patio, Emily and Amber sat on the decaying floor. Emily picked angrily at the peeling paint and rotting wood.

"Emily, what's a dope addict?" Amber asked. "Is Triana crying because her mother is a dope addict?"

"That's what Franco says," the older girl answered flatly. She really didn't know what to think. She remembered one weekend that they visited their mother in Costa Mesa and Rosalie had taken all three girls to Lion Country Safari and what a good time they had. Emily could not picture that person as the same one Franco now accused of being an addict. She chipped off a long sliver of wood and crushed it into the floor.

"Let's go back in now. It's probably safe enough."

The next afternoon, Franco, Kitty and the girls crossed the street in the bright South American sunshine, and headed for Veronica's home.

"Now, keep quiet and let me do the talking," Franco advised sternly. "Keep the girls quiet, too."

Kitty nodded, wisely choosing not to point out that he was the only one who spoke Spanish anyway. Franco had been unusually tense all morning, spending his time inspecting his papers. Kitty guessed that they would leave Salta soon. Maybe Veronica's parents could help them. Leaving such decisions to Franco was best.

The little house was clean and comfortable and Veronica's mother made them feel welcome. She served a steaming jug of coffee and Kitty sat quietly while Franco and the couple conversed. Suddenly Franco's face turned ashen. Kitty tried not to betray her alarm. Soon they said polite goodbyes.

"Coco, the guy," Franco explained, "he's on the Salta police force."

"Oh, no, the Buenos Aires cops are probably after us," Kitty moaned.

"Don't get hysterical about the Buenos Aires cops!" Franco snapped. "A lot you know about anything! He invited us back for dinner tonight. We'll just have to be careful. You and the girls, I want you looking your best. Things are going to work out."

That evening they all sat round the heavy wooden table and enjoyed the best meal they had eaten since arriving in Argentina. The beef was tough, but they didn't mind and even the plain rice was tasty. Another couple named Gladys and Tito had been invited. Kitty instantly liked them. After dinner, Franco went off with the two men and when they returned, all three were smiling. The group visited a while longer then left for the *pensione* with Franco carrying Triana who was half-asleep. Emily and Amber walked briskly along in the cold night air, each holding onto Kitty.

"It worked like a charm," Franco reported enthusiastically. "Better than I thought it would. Tito and his wife are going to help us stay here safely. Isn't that great?"

"Of course," Kitty agreed, "but why are they doing it?"

Franco laughed coarsely. "Why? Because they believe in doing good deeds. Besides, here things are different from the States. People are friendlier."

Franco's tale must have been convincing, Kitty thought.

"Tito and Gladys know a widow who lived some thirty miles outside Salta," Franco remarked. "Arrangements are being made for us to stay with her."

In the little Andean village called Qijono, the air was fresh. The streets, although unpaved, were clean and free of litter. Room and board for all five of them was one dollar and fifty cents a day. The widow was poor, but she had managed to buy two servants, a woman in her late sixties and a young lad of nine.

"It is a good life for them," the widow explained to Franco as she introduced the elderly woman and the boy. "I need them and they need me. What could be better for all?"

Kitty smiled wryly when Franco translated. "I thought that the days of slavery were over," she said.

The widow's house was small but mercifully clean. It was a welcome luxury to drift off to sleep without the raucous noise and foul odors of the *pensione*. Out in the yard, the happy shouts of children playing mingled with the farm-animal sounds. The girls were delighted, especially Triana. There were animals everywhere: chickens, roosters, turkeys, pigs, a horse and a llama.

"Daddy, what in the world is that?" Triana exclaimed curiously when she first saw the llama.

"It's a kind of camel," Franco told her.

"But where are his humps?"

"The ones in Argentina don't have any." Franco tousled her hair. She still cried at night and did not seem to be recovering as quickly as he had anticipated. *She would forget, just give her time*, he thought. It had bothered him to watch his seven-year-old daughter, the love of his life, his obsession, his possession, drag herself around sullenly, watching him with large, sad, inconsolable eyes. He disliked lying to her, but it was the best story he could think of.

"Can I play with him, Daddy? He looks very friendly," Triana said as the llama shifted on a hind leg and stared straight ahead impassively.

"I suppose so, *Penguina,* but don't annoy him."

Triana moved closer to the large animal and stroked its side. "Wow! He's woolly!"

"That's how they get sweaters and blankets around here. They cut off the llama's hair and make fabric out of it," Franco told her.

"It doesn't hurt him, does it?"

"No, he doesn't mind," Franco answered. "They also use him to carry stuff around."

"Oh, Daddy! I just remembered. When we were on that bus, I saw out the window some men with a whole bunch of animals that looked just like him," she pointed at her new friend, "and they had big packages tied all around them. Llamas must be very strong."

Bright and early the next morning, Franco woke, exhilarated. "Everybody up!" he commanded. "Triana! Girls! Wait until you hear what we're going to do today! Come on outside."

Across the road from the house was a beautiful mountain. "See, all the way up there?" He pointed skyward. "Well, that's where we're going to be this afternoon when it's warmer, and you know what?"

The children shook their heads in anticipation.

"Do you know what an echo is?"

Triana and Amber looked unsure.

"Well, it'll be a surprise, then."

"I know what an echo is," Emily announced, hoping for some recognition from Franco. "It's…"

Franco interrupted threateningly, "I said it'll be a surprise. Leave it at that."

Late that afternoon Kitty could hear the beautiful echoes of Franco and the girls calling each other's names high up on the mountain.

"Maybe Argentina's not so bad after all," she said aloud. The servant woman didn't understand a word, but she smiled back at Kitty as she deftly kneaded the mounds of bread dough.

Kitty looked over at the earthen oven in anticipation of the freshly baked bread, then in the direction of the mountain where Franco and the girls shouted their echoes. Living in the country was sounding more appealing every minute. *Perhaps we can learn to like our new life and our new home*, she thought. *We will all be happy here, things will be better.*

As the days passed, Kitty noticed that the girls were beginning to pick up some Spanish.

"I know," Franco snapped when she pointed it out. "Who do you think has been seeing to that?"

"You, of course, Franco." The last thing Kitty wanted was an argument.

"Right, and it wouldn't hurt you to learn a few words yourself!"

Franco was hardly a patient teacher, and Kitty decided that she preferred to start listening more closely to the natives.

Suddenly, there was a big commotion from the yard. Franco and Kitty ran outside. The girls were clinging to high branches in a huge tree, all of them screaming and laughing at the same time.

"Help, Daddy," Triana cried, though she was giggling. "Get us out of here!" Holding them at bay was a huge turkey, squawking his angry threats. The servant boy, Jorge, ran toward the bird, wielding a large stick, a huge grin on his face. "Ay, *muchachas, muchachas*," he hollered up to them as he shooed the turkey away.

"*Muchas gracias*," the girls thanked him, dusting themselves off once they were safely on the ground. Kitty and the girls all laughed. For the first time since they had left the States two months ago, the girls were beginning to enjoy themselves.

Three days later Jorge and the girls were chasing baby chickens. As they chased the tiny, squawking birds, the children neared the swiftly flowing river, which they had all been warned to stay away from. Suddenly one chick headed toward the riverbank. Jorge chased the chick as it tumbled into the turbulent water. Running too fast to check his speed, Jorge fell headfirst into the rapidly moving water.

The girls ran to the house, screaming for help, but by the time they returned, there was no sign of the boy. Even though the grownups searched for several days, the boy's body was never recovered.

The loss of their new friend devastated the children. For days they wandered about the farm, each weighing the meaning of death. Franco pointed out that this was merely an example of what can happen when children don't mind their parents. Slowly the farm animals pulled the girls back to the business of living.

After they had been in Qijono for a little over a month, Franco brought a strange man home with him.

"This is Tony," Franco announced. "He's a *paisano*. He's Italian like me, and he's agreed to help us."

The two men talked for hours in Italian as Kitty tended to the children and listened quietly to words she could not understand, words that she knew would affect her life directly.

Two days later, Franco told Kitty to pack his and Triana's things. They were leaving for the town of Santa Rosa immediately.

"You will join us there in a week or so. Meantime, I got some work for you. There's a family right outside Salta that needs a maid. You can work for them. I'll contact you there."

"What about Emily and Amber?" she asked, realizing that Franco had pointedly left them out of his plans.

"You can either take them with you or leave them here, you figure it out."

The village of Colonia Santa Rosa lies deep in the jungle near the Bolivian border, where the air hangs heavy with moisture and lush green trees and vines cover the hills. Ten days after Franco and Triana departed from Qijono, Gladys and Tito sent an old automobile and driver to take Kitty and her daughters the fifty-odd miles to their new home in Santa Rosa. Kitty kept her face near the rolled-down window of the stuffy old car as it made its way slowly along the narrow main street of the town. It had been a long, tiring trip on winding dirt roads. Kitty wanted two things: a cold drink and a night's sleep. Suddenly, she spotted a familiar little figure walking along the street.

"Girls! Look! There's Triana!" she cried. "Triana! Triana!" Emily and Amber began to shout and wave. When Triana saw them, she burst into tears, and ran at top speed to the car, climbing in through the window as quickly as she could to get to her friends. "Oh, I missed you so much!" she exclaimed, trying to dry her tears. "Wait till you see where we live. It's terrific!"

"Let's see," Kitty smiled, "that must mean lots of animals."

"How did you know?" Triana asked, looking surprised. "And not only that, but there's music and dancing and lots of nice people."

"Sounds like a country club," Kitty said dubiously as she glanced down the road to a large white house.

"Your dad never lets you out of his sight. Where is he?" Kitty asked. "He isn't here, right now. He is returning tonight. A neighbor is watching me," Triana answered.

Their new home was on a large farm called a *fica*. The place reminded Kitty of pictures she had seen of old Southern plantations. Their quarters consisted of two rooms about the size of large closets. Their meals were prepared over an outside fire, a source of delight to Triana and the girls. To them, each new experience was an adventure. Kitty knew this, and tried to hide her own depression by sharing the girls' enthusiasm. She had given up so much. Each day her thoughts turned more and more toward home and civilization. Los Angeles seemed a million miles and years away, yet they had been in this new, unreal world less than three months.

In humid climates, tempers can run short, and Franco's was no exception. Here on the *fica,* the work from sunup to sundown was physically exhausting. Franco was continually irritable. Everyone, even his own dogs, hated the man he worked for. The "Boss" carried a gun on his hip and a whip in his hand for the dogs that often snarled at him as if they wanted to attack.

"Those dogs are not bad," Triana defended them. "They play with us and follow us around everywhere we go. The mother dog even gives me big kisses."

By the time they had lived on the *fica* a little over a month, the girls had become completely acclimated. With characteristic trust and charm, the children had even tamed the boss's dogs. Triana asked for her mother less frequently. Her father had forbidden her to talk about home. When he was present, there were no yesterdays, only today, and the hazy possibilities of tomorrow. There was no Rosalie, no mother, no home, no past.

A month later they were given new quarters in "La Salle," a huge old barn that had lain neglected for twenty-five years. Kitty was ecstatic. La Salle had an inside toilet and a real bathtub. True, she had to heat the water for the tub over a fire in the kitchen, but still, it was a real bathtub. From the time they had arrived, Kitty had seen to it that the girls bathed in anything that would hold water.

La Salle was an experience. The two-story building offered living quarters upstairs. Downstairs, the girls had free reign, although they shared their freedom with snakes, large spiders, and poisonous frogs, which scurried about everywhere.

Behind the big house stood a huge tree that had a rope attached to one of its sturdy branches. As the weeks passed, the weather became warmer and humid. Kitty enjoyed watching the girls take turns swinging on the rope.

Where do they get their energy? Kitty wondered. For her, the heat was too stifling for work in the afternoons, yet the children weren't the least bothered. As they learned new tricks on the rope, each tried to outdo the other. When their competition became too fierce, Kitty would remind them that the Olympics had not yet come to Santa Rosa.

As the weeks passed, happy moments mingled with more difficult and trying times. One steamy afternoon, Triana and Amber could be seen from the big house, clumsily dragging along a heavy, rusty old bicycle.

"I wish I knew how to ride a bike this big," Amber lamented.

"Me too," Triana agreed. "Hey, wait a minute. I'll bet my dad knows how. He can teach us."

Amber considered it. "I don't know, Triana, he might get mad."

"No, he won't," said Triana defensively. "Anyway, he's a good teacher. Look at Paco and Tonio. They speak English really well since he's been teaching them. I'll ask him! Come on!"

The girls ran into the house where Franco was taking his noonday meal.

"Hey, my *bambina,*" Franco smiled. "You girls having fun and staying out of trouble?" He took her in his arms and gave her a great big hug.

"Sure, Daddy, wait till you see what we've found!" Triana and Amber exchanged furtive glances.

Franco frowned. "I hope it's not another rodent. You kids have to be careful with all this wildlife out here. Some of those creatures are poisonous."

The girls found this hilariously funny. "No, no, Daddy, it's not poisonous; it's a bicycle, and we thought maybe you could show us."

"Well," Franco said, "wait until I finish eating and I'll take a look at it."

"Great, Daddy!" The girls dashed happily from the house.

After he finished eating, Franco went outside to inspect the new toy.

"Oh no, no way!" he shouted instantly. "Get away from it, this contraption is filthy, and look at the rust. You ever hear about lockjaw? You could get lockjaw from cutting yourself on a rusty thing like that, especially with animals around here. Some kid on this farm died from it just before we got here."

The girls looked up at him sadly.

"Now get rid of it. I forbid you to even play around with that thing!" Franco wheeled and trudged back to work.

"I guess we'd better do what he said and put the bike back," Amber said disappointedly.

"Yeah, my dad is probably right. We can just leave it here for now and put it away later." They skipped off to play hide and seek, which amused them for the entire hot summer afternoon.

When Emily returned from spending the day with some children her own age at a neighboring farm, she saw the bicycle.

"Wow! I haven't ridden a bike in ages!" Emily jumped on the dusty seat and began riding the wobbling, squeaking bicycle.

"Come on, Triana, hop on. I'll give you a ride. You next, Amber."

"Sure!" Triana forgot her father's admonition and cheerfully climbed on the bike in back of Emily. Off they rode.

Kitty was in the big house mending one of her two blouses, when she heard the screaming. Dropping her work on the floor, she dashed outside. By the time she reached the children, one of the farm workers had pulled Franco away from Emily. Franco had beaten her, slapping, punching and kicking her like she was a rag doll. The ten-year-old cowered on the ground, sobbing in pain.

Triana was nearly hysterical. She threw her arms around Kitty. "It's my fault! I forgot to tell her," she sobbed over and over.

Kitty's face turned white and she thought she would vomit. She pushed Triana aside and rushed over to Emily.

Kitty raged at Franco. "How could you?" she hissed. "You're a monster, Franco."

"That damned kid better start obeying! You hear?" Franco shouted. "Or else!"

The farmhand tried to calm him, but Franco raved on as Kitty rushed her two daughters back to the house.

That night, Triana asked Kitty why her father hated Emily so much. But before she could answer, Franco charged into the room.

"What are you saying to my child?" he thundered, grabbing Kitty by the throat. "Why does she ask a question like that? You're the one who's putting ideas into her head."

"Daddy, Daddy! Please stop!" Triana pleaded, tears streaming down her face.

The two other girls kept their distance, but they both screamed and cried as they watched in horror as Franco beat their mother. Finally, Franco let go of Kitty and shoved her across the room.

"I don't ever want to hear anything like that in my home again! *Comprende?*" he snarled, stomping out of the room.

Kitty composed herself and put her arms around her children. Triana and Amber cried for a while, but Emily stared stonily into space, her own bruises still throbbing along with her mother's.

From that night on, Kitty began to think of a plan of escape--a plan to reach home, her real home. For months, she had blindly obeyed Franco's orders forbidding her to write home or telephone her sister or grandmother. But now it was different. Whenever Kitty had thought about it, her courage had failed her. What if someone saw her? What if Franco was having her watched? Franco had once told her he had had Rosalie watched to make sure she behaved herself.

Whether her plans would ever come to fruition or whether they were just fantasies to ease the pain, she did not really know. She knew that an escape would be difficult, but she began to plan nevertheless. As her life became increasingly difficult with every passing month, these thoughts constantly occupied her mind. Although continually thinking about a getaway, she had no idea how to carry out such a scheme.

As the weeks lengthened into months, the makeshift family enjoyed some good times in Colonia Santa Rosa. Dances were held regularly under clear night skies sprinkled with thousands of stars. These celebrations began after dinner, a few hours after sunset, when the air had cooled. *Criollos*, country folk in colorful garb, hiked through the jungle carrying flaming torches to ward off the snakes and any other creatures that lurked about.

Kitty loved the dances, and although she did not consider herself much of a dancer, she enjoyed watching Franco, who danced expertly. When he danced, he temporarily forgot his problems and the girls could enjoy a rare sense of freedom and fun. She liked to watch her daughters and Triana have fun, allowed to be themselves without any pressure to behave.

Kitty resented the special treatment Triana received from her father, but on these occasions, when Franco danced, he treated all the children much the same.

Men, women and children laughed and danced far into the night, singing their local music and drinking their local wine and yerba mate tea. As the evening wore on and it became late, the natives melted back into the jungle.

When it was time to leave, Kitty and Franco carried the flaming torches. Franco led the way, the girls followed in single file, and Kitty brought up the rear. The girls found the dramatic processions exciting, but Kitty was sure that they would change their minds quickly if they encountered a poisonous snake or a frightening jungle animal. With every footstep, she watched carefully.

As the Christmas season approached, the heat intensified. Only slightly cooler nights followed the days of one-hundred-and-eighteen degree temperatures. Kitty supplied the girls with plenty of newspapers, flour and water paste and a treasured pair of scissors. "For Christmas decorations," she told them. "Use your imaginations." And they did.

"Couldn't buy anything like that in the five and dime back home," Kitty laughed as the pile of crude Christmas decorations filled the table. The girls had made stars, and ornaments of many shapes and colors, and lots of linked chains of variously colored circles.

"But what are we going to do for a tree?" Triana asked. Amber frowned. She hadn't thought about that.

"Problem solved," Kitty assured them as she went into the yard and cut down a small palm. It didn't look like a Christmas tree, but it would do. "Well, sort of," Emily pointed out.

They placed the tree on a table on the front patio. On Christmas Eve, Kitty put one little homemade gift for each of the girls under the tree. They didn't amount to much, but she wasn't going to have Christmas for the girls without at least one package to open. A bright bandana for Emily, a woven necklace for Amber, and a funny little rag doll for Triana.

The girls went to bed happy and excited, but during the night a violent summer storm struck the jungle. Howling winds toppled their little tree. Christmas morning found Kitty and the girls mopping up inches of mud that had flooded the gallery and trying to salvage the soggy little gifts. The girls proved good sports and recovered quickly from their disappointment. They made a game of drying out their gifts and each of them hugged Kitty appreciatively. A week later, Colonia Santa Rosa rang in the new year of 1972.

One hot and muggy morning in January, Emily woke earlier than the others, and called for her mother. "I had a terrible dream, Mom. I was in a big kettle and headhunters were going to boil me alive."

Kitty automatically echoed the age-old reassurance, "It was only a dream," but she noticed that Emily's eyes were glazed with fever. "I don't feel very good, either," the girl added weakly. "I think I felt a little sick last night, too."

Emily's face suddenly paled. She got up as quickly and wobbled into the bathroom, where she vomited for fifteen minutes.

"Now what?" Franco inquired. "It's Emily," Kitty told him, "she's really sick. I think she should go to the doctor in town."

"Can't it wait until tomorrow? We've got a busy day today." Franco looked for any excuse to ignore the little girl's condition.

Kitty flushed. "No, Franco," she said evenly, "we don't know what it is. It could be a poisonous spider bite, or one of those frogs, or it could be something contagious."

The word 'contagious' struck a nerve.

"All right, all right," Franco agreed. He certainly didn't want Triana to catch anything. "I'll see if one of the boys can give you a ride into town. I sure hope it's not too expensive. I'm not made of money, you know."

"Thank you, Franco." The sarcasm was heavy in Kitty's voice as she clenched her hands into white-knuckled fists. *How much more of this can I take?* she thought. Tears began to roll down her cheeks.

Fortunately, the doctor in the village spoke English. Infectious hepatitis was his diagnosis. "She'll be flat on her back for at least a month. Hepatitis can be dangerous in this part of the world."

"What about the rest of us?"

"It's contagious, all right. Keep the other little girls away from her as much as you can." He took three large jars from a shelf and handed them to Kitty. "Give them these vitamins and take a few yourself. These pills should help keep you healthy. In a week or two, I expect some gamma globulin and antibiotics in from Buenos Aires, although they usually send the supplies late this time of year. You could all use a shot or two to strengthen the blood against the bug. Better order some more," he continued to himself. "Might turn into an epidemic. Hope not though."

"Thank you, doctor," Kitty said in a wavering voice. She knew her daughter needed hospitalization, but there was no way to move her. If only they were back in California, if only they had never come to this dreadful, primitive place. She realized the doctor was looking at her inquisitively. "My husband will be in to pay you."

"Oh, sure," the doctor said, "any time next week will do. Oh, by the way, next week you'll notice some jaundice. She'll look kind of yellow, but that's natural with liver infections."

Back at La Salle, Amber and Triana anxiously discussed the situation. "I still don't understand," Amber pouted, "why we can't go near my sister."

"Because it's catching," Triana replied. The image of her mother popped into her mind. "I guess that's why I can't see my mom," she reflected to herself. "I guess drug addiction must be catching too."

"Don't you think the germs can fly around the house and get us anyway?" Amber asked.

"I don't know. My Dad's real worried, so maybe they can. I just hope Emily will get better real fast."

In the sickroom, Kitty stayed at her daughter's bedside day and night, applying alcohol compresses to relieve the high fever and trying patiently to encourage Emily to keep down small amounts of food. The little girl lost several pounds the first week, and, as the doctor predicted, her skin and her eyes soon took on an ugly, yellowish cast.

"Dear God," Kitty prayed, "please don't take her away from me. Please let her live and let us all go home, where we belong."

"Sometimes a mother's prayers are answered," the village doctor said, fanning himself for relief from the searing tropical heat, "no matter what one does, or does not believe in. Your daughter is over the critical stage. She's going to get well." He dabbed at his face with a handkerchief. The humidity was unbearable.

"Oh, thank God!" Kitty beamed. "About your fee, I know my husband is a bit behind in paying." Kitty avoided his eyes. The doctor raised his eyebrows and smiled knowingly.

"I trust he'll pay when he has the money."

Kitty remembered the debts they had left behind in the States. The doctor would probably never get his money. Money, always money. Why did everything revolve around money? She pushed the thought aside. Emily was going to get well. That was all that mattered.

Back at the big house, Kitty found Franco hastily packing. "We're going back to Salta," Franco informed her. "I got a guy coming who's going to take us in his pickup."

Kitty groaned. "Franco, Emily is too sick to be traveling."

"Come on, come on, get busy. We gotta pack," Franco snapped, ignoring Kitty's statement

"When do we have to leave?" Kitty murmured, too exhausted to fight.

"Tomorrow, early in the morning, when it's not so hot."

Not so hot, sure. It is only one hundred and ten, not twenty, she thought. But she did as Franco instructed, hoping the long, exhausting journey back to Salta wouldn't cause Emily to relapse.

CHAPTER NINE

January 1972 to December 1972
Costa Mesa, California
Rome, Italy

During the eight long months since Franco and Kitty had disappeared into the wilds of South America, I concentrated on finding Triana. I wrote to the State Department, to the Passport Office, the FBI, and the Ambassadors of Argentina, Brazil and Chile. I placed ads in newspapers in each country, offering rewards for my child's return. In each country I contacted attorneys to work on my behalf. I sent one a fifty dollar retainer, but he never replied to my letter or returned my money. The others simply replied that they could do nothing to help me locate my child.

Desperate now, I agreed to go with Toni, my friend and co-worker from Union Bank, to San Diego to see a psychic. The psychic told me that he saw visions of a cross, of Franco's protection beneath a cross, of his driving cars to the South. The psychic insisted that Franco was working for a friend who sold cars that he was emotionally attached to a man taller than himself, a man with sandy hair and a moustache.

A year of letter writing, searching and begging for help from every person and agency I could find passed with no news of Triana's whereabouts. Carmen, now living with her sister, Lina, in Rome, professed no knowledge of her son's whereabouts. I knew she was not telling the truth; Franco always kept in contact with his mother, and her small pension was a constant source of funds that he had always relied on.

Christmas that year was bleak and empty without Triana. Worse, Stan planned to spend Christmas day with his boys and could share only Christmas Eve with me. After Stan left early Christmas morning, I spent a sad day alone, thinking only of Triana.

And on New Year's Eve when the champagne corks popped and 1972 was ushered in, my heart drifted to Triana—wondering where she was. With an ache in my heart, and a lump in my throat, I crawled into bed and hugged Triana's favorite toy. I stared at the ceiling, tears rolling down my face, wondering whether I would find her before next New Year's Eve. For the first time, I considered the terrifying possibility that perhaps we would never be together again. I was struck forcibly by the fact that if I was ever going to see my daughter again, I needed to get more aggressive.

Four months later, a group trip to Europe gave me the opportunity to fly to Rome. My plan was to see if I could find any clue to Franco's location, perhaps even hire an attorney.

Once the plane landed, I headed for the American Embassy to tell my story yet again.

"There is little we can do here officially, but I think I can help you personally," the American Vice-Consul told me. "I have a close friend who is an American of Italian ancestry; he works here in Rome as a detective for a company called Wackenhut. I'll call and find out if he can see you today."

He picked up the phone and arranged the meeting.

My excitement mounted. I had heard of Wackenhut as a security company, but was unfamiliar with them as a detective agency. Fifteen minutes later, I was on the bus heading for *Piazza Mincio* 2/15, the office of Detective Cacciato.

The detective listened patiently as I told my story. "During the last few months, I've lost contact with Franco's mother, Carmen. She could be with her son, or just refusing to answer my letters," I told him. "This is not characteristic of her. Even when she wasn't telling me the truth, she always answered me. I can only assume that instructions from Franco have kept her mute. He might even be here in Rome, for all I know. Before I left the States, I wrote to his aunt who lives here. I think she would help me if she had any information."

"Well," the agent reflected, "my best guess is that he's still in South America. But we can start by running checks in France, Spain, and England, and certainly here in Italy. With his linguistic ability, he could go almost anywhere."

Glumly I agreed. "Somewhere in this huge world is my little girl. I only hope she's all right and you can help me find her."

Mr. Cacciato was not very encouraging, but he asked me questions and I gave him all the information he needed.

On the bus back to my hotel, I assessed my trip with mixed emotions. I was disappointed at his lack of encouragement but I had to be realistic. Triana had been gone a year. Did I expect to find her in one short day? Even prominent detectives don't move that fast. I took some small comfort that I had at least hired one of the best international detective agencies. If anyone could find Franco, they could. Still, I would keep up my own search while Wackenhut did whatever they could.

When I returned home, I resumed my mission of letter writing and began corresponding with Wackenhut, hoping for news of Triana. It took the rest of my savings to send a retainer to the detective agency in Rome. I hoped this was not another case of bad judgment on my part.

As the days wore on, I spent the majority of my time at work or Stan's apartment and less time in my lonely apartment.

One evening as Stan and I drove along the Santa Ana residential streets where he lived, Stan turned to me. "Rosalie, why don't you give up that apartment and move in with me? I don't want you to be alone any longer. Besides, we're going to be married eventually anyway." Stan paused, realizing that I wasn't listening. The best proposal of marriage I had ever received hung unnoticed in the space between us.

"Stan, I've got to get her back. She's my whole life," I cried. "He's not going to get away with this! What am I going to do? This is tearing me apart, I miss her so much." I covered my face with my hands and sobbed uncontrollably.

Stan pulled the car over to the curb, and took me in his arms. He held me tightly and sighed. My crisis only added another complication to his already tangled life. I knew that ever since we had met, he had thought about divorce but had resisted filing. He adored his three sons and he understood that they lived for the day he and his wife, Lucy, might reconcile. The pain they would experience from a divorce was a heavy burden he had avoided as long as he could. Stan wiped my tears and kissed me gently.

"Rosalie, I promise you I'll see you through this. I admire your independence and your determination. They are wonderful qualities. I know you can get through this. You'll find Triana; you'll get her back. I'll help you all I can, but you have to go on living, if for no other reason than for the time when you get her back. Come on now and pull yourself together. Just wait till you taste the great wine I've picked out for this gourmet feast I'm cooking you tonight."

My dear Stan; he was the successful problem solver. He believed a solution would be found and everything would eventually be resolved. Control and confidence were second nature to Stan, which was why my situation troubled him deeply.

Moving out of the Costa Mesa apartment that I had shared with Triana was unspeakably wrenching. The decisions to keep or give away Triana's toys and clothing were the most painful I had ever made. Finally, I rented a small storage space. I simply could not part with most of her treasurers. After all, Triana would want them when I got her back.

In May 1972, Stan filed for divorce. We were married on December 9, 1972.

January, 1972
Salta, Argentina
Salta was exactly as Franco, Kitty and the children had left it. Change, if it comes at all, evolves slowly in a languid South American city.

But this time they had a clean, decent place to live. Franco had made the acquaintance of an Italian named Johnny who, together with his down-to-earth, hardworking wife, made them feel completely welcome. Johnny was a warm, good-natured man who loved not only his own children but everyone else's kids, too.

When Franco, Kitty, and the girls arrived early one evening, dusty, tired and hungry, Johnny was outside in the front yard to greet them. The kindness of these people amazed Kitty. She couldn't help but wonder how many of these warm, generous people they would meet and go through in their exile from the States.

"Come in, come in," Johnny welcomed them. "Our home is now your home. Angelica has a fine meal waiting. You can clean up, have a good dinner, and then get some sleep." He beamed at the girls. "Such lovely children."

The small stucco structure had a living room that doubled as a dining and entertaining area, two small bedrooms, a bathroom, and a small kitchen that was also used as a laundry room. The house was a palace compared to the barn in Santa Rosa.

In the morning, there were fresh rolls with plenty of butter and cheese and steaming hot coffee. Even the girls enjoyed the coffee, which had become part of their daily diet.

Johnny's wife, Angelica, divided the chores among her children and herself. "No, let's split the chores fairly," Kitty insisted. "We want to share the household responsibilities. Right, girls?" she said in her newly learned Spanish. Franco has insisted they speak Spanish as much as possible. The children had picked up the language easily, but Kitty still found it difficult.

"Sure," Triana agreed to help, while Amber nodded. "I'm not sick anymore. I can help, too," Emily offered.

"No," Kitty said, "not for a while." Emily's health was still fragile, but Kitty could see that here with nourishing food, cleanliness, and fresh air, she would soon be strong again.

"But, Mom, I'm okay, really."

"Shut up!" Franco snarled, banging his fist down on the table. "Do what your mother says and..."He stopped abruptly, noticing that all eyes were upon him, especially Johnny's. Franco shrugged and smiled charmingly. "Kids gotta do what their parents say, right?"

Kitty was overjoyed. In this house, Franco would have to control his temper and mind his manners.

One evening Johnny walked in with an armload of packages. "Triana, Amber, Emily!" he called happily. "Come see what your Uncle Johnny has brought you!" Kitty and the girls were delighted with the clothes they found in the boxes.

"I hope everything fits all right," Johnny said. "If not, I can probably get others." He hugged his wife, who smiled warmly. Kitty was sure it had taken Johnny a great deal of talking to get Father Buttinelli, from Convento San Francesco, to part with that much clothing. Salta had many poor people and clothing was scarce.

Soon their friends Gladys and Tito began to visit, and several times a week Franco, Kitty, and the girls dined with them at their home. Life in Salta was the happiest time Kitty could remember since they left the States.

It was February now, late summer in South America, and time for Salta's annual weeklong Festival. "You girls are going to have so much fun," Gladys beamed, remembering her own youth. "Wait until you see the Festival!"

And Festival it was, indeed. The streets of Salta were filled with people from all over Argentina. Night after night there was a spectacular parade, which was followed by dancing in the streets till nearly dawn.

"Daddy," Triana said on the third evening of the Festival, just before bedtime, "could we get costumes and march in the parade?" "Costumes?" Franco said. "I'll have to see about borrowing some money. Tomorrow, you can come with me. I'll see what I can do."

"Thanks, Daddy." Triana threw her arms around his neck and gave him a big kiss as she trotted off to bed. Franco stared after her. If she wanted a costume, he would see that she had one.

The next morning, Franco and Triana strolled along the brightly decorated streets of downtown Salta. As they approached the plaza, Triana stopped to look in a window. Just then, a buzzing, snorting noise sounded overhead, and Triana found herself soaked with water.

"I'll get you!" Triana laughed and called out at the backs of the three children as they rounded a corner, making their getaway.

"What the devil was that?" Franco asked angrily.

"It's okay, Dad, it was just water balloons. During Festival Week, we all do it. We throw them at anyone who moves. All us kids do!" Triana exclaimed.

"Oh, I see." Franco calmed down. "We all do, do we?" He was on the run, yet his little girl was beginning to feel at home in Argentina. Sometimes he wondered how it would all end. Perhaps his enemies, or even Rosalie, would catch up with him; that was one thing he constantly worried about. He had no idea when this might happen and it made him nervous.

"Come on, Triana. Here's the place." They walked into a small shop where Triana stared around at big bolts of brightly colored cloth, fancy costumes, and bizarre, angular masks hanging on the walls.

"You look around, *Penguina*; I have to talk to the shopkeeper."

Franco haggled with the proprietor for ten minutes and finally came to terms. Triana would have one of the cheaper masks and a used, faded green costume from last year's Festival. Kitty could clean it up and maybe sew some brightly colored patches onto it. He would pay the man a little now, the rest later. It was the best he could do.

"Come on, Triana." He turned, but she was not in the little shop. She was nowhere to be seen. Franco ran frantically into the street, panic-stricken. He raced through the plaza, poking his head in and out of shops, running this way and that. It was as though Triana had vanished, dematerialized, been seized! Was it possible? Could Rosalie somehow have found them or the other people who were looking for him? Then he saw her, half a block away, talking to a huge peasant woman who had blocked Triana from his view. He ran toward her as fast as he could.

"Triana!" he cried in anger and relief.

"Daddy," she said, waving. She was unaware of his anger. "This is *Señora* Lopez."

Franco grabbed the child and shook her. "Don't you ever run away from me again." He was shaking with fear and trying hard to control himself in front of this stranger.

Triana feared her father's uncontrollable rage and began to cry and to apologize. "But I started to talk to this lady and she was walking. I'm so sorry, Daddy, please forgive me, I guess I didn't realize." Her sobs overcame her.

Franco took his child in his arms. "Do you know," he scolded, "how frightened I was when I turned around in the shop and you weren't there? Do you?"

"I'm sorry, Daddy. I thought it would be okay if I went outside and looked around while you were talking to the man."

"Well, it wasn't." Franco tried to be calm. "Don't you realize that there are bad, bad people around who would like nothing better than to take you away from me? Is that what you want?"

Triana shook her head and began to cry softly.

"Triana, your mother is a really bad person. She just doesn't have her life together at all. It is better for you to be with me and we must be very, very careful, always on the lookout. Promise me, *Penguina,* that you'll never leave me like that again."

"I promise, Daddy," the child whispered. Her voice betrayed the doubt she felt about what her father was saying. Triana's memories, of the closeness and happiness that she had always felt for her mother, were still alive. She could not understand what had happened and she did not comprehend what her father was saying. She wanted to talk about her mother, but Daddy seemed so upset that she dared not ask him about her.

She hung her head miserably. It was all so complicated. Where was her mother, anyway? Was she sick? The burden of trying to figure out such complexities of life was too much.

Triana sighed and Franco hugged her. "Now, *Penguina,* let's go back and get that costume!"

As they walked hand-in-hand back to the costume shop, Triana continued to think about her mother. Could her mother stop loving her in such a short time? There was nothing in her memory that could convince her that was true. Triana felt troubled and confused, but she understood that she must unquestioningly accept whatever her father told her. She had no one to talk to and tell how much she loved and missed her mother. She turned her head away so that Franco would not see the tears in her eyes. She did not need to bother, as her father was preoccupied, wondering how much longer he and his daughter could hide from the world.

Franco's deep fears rose vividly in his mind. He knew Rosalie would never give up; he understood that she was as determined to have her child back as he was to keep Triana with him. At the time, he was more afraid of being discovered by his Italian cronies in the United States than he was of Rosalie finding him. He reassured himself that she would have limited funds and no knowledge of where to start looking. However, the former cronies would never give up and had unlimited funds--their unspoken presence followed him closely, dogging him with soft and inexorable steps.

When the merriment of Carnival week wound down, life with Johnny's family started to settle into a comfortable routine. One day, Johnny brought home a government official from Bolivia. Franco had chosen well when he had made friends with Johnny. Johnny considered Franco an Italian brother and he was prepared to help him in any way that he could.

The official carried a large black, official-looking suitcase. Johnny called Franco, Kitty, and the three girls into the living room. Kitty's apprehension about another stranger entering their confused lives disappeared when Franco explained that the Bolivian was a man whom Johnny had hired to help them.

The Bolivian fingerprinted all of them right there in the house, using paraphernalia from his suitcase. When he had finished, he made out a variety of documents. Instantly they all had new identities: Franco, Kitty, Triana, Emily and Amber had become Luis, Carmen, Lia, Tonia, and Maria, citizens of Bolivia.

"Dad, do we have to call each other by our new names all the time?" Triana asked. She was puzzled. What did she need a new name for?

"Absolutely," her father replied sternly. "You are not to use your old names again. It's a good habit to get into, especially when strange people are around," Franco added nervously.

"I'll try," Triana promised earnestly, as she pondered her new name, Lia. She didn't understand, but she rather liked the sound of Lia. It was pretty and different.

Kitty appreciated the stability that living with Johnny and his family had brought into their lives. Her plans to escape receded and finally she dismissed them. In reality, a risky and dramatic undercover departure had never truly seemed feasible to her.

But the peace Kitty thought she had found was short-lived. One evening, several months after their return to Salta, she heard a wild commotion coming from the front yard. Johnny stomped in, glowering angrily.

"Everything! You do everything for some people, and still it's not enough!" He shouted at her. Kitty rushed past him. Out in the yard, Franco hauled himself up out of the dirt, rubbing a bruised jaw.

"He's crazy, that's what he is!" Franco screamed. "I didn't take any of it, not one peso!" He strode into the house where Johnny stood waiting, his eyes black and snapping.

"You are an ungrateful thief! I want you out of my house immediately. Tito and Gladys will just have to find someone else for you to steal from!"

"Steal? I never steal! I work hard for my money. I teach English!"

"Your money," Johnny snorted. "You spend it before it even reaches your filthy paws. I've had more than enough of you."

But his expression softened as he looked around at the wide-eyed, frightened faces of the children. "Your wife and your children, they have my sympathies," he said sincerely. "Such good little children."

CHAPTER TEN

May, 1972
Outside Salta

The children sat in the back seat, watching the countryside go by as Tito drove over the dusty road. A dazed Kitty slumped in the front seat, staring mindlessly at the passing jungle.

"This place is hardly luxurious," Tito warned Franco. "But our cousin needs someone to mind it for him for three weeks while he goes to Buenos Aires on business. Meantime, Gladys and I will be scouting for someplace else for you. And," he had added, "here no one can accuse you of stealing. There is nothing to steal!" Tito laughed to himself and stole a sheepish glance at Franco.

The place was a tobacco farm ten miles outside Salta. It consisted of a tiny, rickety shack and an ancient, broken-down tractor sitting idly among acres of tobacco plants. Kitty was speechless as she stepped in the doorway of the dark, foul-smelling, empty hovel. There was no furniture, not even a bed.

"Enjoy," Tito's voice echoed as he watched her disappear into the single room that was to be their home for the next three miserable weeks.

Tito would not have asked a dog to sleep in that dilapidated hole. He had no choice; he had run out of places in which to house this strange collection of people. Tito shook off the disturbed feeling he felt over abandoning Kitty and the girls and returned to his conversation with Franco, who was still standing by the car.

115

Emily tossed some of their belongings in the corner, sat down on top of the pile, and stared at her mother.

From outside in the sunlight, Triana's voice rang out. "Carmen, come see what we found!"

Unaccustomed to her new name, Kitty did not respond. She was still staring at the filthy room.

"Mom, that's you Lia is calling," Emily reminded her mother. Kitty took the single step that was all that was required to reach the outside. Triana and Amber grabbed her hand and hurried her toward a shed. Unexpectedly there stood a cow.

"At least we'll have fresh milk," Emily said wryly.

"Well, she's a nice old cow, anyway," Kitty forced a smile.

"She sure is!" Triana agreed enthusiastically. "Let's call her Bessie!"

While Bessie did indeed supply plenty of fresh milk, finding water presented a more serious problem. Daily they had to load huge milk cans on the back of the old gray tractor and laboriously make their way three miles back and forth to the nearest well in order to have water for drinking, cooking, bathing, or washing clothes.

Nightly they collapsed on the bales of pungent tobacco that served as their beds, couch, working and eating area. An oppressive weariness set in. They stumbled doggedly through the days, routinely expecting some new disaster to befall them. They were never disappointed.

One day Triana announced to Kitty in a trembling voice, "something terrible happened. Bessie's dead."

It was true. The tired old cow had stumbled into the small, polluted reservoir on the property and, unable to extract herself, had drowned. That was the end of their fresh milk. They dreaded the owner's return when his greeting would include news of his deceased livestock.

"Great!" Franco sneered sarcastically. "You people better start being more careful, or else!"

Not one of them understood exactly what "or else" meant, but they had been schooled too long in Franco's ways, and they knew his retribution would not be pleasant. They avoided him as much as possible, fearing his constant cursing and violent fits of anger.

Three bleak weeks passed, and Tito reappeared right on schedule.

"Well, it looks like you all survived," Tito chuckled. Nothing ever seemed to bother Tito. "Wait till you see the new place I got for you."

Their new quarters turned out to be the nicest place they had lived in so far. The small, three-acre farm lay out in the country, five miles from Salta. Tito had wangled a deal for them to serve as caretakers. Their pay included free room but no board.

Two priests from the large church in Salta visited them, generously offering assistance in the practical form of food and powdered milk, and clothing for the girls. One of them brought news of work for Franco.

"We spoke with your husband yesterday afternoon," Father Juan told Kitty, settling himself into a worn chair. Father Raymondo sat at the table in the cramped room.

"Father Buttinelli has arranged for him to teach English. Many of the adults and children here in the country will benefit from his services. Of course, they are not rich people and cannot afford to pay much, but, still, there will be some income. The people here are very neighborly. I am sure you will make many friends among the good country folk. And, of course, we will be of as much assistance to you as we can."

"I like it here already," Triana told the priests.

Father Raymondo smiled kindly. "And why is that, my child?"

"Because there are lots and lots of animals. I love animals." All three girls giggled.

"That is good," Father Raymondo said approvingly. "God has put animals on earth to help us; they are his creatures and we must always treat them with kindness."

Triana nodded seriously.

"I have an idea," Father Raymondo said, tapping the top of his head with his forefinger. "How would you girls like to have pups of your very own? There is a family nearby whose dog recently had a litter, and I believe there are two pups left, a brother and sister. I'm sure they would be glad to give the pups to you girls. They would be good protection for you," the priest continued when the girls' cheering had died down.

"Protection from what?" Kitty asked.

Emily hurried to supply some reasonable excuse to convince her mother to allow them to have the dogs. "Who knows, Mom, maybe from some strangers wandering by."

"I'll talk it over with my husband and let you know, Father," Kitty said quietly to Father Raymondo.

That night, Franco agreed to accept the dogs. "Good idea. If anyone approaches the house, I want to know about it. The dogs will see to that."

"How in the world are we going to feed them?" Kitty asked anxiously. "We're just managing to feed ourselves."

"Don't worry, the priests won't let them starve, or us either," Franco replied confidently. "They're good people, real Christians, not phonies."

Kitty thought about the strange assortment of people who had entered her life, many who had rescued them from difficult, uncomfortable, even dangerous situations, and she was grateful. She did not agree with her husband's assertion that they were phonies, but she said nothing.

A few days later, two large mongrel pups romped and played with the girls in the front yard. They were dubbed *Solidad* and *Capitan* and established their territorial rights immediately, refusing to allow anyone on the premises, friend or foe, unless called off by one of the family. The girls were ecstatic and Franco felt secure.

The *piece de resistance* was the house itself. It was new, and the owners gave permission for it to be painted, provided that Franco and Kitty supplied the paint and the labor. The girls, who shared a small bedroom, chose pink for their color, and the rest of the house was to be pale green. The priests gave Franco a ride into Salta to buy the paint. Cheers from Kitty and the girls, along with happy barking and tail-wagging pups, met Franco, upon his return. The next day turned into a painting fiesta, the only mishap occurring when *Solidad* sneaked into the house and put one of his huge paws into a can of pale green paint.

"It's a good thing we have running water here," Triana said as she cleaned her up.

"Well, semi-running water, anyway," said Emily.

"No, kidding," Triana laughed. "Imagine if we still lived in that last place with the tobacco? We would've had to go miles and miles and miles to get enough water to get this glob off *Soli's* foot."

"Yeah, this place is okay, I guess," Emily said. She was very glad that Franco wasn't around very much.

Indeed, Kitty and the girls were alone up to eighteen hours a day on the farm. Franco arose at the break of dawn and made his rounds teaching English. He rarely arrived home much before 11 p.m. What he did in the evenings, no one knew or asked. It was much too peaceful without him.

Winter arrived, bringing with it mild days and chilly nights. A year had passed and their life had finally assumed some degree of normalcy. The girls spoke fluent Spanish now and had made friends with some of the country children. During the day, they played in the yard with Soli and Capi at their heels.

The sun went down early this time of year. Kitty on occasions would call the girls in for an hour or so of studying. She tried to establish some kind of structure in their lives. She didn't want the children to miss out completely on their education. When Franco was home, they were all forbidden to speak English. When he was gone, Kitty spoke only English with the girls. An old *Reader's Digest* and *Time Magazine* served as their only textbooks. She wrote little short stories for them in English and gave them little spelling tests and simple arithmetic quizzes. Kitty knew she was no teacher. She had had very little schooling herself. Perhaps that was why the girls enjoyed their lessons. They were light-hearted and fun.

"I was only in first grade when we left," Triana reminded Kitty, "I don't remember much of it. This is more fun anyway."

Kitty hoped she could teach them enough that they might fit somewhere in the school system if they ever returned to civilization.

One afternoon during a reading lesson, Capi kept interrupting, scratching at the door and whining a high-pitched wail. "I'll go see what he wants," Amber offered. In a few moments she returned to the house, crying. "It's Soli," she said, "I think she's dying."

"Oh no!" Triana cried. She was the first one in the yard, bending over the semi-conscious puppy. The pup's gums and tongue were deathly pale, and blood trickled from her mouth and nose. Now and again she would whine pathetically and try to get on her feet. Capi kept licking his dying companion, trying to revive her, wagging his tail and nuzzling the girls as if begging for help.

"Girls, there's not much we can do," Kitty said. "Go in the house."

The girls buried Soil in the yard under a tree with her favorite bone, and topped the grave with special handpicked flowers.

"Broken bits of glass," Father Raymondo said in a sad tone tinged with righteous anger. "There are evil ones in the area, and your pup is not their first victim. Yesterday two other animals were found cruelly destroyed. We have put up notices and if they are caught, they will be brought to justice."

"Who would want to do such a cruel thing to a harmless, innocent puppy?" Kitty asked. "And to the children who loved her."

"A sick, bothered soul," pronounced Father Raymondo. "I have seen it before. Those who refuse to obey God's laws." His soft voice drifted off helplessly. He did not know quite how to explain the sad event to the children.

"You still have the male pup," Father Juan pointed out consolingly. "Watch out for him."

The girls listened and obeyed. They did not need Father Juan to remind them to care for their beloved remaining pet. But not more than two weeks later, Capi also died. The girls courageously endured the poor dog's agonizing death. Nervously, they tried to comfort each other, but even the bravest of them succumbed to tears. Capi was buried next to Soli. The girls kept fresh flowers on the graves and comforted themselves with the thought that at least the pups were together.

Around this time, Triana began to walk in her sleep. Sometimes she would try to leave the house, so the door had to be kept firmly locked. Mistaking her for a prowler one night, Franco almost hit her with a lamp. Fortunately, Kitty turned on the light just in time. The behavior persisted. Perhaps the close deaths of the two puppies, or her father's inconsistent and erratic behavior, her unanswered questions about her mother, and the constant moving were all simply too much for her subconscious mind to absorb. Whatever the reason, both Kitty and Franco were alarmed at her wanderings.

With the pups gone, the local snakes resumed their brazen trips through the yard. One afternoon while she was hanging the laundry, Kitty caught sight of a slight movement in the nearby tall grass. She froze. Not ten inches from her feet an ebony serpent was coiled and ready to strike.

"Girls! Someone!" Kitty screamed as she struggled to remain perfectly still.

Emily and Triana appeared at the front door.

"Move very, very slowly," Kitty said as softly and evenly as she could. "Get a shovel. Come around behind me and hand it to me very carefully."

"Why do you need a shovel?" Emily asked.

"Don't ask questions. Just do what I said!" She held her breath as long as possible, never taking her eyes off the coiled snake. She tried to quell her panic. Finally, she heard Emily's footsteps approaching. Slowly she moved her right arm and felt the shovel in her hand. Slowly, slowly she moved forward and struck the coiled creature with as much force as she could muster. Her aim was true and there was one less black snake in Salta Province.

The girls rushed toward Kitty, Emily and Amber hugged their mother tightly. Trembling violently, she laughed and cried with relief. The danger was over and the girls ran off, waving at her and laughing.

"And you be careful, too! There are a million of those slimy creatures around," Kitty called after them. Kitty immediately placed a new request with Father Raymondo for any new puppies he might encounter.

The weather warmed and Kitty took care to limit the girls' strenuous activities during the stifling afternoons. One morning,

Triana persuaded Franco to take her, Amber and one of the neighbor children into town.

"Our friend Carla says there's a street with a movie house downtown where they show Donald Duck and Goofy and Mickey Mouse, and we'd sure love to go! Will you take us with you, Dad?"

Franco stared down at the wide-eyed, pleading Triana and relented. He agreed to drop them off at the movie. He could teach English for a couple of hours, swing back into Salta, and pick them up.

As the months had passed, Franco had begun to feel more secure. But the old sense of apprehension had not totally left him.

"You must promise not to talk to anyone," he admonished them. "You just stay in the movie house until I come pick you up. There are still plenty of people, bad people who want to take you away from me. How much does this cost, anyway?"

"It's free, Dad. Free for poor children."

Franco's pride bristled. "Poor, huh! Well," he pushed the feeling aside. "All right, if you really want to go, get ready and I'll take you."

"Me, too?" Amber asked.

"Sure, why not." Franco cared little for the two other children, but he tolerated Amber, because of her affection for Triana. Emily was a constant annoyance and irritation to him.

Franco let the girls off on the street that housed four different movie theaters, each more decrepit than the next. "Have a good time, and remember what I said!" Franco called out as Triana, Amber, and the neighbor child ran down the street.

"Are you sure you know which movie house it is?" Triana asked Carla.

"I'm not positive, but I'm pretty sure it's this one. The reason it is free to us is that we slip past the booth. They very seldom catch us."

Triana looked at her friend with wide eyes. She had told her dad a lie and she wondered if he would be angry if he found out. No cashier attended the booth, so the children walked in and took seats in the darkened theater as quickly as they could. As their eyes became accustomed to the dark, they could see a few other children in the movie house and several adults slouched in the old wooden seats.

"I hope it is Goofy in Spanish," Triana whispered to Amber.

"Shhh," Amber chided. "Your dad said for us to never talk in English around other people."

Suddenly the screen lit up with an image of a woman standing alone on a deserted road. A car pulled up, and the woman got in. The car drove off into the distance. The scene changed abruptly to a clearing, showing the abandoned car parked on the shoulder. Heavy breathing and moaning could be heard from the scratchy, barely audible soundtrack. Then, suddenly, the larger-than-life figures of the man and woman appeared on the screen, their naked, sweat-glistened bodies exposed in full view. The eight-year-old girls gasped.

Triana recovered first and managed a hoarse whisper; "My dad will kill us if he finds out that we watched this."

"No, he'll kill us, not you. Let's get out of here and wait for him outside," Amber urged.

Triana tapped Carla on the shoulder. "We're leaving. Come on."

"No way," she replied, "the good part's just coming on." A new, even more explicit scene appeared.

"See," Carla said. "You can leave if you want to but I'm staying."

The girls' fear of reprisal, mingled with revulsion and disgust, sent them charging blindly out of the theater into the harsh, afternoon sunlight.

"We can wait out here as long as we don't talk to anybody," Triana said, "and let's never even think about that movie, okay?"

"Okay," Amber replied, "But Carla shouldn't be in there either."

"I know, I know, but we can't say anything about that either, please!" Triana pleaded.

"Okay, sure," Amber agreed pensively. Shocked as she was at seeing such a scene in a movie theater, living in such close quarters with her mom and Franco had been a sexual education in itself. Amber's curiosity about the lovemaking in a car had been aroused and she wondered if perhaps she should have stayed and watched.

Franco picked them up and took them home. On the way home the girls whispered to each other about the movie and what they were going to say. They made up a story to satisfy Kitty when she asked what movie they had seen. For a while, she believed them, until one of the neighbors volunteered the information that the theater specialized in pornographic movies. Kitty vowed to forbid future unsupervised jaunts into town.

"Just another rotten part of living in this wilderness," she sighed, wondering again for the thousandth time if she'd ever get back to civilization.

Why had she ever agreed to this madness of running and hiding? Running from what? Hiding from whom? What was Franco so afraid of? Rosalie? Some unnamed enemies from the States? Or was it some other, deeper inner drive? She remembered Franco's return from a trip to Chicago with a wild tale about witnessing a mob killing. She had pushed it aside as another one of his fabrications. Now she wondered. Could there have been some truth to it? Where had he gotten that large sum of money he had flashed under her nose? Heaven only knows what he spent it on, certainly not on her or the girls, but she had seen the money. The crazy things he told her about his efforts to earn money aroused her suspicions, too. Were they running from something much bigger than bad debts and child stealing?

Kitty could not develop a rational explanation for the turmoil and tragedy in which they were embroiled. Franco was an extremely complex man. She never knew whether he was telling the truth or whether he was merely enjoying the recital of some fresh fantasy.

CHAPTER ELEVEN

April, 1973
Rome, Italy

Franco's mother sat at one side of the huge oak desk, a dozen letters spread out in front of her, while Father Celsari, the young Italian priest, paced the room. He stopped in front of the big window and adjusted the Venetian blinds so that sunlight fell across the rectory office but not into his eyes. From outside, the street noises of a bustling Rome afternoon invaded the sanctuary. The dilemma his devout parishioner had placed in his lap required priestly advice. When she came to confession, he had listened to a tale of intrigue fit for the Italian cinema: bad debts, unfit motherhood, child stealing, escape into the South American jungle. Carmen's son played the leading role, forever the blameless and bereft victim. Franco consistently disclaimed all responsibility for his conduct.

"I've been receiving letters from him," Carmen's voice interrupted. "He is in some wretched part of South America, poor boy. He complains that his life is rough, but that he and his new wife are managing, and that he has little Triana with him. He has told me how the child's mother, Rosalie, was unfit as a mother and he has asked me to refuse to communicate with her. I know she is still looking for the little girl; she is a strong-willed woman. She writes to me, too. In her letters she says her heart is broken." Carmen sighed. The situation overwhelmed her. "I understand, Father, I understand," she continued. "I am a mother, too. But I must be true to my son. I tell her that I have not heard from him. But that is a lie, a sin. God does not forgive a lie. Father, what am I to do?"

Before the priest could answer, Carmen went on. "And now my son says that his new wife is not a good mother either, and that he wants me to come to live with them, somewhere in South America. He will telephone me next Thursday evening and tell me where he is and where I am to come. He says he needs me to take care of his little one, but I don't know if I can live in such a place as he describes. I am an old woman; I have worked hard and had little money since my dear husband died. To live on dirt floors in barely four walls seems too much to ask."

The old woman sighed again. She seemed to be talking more to herself than to the priest. "Ah, he is my son and I will do God's will. I will join him if he wishes. He cannot come back here; the police are after him, and he cannot go back to the United States because the child's mother will have him arrested."

"I know," the priest interrupted as kindly as he could. "You've told me about his problem."

"Father, what am I to do?"

The priest walked around the desk and sat down. He reached for his pipe in the ashtray and lit it. He had made his decision.

"One thing you can do, *Signora*, is to go to your son, stay for a while, and persuade him to contact the child's mother. They will have to come to some agreement."

"Father, I have tried. Do you really think I haven't tried? But he says she is unfit."

"And what about you *Signora*, what is your opinion? You know her. Do you believe she is unfit?"

Carmen wrung her hands. "She didn't seem so, but what do I know of it? He knows her better than I."

"Come now, *Signora*. First he says the child's mother is unfit; now he is not satisfied with his new wife's ability." He leaned forward and spoke gently. "Perhaps, Signora, the problem is with your son."

Carmen stared at the priest in disbelief. How could he say such things? If only he knew her son, he would realize his mistake.

"But I don't know if he'll listen to me anyway," she sighed. "And

I'm so old; but if that is my duty, I will go to the jungle to live. I love my granddaughter Triana dearly, but in South America there are such burdens." She looked upward. "I am sure God will guide me."

"Of course, *Signora*, look to God for direction. He will guide you. The final choice is God's. That is my advice. But," he added, "I'm sure you will choose to see the child returned to her mother where she belongs."

Carmen gathered up Franco's letters, thanked the priest mechanically, and slowly walked home. "This young priest," Carmen said to herself, "what does he know of the life that a mother has to bear; what does he know of love for your child?" Her choice was now clear. She could not refuse her son when he needed her. At home, she hid Franco's letters, as he had instructed. She was not even to show them to her sister, Lina, through whose kindness and generosity she would obtain the money for the trip. While Lina did not always approve of Carmen's relationship with Franco, she loved her sister too dearly to refuse her the money.

After several conversations with Lina and the priest, however, Carmen was convinced that Triana should be returned to her mother; that would be the main purpose of her trip to South America. She agreed that she would report her progress to her sister through the priest.

On Thursday evening, Franco called Rome. "It's all set, Mama," he said. "You will receive a letter of instruction from a priest telling you where to go first. His name is Father Buttinelli. He will contact you within a week." Franco was afraid to be more specific. He could not be sure who might be listening to his phone call. "Will Lina give you the money for the trip?"

"Yes, she will," said Carmen, not adding that the money was conditional upon Carmen ensuring that Triana be returned to her mother in the States.

"I love you, Mama," Franco added.

"I love you too, Francesco," she answered.

The line clicked; the call was over.

A week later, Carmen met the young priest at the *Convento Ara Coeli* where he delivered the letter of instructions from Franco. The plan was very simple: she was to be ready to leave on Tuesday next. A friend of Franco's would pick her up at ten a.m. and take her to the airport. Further instructions would be given to her at that time.

As Carmen packed, she carefully considered Franco's letter. Franco was taking no chances. He trusted no one and now it seemed that he didn't even trust his own mother. Was her sister right about her son? Had he been struck with the same deadly illness that had killed her beloved Vittorio? No, that could not be. Vittorio had been well at the time she had conceived.

April, 1973
Salta, Argentina

"Gypsies! Gypsies! Watch out!" A woman's shrill voice shouted nearby.

No sooner had Kitty stepped out the door than she froze, aghast. Before her stood a dozen of them; the band included women, small children and teenagers, one of whom dragged a half-dead chicken along by its neck. A tall, gangly youth held a struggling Triana by the arms while a hefty women, obviously the leader, stepped forward, opening a tied bandana from which fell paper money and coins.

"How much you want for the girls?" She smiled, revealing large gaps between her remaining rotten teeth. "We got plenty money."

Kitty picked up a broom and charged ferociously toward them. "Let her go! Let her go at once!" She screamed as loud as she could. The startled teenager obeyed, and Triana ran quickly to Kitty's side.

"All three of you girls--in the house!" Kitty commanded.

"Hey, lady," the Gypsy woman said smoothly. "Don't get so excited. We'll give you a good price. How much you want for all three? We'll take good care of them."

"Get off this property!" Kitty shouted hoarsely, waving the broom menacingly. "And don't you ever come back again!"

The other women in the group stared at Kitty, moving their fingers around mysteriously. High-pitched, chant-like sounds came from their lips. The leader snarled, "A curse! We put a curse on you! You get very sick, you die."

"Get out," Kitty repeated, brandishing the broom. Slowly they began to back off. "We will be back," the leader hissed. "And then we kill you and steal the girls! You die!" she jeered. "*Adios*."

Kitty watched them lurch off into the dusk and ran to the house.

"Are you all right, girls?"

"Sure, Mom," Emily said, feigning confidence. "What was that all about? What a bunch of creeps."

"Now look," Kitty said sternly, "If any of you ever see them again, I don't care how far away they are, you come into this house immediately and tell me. Do you understand?" Her hands trembled uncontrollably. The girls saw the fear in Kitty's eyes and they promised.

When he heard how close he came to losing Triana to the gypsies, Franco began to rage, "Can't you keep an eye on these kids? You have nothing that's more important than watching Triana. If anything happens to her, you'll have hell to pay. Do you hear me? You are unfit as a mother!" Franco tossed every piece of furniture he could touch against the opposite wall as he called Kitty every filthy name that came to mind.

Kitty and the children cowered in the far corner, trying to stay out of the range of the flying objects and Franco's insane rage.

After Franco stormed out of the house, Kitty and the girls picked up the various items scattered about the room and righted the wooden table. Franco's fury was becoming a constant in their lives. He seemed upset more days than not.

A week later, Father Raymondo and Father Juan stopped by with some provisions. Kitty told them about the Gypsies.

"To say that the Gypsies are a strange people is an understatement," Father Raymondo explained. "Their way of life is one that only they can comprehend. They have lived in this fashion for centuries and they cling to their beliefs and their traditions tenaciously. There is not too much anyone can do to stop them. Most people just stay away from them."

"We certainly intend to," Kitty agreed, but the memory of the experience shadowed her eyes.

"You see," Father Juan continued, "the Gypsies love light-colored children, like yours, and are willing to pay dearly for them. Their intention is to marry them to their own dark children. It is the blue eyes and the blond hair that attracted them, but they would have been willing to take dark-haired Triana as part of the bargain."

"My God." Kitty shook her head in amazement.

"Now to a more pleasant subject," Father Raymondo interjected. "Tomorrow, we will visit you again, and we will have a surprise that you will enjoy immensely."

"What is it, Father?" Triana asked enthusiastically. "Is it an animal? What's the surprise?"

"Never mind!" Father Raymondo held his hand up. "If I tell you, how can it be a surprise?"

The next day, the priests delivered three welcome gifts: *Michi, Gordo,* and *Negra*, a trio of delightful kittens who immediately followed the girls around the yard. Even the snakes seemed to understand and remained a safe distance from the house.

"They're not more than eight weeks old; you'd think the snakes would try to make a meal of them," Kitty worried. "Yet not one snake has come close to the house since their arrival, look how much bigger we humans are, and the snakes couldn't care less. It was a mystery, which Kitty promised herself to solve if she ever got home. She shook her head. If I ever get back home, I'll never want to see another snake as long as I live, even in a book!

December 1972 to May 1973
The suburbs of Salta

Another South American spring dragged to a close. Soon it would be summer with another Christmas. Kitty lay awake in bed, hoping this Christmas would be one with less perturbation and violence from Franco and a more stable environment for her and the girls.

At four-fifteen a.m., there was a sharp knock at the door. Franco rose to open it, and there in the doorway, to Kitty's utter amazement, stood Franco's mother, flanked by Father Buttinelli.

"Nona!" Kitty gasped. "What on earth?"

An exhausted and pale Carmen smiled wanly. "He didn't tell you?"

"No, no, Mama, I didn't say anything. Kitty, put on some coffee. What's the matter with you? And wake up the girls! I wanted it to be a surprise for everyone."

"Nona!" Triana rushed into her grandmother's arms. "Oh, Nona, I'm so happy! Will you stay, will you, Nona, please?"

The children were overjoyed. Sleep was forgotten as each of them attempted to relate the experiences of more than a year and a half in a matter of a few hours.

"Well, I came at a good time," Carmen said. "It can't be too hot here in the winter, is it?"

"Mama," Franco said, "the winter here is over. Now it's going to be summer. But the heat's not that bad, you'll see."

The temperature stays at one hundred eighteen, day and night, Kitty thought. *He doesn't care about anybody but himself. How could he do this to his own mother?*

Indeed, Carmen had a difficult time adjusting to life in Salta. As the months progressed, the sweltering heat and exhausting humidity grew almost unbearable for her. One of the girls' favorite activities was to have Kitty flood the kitchen floor. They would then get down and slip and slide around in the cool water. It was the only available relief from the oppressive, stifling heat. The first time Carmen witnessed this procedure, she was horrified.

"God in Heaven, water all over the floor! We live like savages, savages!" She shook her head in disbelief. After a while, she began to accept the fact that, flooding the floor notwithstanding, they were not savages but civilized people adapting to a difficult environment with its uncertainties and surprises.

Early in March, Franco marched into the house with the latest bad news. "The owners want us out. We've got one week to get off the property."

"But why?" Kitty asked.

"Why? Franco snarled. "Because they're idiots, that's why!"

Kitty and Carmen exchanged glances. Kitty wondered what trouble Franco had gotten them into this time.

Father Buttinelli helped them find their next lodging, a house with two small rooms and three makeshift interior walls. It was a half-mile outside of Salta. One room served as a combination bedroom, kitchen and toilet, which was occupied by Kitty and Franco, while the second was used as a dormitory where Carmen and the three youngsters slept. Carmen thought she would lose her sanity.

"How can you stand living in these filthy, overcrowded conditions, Franco? You must think of your family."

"Mama, what am I to do?" Franco whined. "What am I to do when I am forced to take care of so many people? And with no money!"

"Oh, it's not so bad, Nona," Triana assured her as she helped her grandmother to their sleeping room.

"Some of the other places were a lot worse," Amber agreed. As the girls prepared for bed, they painted a picture too dark, too gloomy, too dismal for Carmen to absorb. They recited every grim detail, from the original *pensione* to the bed-less, water-less tobacco farm.

"We even saw a dirty movie once." Amber blurted out. A look from Triana silenced her. "Part of it, anyway," Amber added sheepishly.

Carmen sat up from the thin, torn mattress where she had been lying while the girls talked. "What?"

Triana, embarrassed, kept her eyes on the floor.

Amber continued rapidly. "You see, Franco and Mom didn't know anything about it, and we thought it was going to be Goofy in Spanish."

"It's true, Nona," Triana admitted quietly. "It was a mistake and we left right away."

"You poor, poor children," Carmen sighed. "What kind of a country is this where they let children in to see dirty movies?"

"Nona, please don't tell Daddy. He'll only get mad and it was a long, long time ago."

Carmen understood. "I won't say anything, darling. Don't worry.

Now say your prayers and go to sleep. It's time for bed." She kissed her granddaughter and the other two girls. "Goodnight, children."

Carmen was awake most of that night, trying to reassure herself that she had done the right thing in coming to this strange, unhealthy place. She prayed, and said her rosary over and over again.

Six weeks later Father Buttinelli found the family a better place to stay. Only five or six blocks from downtown Salta, the house had two bedrooms, a real bathroom, cold running water and a living room-kitchen combination.

Carmen provided a calming effect on Franco. His usually frequent temper flare-ups were fewer when his mother was present.

Occasionally Kitty and the girls rode the bus into town and spent the day at the park. These days were happier ones and even Carmen settled in. She could walk to the church each morning for her prayers and she took a job cooking for the priests.

One evening, Franco came home loaded with packages and a startling plan. "Girls," he announced, "it's about time you got some education, and today I enrolled all three of you in first grade."

"Huh?" Amber said. "School, yucky!"

"What's in the packages, Dad?" Triana wanted to know.

"School clothes!"

The girls had to wear white pinafores over their own clothing as a school uniform. Kitty thought they looked wonderful. Now they would be getting a real school education. Both she and Carmen were happy and relieved.

"How did you manage this?" Kitty asked Franco.

"Tito's old lady. She has a sister who's a teacher, and she got the kids in. It's not that easy to do, you know, but I talked to Tito and, as usual, he came through. And who do you think talked me into it? Mama, that's who." Carmen smiled shyly at Kitty, as Franco came over and put his arms around his mother.

"She's the best--a real mama, Kitty!"

Kitty looked away. There was no use getting into an argument. Franco never listened to anyone. It was difficult to believe he had paid even this much attention to his mother.

The girl's schooling lasted all of two weeks. One morning at breakfast, Franco suddenly changed his mind, "I don't trust that school, and I don't want you girls hanging around with strangers every day. It's not safe. No more school."

"Now, Francesco," his mother began. She stopped abruptly as Franco pounded on the table, his eyes flaring with anger.

"Mama, you don't understand, you don't understand at all. There are all kinds of evil people around. Why, right now one of them might be plotting to get to me by taking Triana. Not to mention certain rotten people from the States." He gave his mother a hard stare.

"As you wish, Francesco," Carmen conceded lamely.

"Well, it's not all right with me!" Kitty banged her coffee cup down sharply. She could no longer contain her anger at Franco's childish insistence that his every whim be gratified. His paranoia was worsening with each passing day.

Franco flew into a rage. "Who the hell do you think you're shouting at? I'm the one who supports this family, and I'll be the one to make all the decisions."

A terrible fight ensued. Franco stormed out in a rage. Kitty ended by sobbing wildly and herding the terrified girls into their bedroom. But finally, with stoic obedience born of experience, she folded the white pinafores and put them away. The girls stared at her in melancholy silence.

"Oh, come on now, girls, we'll continue our lessons at home," Kitty reassured them. "After Franco leaves for work," she continued, mustering up a smile. "As soon as he leaves the house, we'll start our studying. You'll see. Everything will be just fine."

She dried her eyes and comforted the confused and frightened children. But Kitty knew somehow, someway, she had to find a way to get her girls back to the United States.

A week later, Kitty decided to approach the subject of her and the girls going home. Surprisingly, Franco consented and asked Carmen to see if Lina would send money for their trip to the United States. Kitty assumed that now that Carmen was there she was disposable, no longer needed. This suited her fine.

Franco was tiring of Kitty, he didn't care if she left; she could be replaced on any street corner. And this could be a chance to get his hands on some money from his aunt and to hell with Kitty and her girls, they could hitchhike back to the States.

Several days after her plea to leave, Kitty found Carmen sitting at the chipped wooden table writing a letter. "Are you writing to your sister?" Kitty asked. "I have wished for so long to write to my family."

"No, I wrote to Lina four days ago. This is to a priest friend of mine," Carmen answered.

"Will Franco let you mail that?" Kitty asked in amazement as she looked around for her husband.

"No, I am hardly so foolish as to try to mail my own letters. I simply take them to the church. I give them to Father Buttinelli, who sends them to Rome in a mail pouch. He asks to have the letter mailed from there, or he flies to Rome every three weeks and delivers them personally to my friends and my sister. I've been writing letters since I got here. In fact, that was how Franco corresponded with me before I came." Suddenly Carmen realized from the shocked expression on Kitty's face that her son had never allowed Kitty to correspond with anyone. "Do you want to write to someone, my child?" Carmen asked sympathetically.

Kitty's eyes filled with tears. "Oh, yes, Nona. I've wanted so much to write to my sister in Montana, and my grandmother in California; I begged and pleaded and fought with Franco, but he absolutely forbade it. They may be able to send some money, and I'm so homesick."

Carmen's heart went out to the tired, unhappy woman.

"Well, you write your letters, Kitty. I shall see that they get to the priest. I don't know how long it will take, but they will be mailed from Rome and eventually they will reach your family. Your poor family, they probably don't know whether you are dead or alive."

Kitty threw her arms around Franco's mother and cried. Maybe soon her ordeal here would be over; maybe soon she and her children could go home.

Three weeks later, on Sunday afternoon after mass, Father Buttinelli called Carmen, Kitty, Franco and the girls into the anteroom of the church.

"I have something important for you from Rome." The priest took out an envelope. "It is for your trip home, *Señora*," he told Kitty, "for your trip and for your two daughters."

Franco smiled, assuming the envelope contained a bank draft.

"Thank you, Father," he said, reaching for it.

"This, my son," the priest said sternly, "is not for you."

Franco stopped in his tracks, his face falling as the priest opened the envelope, removed the nontransferable airline tickets Lina had sent, and handed them to Kitty. Since she knew Franco very well, Lina had attached some conditions when she sent the tickets. They were to be given directly to Kitty by the priest and they were non-refundable tickets in order to ensure that Kitty and her girls would actually return to the States as they wished. And there was money for Carmen that was to be given to her later, in secret, to see that Triana was returned to her mother.

Red-faced, and visibly shaken, Franco stepped back. When Kitty had spoken to him about leaving, and his mother had offered to ask his aunt for the money, he had not expected it to turn out this way, he hadn't anticipated this development. Lina had completely thwarted his plans.

"Your wife and her daughters want to go home to the United States, and home they shall go," the priest repeated adamantly.

"I pleaded with Lina to send the money for them," Carmen explained softly as she nervously fingered the beads of her rosary.

"She's my aunt!" Franco shouted hoarsely. "She's never lifted a finger to help me, but she sends tickets that must be worth a thousand dollars to help this bitch?" Frustrated, Franco stomped around like a child in a tantrum.

"My son, you watch your language here!" the priest ordered.

"Francesco, you will not talk like that in the house of the Lord, and in front of your children," Carmen said. "I am truly shocked at your behavior. Your action angers me, my son. For you to display such misconduct in front of your child and a man of God hurts me deeply, Francesco."

Franco stalked out, slamming the door behind him.

CHAPTER TWELVE

May, 1973
Irvine, California

"**S**o, unfortunately," said the voice on the phone, "it was just another blind alley. But don't worry; we're still working on it."

"Thanks, Jack," I replied, dejected.

Hanging up the phone, I looked around the rented Irvine house in which Stan and I had been living since our marriage in December. Twelve months had passed since my trip to Rome. As the weeks dragged on, I had spoken regularly with the Wackenhut detectives in Rome, as well as their Los Angeles representative. The little information they had gleaned proved to be hardly more than what I had found out on my own. I picked up their latest report:

Rome: 1968--Franco was sentenced to three months imprisonment for defrauding the Diner's Club.

Paris: Subject could have entered France without entrance having been noted by police. Although he would have been required to register with police as a foreign resident, many foreigners do not do so and are consequently seldom caught.

Brazil: No record of either entry or departure.

Buenos Aires: Braniff International keeps records for thirty days only. Police keep arrival records for one year. Ministry of Records showed arrival of Franco and party on May 31, 1971, giving their address as a hotel. Upon inquiry, the hotel informed the investigators that the entire group disappeared the next day, leaving two trunks of personal belongings behind.

The report continued with pages of technical information pertaining to Wackenhut's investigation of Franco's various escapades. Wackenhut considered the case closed and had so advised me in their final report. I folded the letter and investigation report, adding them to the mountain of correspondence from the last two years.

Included in the report was their bill for fifteen hundred dollars. It would take a few months to pay the bill in full. However, no matter how we struggled to make ends meet, and pay for the expenses of my pursuit, I could not give up my search for Triana. Somehow the bills would be paid.

Two days after I had received the letter from Wackenhut, I was busy at the typewriter writing still another desperate plea for information when the phone rang.

"Rosalie?" the excited voice said. "This is Lea. I think I have some wonderful news for you!"

It was some months since I had heard from Kitty's sister, who lived in Eastern Montana. She had been as worried about Kitty as I had been about Triana. Lea and I had kept in touch since the whole ordeal had begun, but so far she had been unable to offer any real assistance. Now my pulse quickened.

"What is it? You found them?"

"Well, no," Lea answered. "But I just got a letter from Kitty, the first one I've had in all this time! She says that everything is pretty terrible and she wants to come home. She doesn't say where they are. She asks me to send money to a Father Romanelli, at the oh, God, I'll have to spell this out for you." Lea spelled out the *Convento Ara Coeli, Scala dell'Arco, Capitolena*, Rome, Italy

"The postmark, Lea, look at the postmark."

"Oh, you're right. I was so happy to get the letter that I didn't even think of that."

I waited impatiently while papers shuffled on the other end of the line.

"Rome!" Lea exclaimed. "The postmark says Rome!"

"Rome?" I murmured, more to myself than Lea. "Okay, Lea, can you send me a copy of both the letter and the envelope?"

"I'll do better than that. I'll send you the letter itself with the envelope. I'll get it right in the mail today."

"Oh, God, I can't thank you enough, Lea. Thank you for being such a good friend, when you haven't even met me." I was crying and I could hardly get the words out. "Thank you so very much. I'll let you know what happens."

I immediately dialed the overseas operator to put through a call to the Wackenhut office in Rome. Miraculously, the call went right through, to Mr. Cacciato.

"I think Franco is in Rome," I told him. "You check it out, and as soon as I can make arrangements, I'll catch a plane!" I filled him in on the rest of the details and hung up.

Stan was somewhat taken back on my insistence that I must fly to Rome. But, he knew how important this was. We would charge the ticket on one of our cards and I could take what cash I might need for the trip. I hurriedly began to make the necessary arrangements.

It had only been a few weeks since I suspected I was pregnant. I had decided to put off telling Stan, because I was uncertain of his reaction.

When we first met, we talked about having children. Stan insisted that having additional children would be impractical for us since we already had four children between us.

"I love children, but I don't think that I've got enough time in my life to parcel out more of myself for any more youngsters," he said.

With my history of miscarriages, I also wanted to be a little further along before I told him. Now I hoped that the excitement of this sudden trip to Rome wouldn't bring on another disappointment. I had to go, even if it cost me this child just beginning to form in my womb. Still, I knew it wouldn't be fair to withhold the news any longer. Stan had a right to know.

On the way to the airport, I told him.

"I really want this baby," I confided, "but if you don't want another child, then we will have to make a decision when I return. Stan, please think about this carefully."

Stan was shocked. "How far along do you think you are?"

"Over two months, I think," I replied. "I haven't seen the doctor, but I'm sure I am pregnant. Heaven knows after nine miscarriages I know the feeling."

"Rosalie, how could this have happened?" Stan said incredulously. "You have an IUD. They're supposed to be foolproof."

"First of all, Stan, nothing is foolproof. Women have gotten pregnant using every conceivable protection available. However, at the doctor's suggestion, he removed the IUD. He said I had had that thing far too long. I had intended telling you at the time; I thought I would have time to investigate new methods of contraception. The pill is out because I have a reaction to them. And, later I thought I could convince you that our having a child would be a great thing. I thought we would have more time. I was wrong, but I'm not sorry."

I had wanted to tell Stan that I wanted another child more than anything else in the world--a child that was part of both of us, a bond, a family.

Stan felt betrayed--this had not been in his plan. He did not need additional problems, additional responsibility, and everything I said sounded like an excuse. I decided to drop the subject until I got back. Upon my return, I hoped I could convince him that a baby would be a wonderful thing for us both.

What I didn't know at the time were the thoughts in Stan's mind as he watched my plane fly away toward Rome: Did I think that I could keep hopping all over the world searching for Triana while I was pregnant? What was I going to do when the baby arrived? Would I devote the necessary attention to the new child or take off at a moment's notice, to go God-knows-where on another quixotic search? I was sure Stan pondered the situation as he walked back to the car and drove home.

May, 1973
Salta, Argentina

The last few days in Salta were a maelstrom of extreme happiness and sorrow for Kitty. She moved about as if in a dream, overwhelmed by feelings of unreality. On one hand, she felt ecstatic at the prospect of going home with her children, but she could not deny the gnawing feelings of sadness tinged with guilt that gripped her whenever she looked at Triana. These past years she had blamed Triana for Franco's harsh treatment of her two daughters, even though she knew it wasn't Triana's fault. Now that she was leaving she felt afraid for Triana. What was going to happen to her? Would Franco take out his frustrations on her when Kitty, Amber and Emily were no longer there? Kitty truly believed that Franco had gone over the edge. He behaved like a madman. What was to become of Triana? Nona would see to the little girl's needs, but how long would her grandmother stay? With considerable effort, Kitty pushed the feeling aside. She was going home. She was powerless to do anything about Triana.

Soon the day of departure arrived. The family gathered at Gladys' sister's home. The three girls and Kitty hugged each other tightly, crying hot, bitter tears. As Kitty left, she took Triana in her arms.

"Triana, I don't know how or when, but when I get back to the States, I promise you I'll do everything in my power to get you back home where you belong, with your mother."

"But Kitty, my mother is d...."

"I love you, Triana," Kitty interrupted. She kissed the little girl one last time and got into the car.

Triana stood waving at the old automobile, feeling lonely and frightened, as she watched it become smaller and smaller in the distance. Finally, it disappeared entirely. A strange, isolated feeling came over her as she ran back into the house weeping out of control. Moments before the house had been alive with the presence of the three people she had come to know as her family. Without them, everything seemed empty and dead.

Franco found her alone in her room, crying softly. "My *bambina*, why are you so sad? Just think, it's just you and me now."

"Oh, Daddy, I'm going to miss them so much." Triana could not stop crying.

"Say, how about you and me going shopping? I think there is a doll that needs a new home." Franco had discovered the money Lina had sent to Carmen for Triana's fare home. Although she had resisted initially, Carmen had finally given in and handed him the money. She was unable to refuse her son, no matter what he asked. Her best intentions vanished when Franco made a demand. The promises she had meant to keep sailed away on the empty air.

"You mean the big one that I have been wanting?" Triana asked, brightening up a bit.

"Yes, the big one that can walk. You want it? We had better go get it before someone else does." Franco stretched out his hand for his daughter's.

June, 1973
Rome, Italy

When the jet landed in Rome, I took a cab to the *pensione* where Mr. Cacciato had made reservations for me.

The *Amati* was located on *Via V. Veneto*, 155. I checked in and called the Wackenhut office.

My room was a seven-by-ten rectangle with a bed smaller than a normal twin. A tiny window looked out onto a side street. The walls were empty and the only other convenience was a small closet that was barely adequate for the few essentials that I had bought. The shared bathroom facilities were across the hall. However, both the room and the bathroom were immaculate, and the accommodations included a Continental breakfast.

The next morning I caught a bus to the Wackenhut office at *Piazza Mincio* 2/15 where I had arranged to meet with Mr. Cacciato at nine-thirty a.m.

"We have had surveillance at the *Convento Ara Coeli* since you telephoned me. However, we are certain that the sanctuary does not take in laymen as boarders. So we think the Allateres are not on the premises." Mr. Cacciato explained to me. "Although we haven't found Franco," the detective went on, "we did contact his aunt, and she's agreed to meet with you."

I had only met Franco's Aunt Lina when he and I were first married, although I had communicated with her several times since then, asking for her help in locating Triana.

"I'll go as your translator," Mr. Cacciato insisted. "She need not know I am an investigator, as it might deter her from talking."

Lina had always written through Carmen, a priest, or a friend who spoke English. She had never needed to use a language other than French or Italian. Her only slight need for English was her communication with me, and that had been in letters and a few written notes.

"*Comenici*, Rosalie," Lina greeted us at the door. "*Como domo du es.*"

Italian cakes and espresso were served. Once we were comfortable, Mr. Cacciato took over the translation.

"I really appreciate your seeing me," I began. "I'm desperate to get my daughter back. And I haven't heard from Nona. I haven't been able to get in touch with her for a while."

Lina sighed. "It is always so difficult to determine loyalties in a situation like this." She stared directly at me as Mr. Cacciato translated.

"I don't want to make any trouble for anyone," I said sincerely. "All I want is to get my daughter back."

"I can understand that." The older woman paused. "However, one of the problems is that my sister Carmen has told me that you are an unfit mother."

"Unfit!? What do you mean unfit?" I couldn't believe that Franco's mother would say such a thing. I struggled to find my composure. "Unfit in what way? What did she accuse me of?"

"Carmen told me that your being unfit was one of the reasons Franco took your daughter." Lina leaned forward. "She said that you allowed the child to travel from home to school and back, unsupervised. This is definitely unsafe. Here we would never allow a child to do this."

I leaned back in the elegant, upholstered brocade chair and shook my head, trying to stay calm as I sipped the strong Italian coffee. What kind of a trumped-up story was this?

"Lina, you don't understand," I explained. "In some parts of the States, in the smaller towns, it's perfectly safe for children to walk to school. I'm sure here in Italy in the small towns, it's equally safe for the children. All Triana had to do was walk across a small park and one short block to school. They have crossing guards and all the neighborhood children walked the same route. In fact, they all walked together. There has never been the slightest problem for any of them. We lived in a very nice area where there was absolutely no danger. Here in Rome, I'm sure it's like our large cities, where you must escort your children everywhere, but in Costa Mesa, it is perfectly safe. Believe me, Lina, if it weren't safe, I would never have let Triana walk to school!"

After the detective translated all of this, he confirmed he had also lived in a small town in the United States where the children were safe. However, now that he was living in Rome, he understood Lina's concern.

She nodded. She watched me carefully as I spoke, and her eyes acknowledged that I spoke the truth.

"All right," she said after a few moments. "I will give you some information, though I don't know how helpful it will be."

I listened attentively, ignoring the cramp that was forming in my stomach.

"My sister Carmen is with Franco and your daughter. Carmen has written to me, telling me that conditions are unspeakable and that she is very unhappy. She would not say, however, exactly where they are, but it sounded very primitive indeed. The letters have always been postmarked Rome, but that can be easily arranged, you know."

Lina got up and began to move around the room nervously. "Then, the letters stopped coming. Needless to say, I began to worry about my sister. Then one day, a priest who had come from South America called me and said that my sister was all right and that I should not be concerned. And I'm afraid that is all I know."

She walked over to the window and looked out. When she turned back toward me, she had decided to tell me the rest of the story.

"Perhaps I should tell you this. Franco's new wife, Kitty, and her two daughters were with them, but Carmen wrote that Kitty and her girls wanted desperately to go home. I am not a poor woman, you see, and so I decided to help them. Through the priest who called me, I sent tickets--non-refundable, I might add--to allow this unfortunate woman and her children to return to America, where they belong. I have not heard whether the tickets were used." She paused. "Rosalie, I also sent Carmen some money to see that your child was returned to you. Perhaps the money was used for some other purpose."

"Lina, I don't know how to thank you! Now maybe I can track Franco down through the priest. He must know where they are," I exclaimed joyously.

Lina smiled as she wrote down the name of the priest. "Father Jeremiah Buttinelli, or perhaps José Buttinelli, I'm not sure. I think the priest said something about a town called *Maiaj* or *Maij*. I am not certain. Also, this is a name and address of a priest here in Rome that is a good friend of my sister. His name is Father Giulio Celsari." Putting down the pen, Lina took my hands. "It is the right thing for me to do, to help you. You see, I cannot believe that any mother who would take all this trouble to find her child could possibly be unfit."

She picked up the paper to hand it to me. "Oh, one more thing," she wrote down another name and a phone number. "This man, Aldo Bernabei, is supposed to be a friend of Franco's. He may also know of his whereabouts."

She took my hands once again. "Good luck, my child. I hope you find your little girl. I will help if I am able. I never did like Franco."

"Thank you, I'll write to you and let you know when I find out anything." I took the small, thin woman in my arms, hugged her and kissed her goodbye.

Mr. Cacciato and I made one other stop, at the *Parrocchia dell'Immacolata*, to talk to Father Giulio Celsari. Father Celsari was very friendly and cooperative. He stated that he had known Carmen only since the fall of 1972, at which time Carmen had come to him about a problem concerning her son. He believed her to be a very intelligent and religious person. He revealed that Franco and Triana were in South America, and later he mentioned the Republic of Argentina. To the best of his knowledge, Kitty and her two children had returned to the United States, however he was not positive of that fact. Father Celsari said that Carmen had told him that Franco was mentally unstable, and that Kitty and Franco had separated permanently. As far as the priest knew, he was sure that Carmen fully intended to deal with her son and see to it that Triana was returned to her mother. The priest was aware that Franco was in deep trouble and wanted by the police in the United States.

Through his conversation with Mr. Cacciato, the priest requested that I stay calm and not to make efforts to locate Triana in South America, since Carmen would see to it that she was returned. Carmen did not want anyone to interfere with her plans to return Triana. In particular, she wanted to avoid exciting Franco and running the risk of some dangerous action on his part.

"Kitty wrote to her sister in Montana," I told him. "The letter was mailed from Rome. She asked for money. Do you know who mailed the letter?"

Mr. Cacciato translated the priest's reply for me. "Father Romanelli is a friend of Carmen's. I think he must travel to South America and bring back her messages. The letter sent to Kitty's sister in Montana was probably brought back by him."

"Would you be willing to call Father Romanelli and ask where the money is to be sent if Kitty's sister can send some?"

My heart began to pound as Father Celsari agreed to telephone Father Romanelli at the Convento Ara Coeli to obtain further information.

He kept his word. Father Romanelli affirmed that the money was to be sent to Kitty, in care of himself and he would see to it that it was transmitted to the Allateres in Argentina.

Franco, Triana, Carmen and possibly Kitty and her two children were definitely in Argentina.

While Mr. Cacciato dealt with another client in his inner office, Mr. Cacciato's daughter and secretary, Julia, and I pored over a map of Argentina. While I scoured one end of the map, Julia searched the other. We were looking for the town called *Maiaj* or *Maij*. When no such town was found, Julia placed a call for help to the Argentinian Consulate in Rome. The call proved negative.

"Okay, we have the name of the priest who came over here from Argentina," I offered. "Let's try that."

My mind raced ahead. I knew the answer was on the map in front of me. Someone here in Rome must have the information. "Let's call the Vatican and see where this priest Father Buttinelli is assigned. They must have a record of their priests' locations."

Julia looked at me in amazement and picked up the phone. She called the main operator of Vatican City who connected her with an office that had access to the latest directory of missionaries in Argentina. This directory dated back to 1961 and disclosed one listing for a Jose or Giuseppe Buttinelli in the *Consiglio Diocisiano* at *Jujuy*, Republic of Argentina. No reference to *Maiaj* or *Maij* was found in this directory. We also learned that Father Buttinelli was at one time assigned to *Convento Ara Coeli* and, upon his visits to Rome, stayed at the church.

When Julia hung up the phone, both of us were wildly excited. We had found the missing link!

"We have to calm down and think." I tried to steady myself. "Now what we have to do is call the Convento Ara Coeli without their knowing who we are. I've got it!" My heart pounded with excitement. "We know Father Buttinelli was here approximately two to three weeks ago. He must have brought the letter from Kitty at that time. He must have traveled through Buenos Aires, right?"

"If you don't get to the point, I'm going to die with suspense," Julia said.

"Since you speak Italian, you will have to make the call. Say that you traveled from Buenos Aires, or better yet, to be safe, you traveled from Argentina to Rome with Father Buttinelli. Tell them that you became friends; say that he gave you his address in Argentina and you have lost it, and you want to write to him, and could they please give you his address?"

As she made the call, I listened carefully even though I didn't understand a single word. Everything was riding on this one phone call. The call went on forever. Finally Julia hung up.

"Well," she said, "Father Giuseppe Buttinelli has recently been transferred from the convent at *Jujuy*, to the *Convento San Francesco*, Salta, Republic of Argentina." Julia wrote the information on a piece of paper. "I think we have just found your daughter."

Julia came around the desk and hugged me. In a few limited, tense hours, we had developed affection and respect for each other.

"Before I leave, could you make one more phone call for me? Could you call this man and ask him to meet me at my *pensione*? He is a friend of Franco's. I want to see if he will help me." I handed her the name and phone number of Aldo Bernabei. "See if he can meet me around seven this evening." Julia made the call and Aldo agreed to meet me.

"Julia, you did so much for me, I can't thank you enough for your help." I gave the slender, pretty girl a hug, accompanied by the customary Italian kisses on both cheeks.

"By the way, if you ever want to work as an apprentice private eye, let me know. I'll put in a good word with my dad!" Julia said laughingly, as she walked me to the office door.

"Thanks, but, I think I'll retire as soon as I get my child back," I called back as I descended the stairs. My spirits were the highest they had been in a long time.

Late that evening in the dining room of the *pensione*, Franco's friend, who spoke English fluently, sat across from me, sipping the strong Italian coffee I had ordered.

Aldo eyed me curiously. "Yeah, I'm a friend of Franco's. I worked with him when he lived in Italy."

Though the man was clean, neatly dressed, and polite enough, I sensed early on that he had no intention of helping me. When he answered, "I don't know" to my every question, I knew that I was wasting my time. After forty-five minutes of nothing, I politely thanked him, wondering why the man had agreed to see me. Perhaps it was merely curiosity, or perhaps he wanted to learn how much I knew. I was very careful, and made sure his time was as wasted as mine.

Two of the five days my economy ticket allowed me had come and gone. I still had three days to go before I was scheduled to fly home. If I left any earlier, I would have to pay full fare. The day before, I had discussed with Stan the possibility of being finished earlier than expected. We had agreed that it would be considerably cheaper for me to come home as scheduled, so I found myself with time on my hands.

On the first morning, I had met a couple and their young daughter who were also staying at the *pensione*. For the next two days, we ate our meals together. When they heard that I would have some free time before my return, we planned to do some sightseeing together.

"Have you seen Tivoli?" I asked.

"No, we toured Rome yesterday. How far is Tivoli from Rome, and what's there?" Doris asked.

"When I saw it some twelve years ago, it was one of the most magnificent sights I have seen in Italy. It is the palace of the *Villa d'Este*, home of the famous fountains. It's truly something that you should see. I think the bus trip should take no more the twenty or thirty minutes."

I thought back to when I was a young bride who had been so enchanted with the beautiful villa and its gardens. It seemed like an eternity since I had last seen those beautiful fountains.

"Would you like to join us and give us the grand tour of your magnificent fountains?" John asked.

"I would love to see them again."

The tour of Tivoli and the Villa was a delightful, relaxing day. Their daughter was a year older than Triana. I could not help comparing my child to this charming girl. Was Triana taller, darker, thinner, happier, or sadder? Through the mixture of pain, sorrow, and happiness that swirled within me, I clung to the child as though she could fill some small part of my hollow loneliness. Doris and John were delighted to have me as their guide and were charmed by the beauty of the Villa and the fountains.

As soon as I returned to the *pensione* I realized my body, not just my heart, was crying in agony. I had been ignoring a cramp in my lower abdomen. In the bathroom, I discovered spots of blood in my underpants. My heart sank as I made my way to my room to lie down on my small bed. The memories of the pain and sorrow of my prior miscarriages flashed through my mind. I did not want to lose this baby.

Reaching for the phone, I dialed the front desk and told him that I had a medical condition that required care. The head desk clerk came to my room right away. He took one look at me and placed a call to his wife's doctor. The doctor agreed to look in on me after his office hours.

He came as promised, examined me and gave me a shot. Then he sent one of the young men that worked at the *pensione* out for medicine and ordered me to bed for the remainder of my stay in Rome. When he left, I placed a call to Stan. After what seemed forever, the operator rang to tell me the call was ready.

"Hi, honey," I began. "So much has happened, I don't know where to begin."

"Did you get a solid line on where Franco and Triana may be?" Stan inquired.

"That's the best part. I have an address in Argentina where I think I can locate him. At least I know he's been there recently. You just wouldn't believe the unbelievable chain of events that have literally dropped everything I wanted right into my lap," I hurried on breathlessly.

"I'm so glad. I was so afraid that you'd face another disappointment. I just don't want to see you hurt and depressed any more." Stan's warm, compassionate voice comforted me. "And how are you feeling? Any problems? I've really been worried after what you told me at the airport. Pregnant ladies aren't supposed to be going on eight thousand mile detective journeys. Seriously, honey, have you been all right?"

When I heard the tenderness in Stan's voice, I felt sure that everything was going to be all right between us. The pent-up worries and the excitement of the day welled up in me, and with tears streaming down my face, I told Stan how I felt. He reassured me that he was happy about the baby.

"Rosalie, are you sure you don't want me to come over there? Are you really up to making the trip back by yourself?"

"Stan, I'll be just fine. This thing today isn't all that serious. I'll just rest the next couple of days and make sure that I don't overdo it.

I'll take a cab and make sure someone else carries my luggage. Don't worry," I reassured him.

"Well, I can't help but worry. You know yourself well enough that usually I rely on your judgment. However, you do have a tendency not to know when to quit. Just, please, don't get involved in anything more that might endanger you or the baby," Stan implored.

"I promise not to do any second-story work before I leave. Seriously, I'll be careful. Take care of yourself. I love you," I added with a light-hearted laugh.

"That sparkling laugh doesn't fool me for a second. I'm serious-- take care of yourself, do you hear? And, I love you too, darling. See you in a few days." Stan hung up.

For the remainder of my time in Rome, I rested. The flight home was not full, so I was able to lie down for the entire trip.

In Los Angeles I dashed into Stan's arms. On the way home I filled him in with all the details.

"Sounds good, hon," he said. "Sounds like you will be heading for South America. But first I want you to check with your doctor and then, if he says it's all right, it's okay with me. You should have Triana back very shortly. Where did you say it is in Argentina?"

"Salta," I said. "Salta, Argentina."

CHAPTER THIRTEEN

June, 1973
En route to Argentina

Slumped in my cramped airline seat, I stirred in my sleep, dimly feeling the plane's descent to Buenos Aires.

"Will we be landing soon?" A woman seated some rows in front of me asked a passing flight attendant.

"Fifteen minutes," the girl replied. "We've got some turbulence up ahead. The captain thought it would be more comfortable for everyone at a lower altitude." She continued toward the rear of the cabin, glancing down at me just before I glided back into a slumber. "How sad she looks," I heard her say softly to another flight attendant.

In my dreams, my mind was moving crazily back and forth over the years since Triana's birth. Everything seemed jumbled and out of kilter. My visions were distorted and painful as I twisted uneasily. I saw Franco smirking as he mocked my pain. He held Triana's hand as they faded in and out of a gray murky fog. The image keep repeating itself over and over in my dreams as I reached out in vain, just short of Triana's outstretched hand. The distress of the knowledge that somehow I could have prevented this pain and kept Franco from taking Triana, was more than my soul could accept. If only I had realized that his assurances had no meaning, they were only words of appeasement to gain my trust; if I had not trusted in his promises, or him swearing on the life of his mother, I could have my child safe at home. The images, the words and the visions kept repeating over and over in my dream. How foolish I had been.

Kitty's face floated into my mind and I wondered if I would find her and Franco still together. I held her equally responsible for my misery. Surely, she was as guilty as Franco. She could have kept Franco from taking Triana! She could have warned me what he was planning. She could have refused to participate in stealing my daughter.

I had liked Kitty; she seemed like a good person, a good homemaker. I had trusted Kitty and Carmen with Triana's after-school care, first in pre-school and then first grade. I had included her two daughters in several of our weekend adventures. Why was it, I wondered, that I so often liked and trusted women who eventually betrayed my trust? First Nona and now Kitty.

Suddenly I was awakened as the cabin lights came on and a bell rang softly, signaling that the pilot was about to make an announcement. Dimly I heard the pilot explain in English and then in Spanish that we would land in Buenos Aires in a few minutes.

As he talked on, I paid no attention. Somewhere below was my daughter. There was so much to do when I landed. Was I up to the job ahead? I would soon step off the plane into a country where I did not speak the language; had no definite plan and I had no one to help me. I was alone.

The jet continued to plow its way toward Buenos Aires, bringing me closer to what I believed would be my reunion with Triana. What would my child be like? Would she be the same? How ridiculous! I needed to prepare myself carefully for the changes that would confront me. Children her age grow so much in two years. No matter, she would still be my Triana. I closed my eyes and tried to imagine what she would look like now. Out of my carry-on bag I retrieved Triana's last picture. I held her first grade school portrait close to me; it was my constant companion.

In Buenos Aires, I checked into a hotel, threw my unopened bag on the luggage rack, and headed immediately for the American Embassy.

"Perhaps you can help me," I said to the Consul General, a Mr. Bishton. "I need the services of a good English-speaking attorney."

The Consul General made the necessary arrangements, and two hours later I sat in the office of my Argentine attorney, Dr. Alfredo Errecondo. He was a tall, impressive, sympathetic young man in his mid-thirties who listened attentively.

"It will take two days to prepare the proper legal papers which you must take with you to Salta," he said. "I have an associate there; I will call him at once so that he will be ready to help you."

"Will there be difficulties getting the documents to allow me to take Triana back to the States?" I asked. After the long months of stumbling blocks, red tape and disappointment, I had grown cautious and skeptical.

"No," he reassured me, "I foresee no difficulty. With the legal papers you already have, the most time-consuming effort will be to translate these documents into Spanish. Once that has been done, an official seal is needed to legalize them here. But don't worry; I will take care of everything. By the time you reach Salta, there will be other necessary documents to be prepared for local jurisdiction. Dr. Alias D'Abate will handle that end of it when you arrive in Salta."

The lessons of two years and three months had not taught me patience. "Is there anything I can do to help expedite things?"

"*Señora*, here in Argentina things move much slower than in the United States. There are certain procedures only an Argentine can handle. Please be assured that my colleagues and I will do everything we can to speed the process up." Dr. Errecondo took my hand. "I have to tell you, that you are one of the most beautiful women that I have had the pleasure to serve. It is apparent that you have suffered a great deal, and my heart recognizes your pain. I intend to see that this matter is handled as quickly and as painlessly as possible. You will have your child back and be on your way home very shortly."

I gently slipped my hand loose from his touch and walked to the window.

"Are you sure it will take only a few days?" I asked. "I am so afraid that Franco will find out that I am here. If he does, he will leave immediately."

"Of course, I understand. I will complete all the documents as soon as possible. I realize it is very difficult for you to wait."

Neither of us spoke for a moment. I stood with my back to him, staring through the window at the busy street, wondering what I would find in Salta, and whether or not Franco and Triana would be there.

I felt him step towards me. He spoke gently.

"*Señora,* I have some friends here in Buenos Aires that I would like you to meet. The gentleman was a respected attorney until the present political system gained power, but he was on the wrong side of the system and now he is forbidden to work. Both he and his wife speak fluent English and are very charming people. I will call them and see if they will invite you to tea. They are very good friends of mine and I know they will be delighted to have your company." He hesitated. "I mean to help you pass the time. May I give them your number at the hotel?"

"Thank you. That is very kind of you. I'm staying at the Gran Hotel, on *Marcelo T. de Alvear*. Dr. Errecondo, you will call me if there is any news.. anything?"

"I will call you tomorrow and let you know how we are progressing," Dr. Errecondo promised as he escorted me to the outer door.

As Dr. Errecondo had anticipated, the Ugarte family made me feel at home in Buenos Aires. They took me to lunch and to the city's famous and elegant Calle Florida for shopping. I guessed at her proper size and bought some clothing for Triana. We drove along the clean, modern streets, lined with jacaranda trees, beyond which stood tall, balconied apartment buildings and spacious mansions.

"Buenos Aires really is a lovely city," I complimented my hosts.

"Yes, thank you, we love it, but sometimes living in such a lovely place has its price. The political instability has created many unseen problems." The woman smiled wistfully.

The next day the couple showed me around the Boca, the Italian section, which featured winding cobblestone streets and quaint, colorful little houses. The size of the large Italian section in the middle of Buenos Aires surprised and disturbed me. Franco must have plenty of contacts here. That evening, the Ugartes invited me to dinner at their home with their children.

The Ugartes had four youngsters. The next to the oldest, a boy of seventeen, had said very little over dinner, but anger poured out of every word he did speak.

"So you see," *Señora* Ugarte explained over an after-dinner cordial, "we are now on the wrong side of the political tracks. My husband is a very fine attorney, but he has been, how shall I put it... retired."

Señor Ugarte smiled wryly. "It is a shame, we are limited to such a small salary now, and it is very difficult for our children to understand. They are much more rebellious than we were. They do not hesitate to show their anger in public. It provides them with some release, I suppose. Still, all we can do is wait it out, and hope that our children escape arrest."

"It's easy for you to be passive. You are used to being pushed around. I intend to fight back." The oldest boy jumped up from the table and walked rapidly out of the room.

"If our son seems disturbed," Mrs. Ugarte explained, "it is because he is going through a terrible depression. Please excuse him."

"A political depression," Mr. Ugarte added grimly. "As you well know, when one has children, one also has problems, even though it is not always the children who cause the problems."

I agreed completely. My heart went out to the young man.

When the Ugartes bid me farewell at the hotel, they shook my hand warmly and wished me good luck on the journey to Salta. I longed to do something to help this kind and gentle family. I could not imagine being entirely at the mercy of the government, unable to work if you lacked the proper political affiliation. My appreciation for the United States soared. I realized how lucky I was to be an American--how lucky I was and how little I appreciated my country. Seeing others who did not have the same privileges was eye opening.

The next morning Dr. Errecondo, who had decided to accompany me to Salta, picked me up at my hotel. We drove to *Ezeiza* Airport, where we boarded a small propjet for Salta.

Once we were settled aboard, Dr. Errecondo explained the

situation. "I have done all I can do here in Buenos Aires. Now we must have the rest of the papers prepared in Salta. It should take no more than a day. Everything involves red tape, however; there are districts for this, districts for that. Even in Buenos Aires, it is complicated and time-consuming, as you have seen. I hope the wait was not too difficult for you. Did my friends call you?"

I smiled. "Your friends were most generous and took very good care of me. Thank you for your consideration. And as for red tape, we wade through it in the States, too."

I settled into my seat and actually enjoyed the flight to Salta. I was flying toward Triana.

"My associate will meet us at the airport," he smiled. "After lunch we will go directly to his office to complete the papers. You could have your baby back in your arms this very day."

Suddenly the ease and confidence with which he spoke alarmed me.

"I hope you understand," I cautioned him, "that my ex-husband will not give up my child easily. We will have to take him by surprise; he will try to run if he has the slightest suspicion that I am near."

"You are not to worry about a thing. It will be handled with the greatest of care."

The confidence with which Dr. Errecondo spoke calmed me, but his naiveté worried me. He did not know Franco as I did. However, I wanted so desperately to allow someone else to assume the burden of these last two years, if for only an hour or two, that I eased my mind and dozed for a short time.

Once in Salta, Dr. Errecondo, Dr. Alias D'Abate and I stopped at a small restaurant, which served the best American food in Salta.

"Beefsteak!" Dr. D'Abate proclaimed loudly. "You must try what we are most famous for!"

Dr. Errecondo translated for me, but his tone reflected his doubts about Argentine beef. He had traveled to the United States and been introduced to our tender American steak.

"Please," I said to Dr. Errecondo, "you order for me as I neither understand the menu nor what Dr. D'Abate is saying. If he insists on the beefsteak, I will be glad to try it."

The beef arrived. Trying not to offend Dr. D'Abate, I attempted to chew the tough, leathery meat. *Argentineans must have the strongest teeth in the world,* I thought. Dr. Errecondo winked as he translated Dr. D'Abate's next comment.

"Here in Salta, it is my personal opinion that we have the best beefsteak in all of Argentina! But perhaps I am prejudiced."

That was a statement with which I could readily agree.

"Ah," Dr. D'Abate spoke to Dr. Errecondo, "I can tell by the beautiful *señora's* expression that she, too, is in love with our beefsteak."

Dr. Errecondo's quickly changed the subject. He knew it was the toughest piece of meat that I had ever tried to eat.

"How long do you think it will take to complete the papers?" Dr Errecondo asked. "I need to get back to Buenos Aires this evening."

"We will go back to my office and get started right away. I have already called the judge. She will meet us as soon as everything is ready. I don't think it will take more than three or four hours," Dr. D'Abate said as he picked up the check and paid the bill.

At Dr. D'Abate's office, the two attorneys conversed in Spanish for a long time. Occasionally, Dr. Errecondo translated bits and pieces, but a word or two in English every half hour was hardly adequate to satisfy my curiosity or quell my apprehension. My confidence and calm faded.

Dr. Errecondo finally explained that the work required two more hours. He suggested we leave and return in time to meet the judge with Dr. D'Abate.

"Did you make it very plain that we need to be careful about Franco?" I pleaded with Dr. Errecondo. "That he will run if he suspects that I am here? Please make sure that he understands this. It is very important."

"Please don't worry; we will take care of everything. You are not to worry your pretty head. Your ex-husband will not run from the authorities. Here," he said proudly, "he will have to obey the law." My clenched fingers and nervous expression had not escaped his notice. "Please relax, *Señora,* these matters take time. How about going for a sightseeing tour of beautiful Salta?"

"I'm a nervous wreck and you want to sightsee?" Then I looked at the warm gentle man of whom I had grown fond, and relented. "I guess it's better than sitting on our thumbs for two hours. But I'm so afraid that by some chance we will run into Franco."

We took a taxi out of town, and up a winding hillside, stopping at an observation point from which we could view the entire city of Salta. "What a beautiful city! It's the perfect shot for the travel brochures." I sighed as I looked out over the beauty below. "Somewhere down there is my Triana."

The town was much larger than I had expected. Salta, like most towns, had a small upper-class area; most of the city, however, was poor. Even so, the town was very lovely.

"You'll have her back this very day, if all goes well." Dr. Errecondo reassured me.

Dr. Errecondo and I sat on a rock wall and talked for over an hour. I learned about his wife and children, his devotion to his job, to his family and to the arts. He not only practiced law but also worked for a bank as legal advisor. His wife was a true Argentine beauty. They already had two children and he confided to me that his wife desired another. I shared details about my life in the States and of my pregnancy.

As we rode back through the streets of Salta, I sat as low and as far back as I could, unable to suppress my fear of bumping into Franco.

The papers were still not finished and my impatience surfaced immediately. This day had turned into the longest twenty-four hours of the entire ordeal; the endless documents, the checking of every detail, the addition of still more documents. I wanted action but I wanted caution, too.

Finally, we approached the courthouse. Again, I raised the importance of not alerting Franco.

"No offense. I know you both are fine attorneys, but I can't believe that Franco is about to obey any laws. Our only chance is to take him by surprise."

"There will be no problems. Even your Franco is not above the law down here. If there is any problem, we will handle it with ease. You will see," Dr. Errecondo assured me. "Just rely upon us."

After a mercifully short wait, we were admitted to the small room that served as the Judge's chambers. The judge and her clerk perused the papers quickly. When they had finished, she began an endless conversation in Spanish with the attorneys while I sat in yet another frustrated silence, knowing that my destiny and Triana's were to be forged without my participation. Dr. Errecondo translated very little. The knot in my stomach grew larger as I searched their faces. I was the expert in the group on Franco's behavior, yet I was not a party to the decision.

After an hour, everyone got up and started to leave the building.

"Dr. Errecondo, where are we going?" I asked in an agitated voice.

"The judge has decided to go to the church and demand that Father Buttinelli bring your daughter to the church."

"Oh, God! No!" I objected. "You have got to believe me. Franco will run. You must understand! He'll take my daughter and run away, and I may never find him again!"

Dr. Errecondo would not listen. He smiled at me patronizingly. "Calm down, Señora. Please trust us. We know what we are doing. It will turn out well. You will see. Where else is he going to go?"

I shuddered as I pictured a map of South America, with its myriad towns, many of them surrounded by miles of wilderness.

Just outside the church, my fears again got the better of me.

"Please," I begged. "Dr. Errecondo, you must make them understand that this is not the way to go about this."

Dr. Errecondo again spoke confidently. "You are not going to lose your child. We're going to get her back. I'm not going to let them do anything that will jeopardize the recovery of your child."

Looking into his eyes, I knew he meant every word. But the knot in my stomach persisted. They did not know Franco.

CHAPTER FOURTEEN

June, 1973
Salta, Argentina

Father Buttinelli, Father Raymondo and three other priests greeted us as we entered the church. They listened attentively and nodded while the judge explained the situation.

Father Buttinelli spoke gravely. "I have not seen the gentleman you speak of for some time. However, we can take you to his last address. Father Juan will escort you."

Dr. Errecondo translated for me, Father Juan nodded, and we left for Franco's previous lodging. All of us, that is, except Father Raymondo.

The attorneys, the judge, and her clerk appeared calm and confident, but fear choked my breath tight in my lungs.

Three blocks from downtown Salta, out of our sight and knowledge, Father Raymondo spoke authoritatively to Franco. Father Raymondo, who had fallen under Franco's spell, had not said a word during the interrogation. He had decided to play the hero and bring Franco to the church himself.

"So, Franco, you must now come with me to the church; we cannot disobey the law. We did not want to send them here to your home. It is better that you bring the child and meet them at the church. Please come with me now and get it over with."

Father Raymondo put his hand on Franco's shoulder. He saw Franco's trembling hands. "Come, my son. Go and get Triana and her things. We must be going."

Franco turned immediately and went into the bedroom. Father Raymondo spoke directly to Carmen.

"So you see, *Señora*, it is for the best. The child will be reunited with her mother, and perhaps your son can work out his difficulties with the authorities and you can go home to Rome. This is your wish, is it not?"

Carmen nodded. She sighed and thought about her intention in coming to South America: to see that Triana was returned to Rosalie. She had never been able to carry out that task. She had weakened when she had seen the love her son displayed for his child. Now she had no choice.

"You are right, Father, but it will be difficult on my son." Carmen looked toward the bedroom door. "Perhaps I should help my son and my granddaughter get ready."

She rose and went to the bedroom. What she saw was an open window and an empty room. Franco and Triana were gone.

"Father, he has taken the child and run off," Carmen cried.

"What!?" exclaimed Father Raymondo. "Oh, no! Why? Why would he run away like that?" Father Raymondo repeated the phrase several times as he and Carmen walked to the church. Carmen remained silent, as her fingers worked the beads in her Rosary.

Back at the church, the Judge berated Father Buttinelli.

"Father Juan has taken us on a wild goose chase. There was no sign of Mr. Allatere at that house. The owner stated that he and Mr. Allatere had gotten into a fight and the entire family had departed several months ago. I suspect that you know where Mr. Allatere is and you are protecting him."

I stood watching the two attorneys; the Judge and her clerk attack the priest. I did not need to speak Spanish to understand. I knew that my child was lost to me once again. As tears began to stream down my face, I saw Carmen enter the large church door.

"Nona!" I screamed. I turned to Dr. Errecondo. "I told you this would happen. Why wouldn't you listen to me?"

"Rosalie, Rosalie," Carmen began, "I am so sorry to see you under such terrible circumstances. My son has run away with Triana. I couldn't stop him."

Carmen approached me. By this time I was sobbing hysterically. She took me in her arms and tried to comfort me.

The Judge continued her harangue at the priest. "You may go to jail for this, you realize, especially you, Father Raymondo, especially you. You are not above the law here, either. I want all of you out searching for him," she ordered. "This Franco Allatere is not to escape again. I will personally hold all of you responsible for what happens."

"Your Honor," a crestfallen Father Raymondo interceded, "I went to Franco's place of residence and was going to bring him and the child back here, but."

"But what? The judge demanded. "I will tell you what; you disobeyed the judgment of the Court, and I will not stand for it. DO YOU HEAR?"

The crestfallen priests stared silently at the angry Judge, knowing that she could indeed carry out her legal threats. They did not doubt that she meant every word. Dr. Errecondo translated the entire conversation, hoping to relieve the pain he could see in my eyes, but I saw the guilt in his. He looked away.

Dr. Errecondo and the judge spoke together for several minutes. The Judge, her clerk, and Dr. D'Abate soon departed. They left Dr. Errecondo and me alone with Carmen.

Dr. Errecondo put his hand on my shoulder. He knew no way to relieve the anger he felt. "The judge wants you to check into a hotel," he said. "They are going to set up a roadblock around the town and send out the special police to look for them. There is nothing else you can do but wait."

I pleaded with Carmen. "Carmen, do you know where he has gone? Are they with Kitty and her girls?"

"No, my dear child, I do not know where my son has taken Triana. If I did, I would try to convince him to return Triana to you. My son has been very unhappy running all these years. God knows I have tried to talk to him, but it has not changed him." Carmen's head drooped as she talked. "Kitty and her girls are back in the United States. They have been gone two weeks now. It's just Franco and Triana."

"Nona, I need to check into a hotel for the night. Maybe by tomorrow we will find Franco. Can I come and visit with you later on this evening?"

"Certainly, my child." Carmen took out an old pen from her purse and jotted down the address. "I'm so sorry," was all Carmen could say. "I'm so terribly sorry, my poor child."

The Hotel Plaza proved to be the finest hotel Salta had to offer. I was startled to find such an establishment in this remote South American town. However, its amenities brought me no pleasure. Dr. Errecondo told me of his decision to spend the night, to see the matter through on the following day. He checked us into our rooms and we departed to see if Carmen had received any communication from Franco.

As Carmen opened the door, it was apparent that she had been crying. She gave me a hug and kissed me on both checks, and showed us into the small cramped room. She had not heard from Franco. I looked around; it was an ugly, tattered house.

"How could he force our child to live this way? How could he do it?" I was furious. "How could you live this way, Nona?" I asked as I watched a large cockroach crawl across the dirty wood splintered floor, Carmen looked away.

"But, Rosalie," she protested, "they tell me this is one of the best living arrangements they have had. You should have seen the last place; in fact, you did see it. It was the filthy shack the priest took you to. I have tried to do my duty. I have put up with it all. It is God's Will and I will not complain."

I asked to see where Triana had slept and was shown to the bedroom she had shared with her grandmother. Tears of anger and frustration were my only response.

"Here," Carmen handed me some papers, "here are some pictures that Triana drew. Aren't they nice? You can have them."

As I held my child's drawings, my hands shook. "I haven't seen her in over two years. I don't even know what she looks like," I cried.

"Sit down, my child. Let me tell you as much as I can about her. She's a fine girl. She goes by the name of Lia Parini. Franco has taken a new name." Carmen told me how bright Triana was. There I sat in the house where my daughter had been that very day, touching things Triana had touched, holding in my hand pictures that my child had drawn, perhaps only a few hours ago.

Carmen returned to Dr. Errecondo, leaving me alone with my thoughts in the tiny bedroom. I sat on the edge of the small cot. One by one, I absorbed each of the drawings, and finally wept so pitifully that both Carmen and Dr. Errecondo rushed to the room.

Dr. Errecondo tried to comfort me. "Come, there is nothing more we can do here. You must have some dinner. You will feel better after you have had a good night's sleep."

"Carmen, will you come to my hotel and stay with me tonight?" I asked. "You can come and have some dinner with us. Will you, please?" I pleaded with Carmen with such emotion that she could not refuse. I needed Carmen; she was my only connection, to Triana. She had touched my child, talked to her, laughed with her and I needed that link.

"I will stay with you tonight, but please, I cannot eat. I will wait for you in your room. I will be there if any calls come in, in case there is any news of Franco and Triana."

The next morning at the church, Father Raymondo recounted his most recent encounter with Franco. "I found him," he said sadly, "and I tried to impress upon him again the importance of obeying the law and surrendering the child. But he just screamed and raved at me and ran off. I could not convince him to come back, to turn himself in."

"Well, at least the priest is being honest," said Dr. Errecondo.

"Of course he is honest," said Father Buttinelli. "He is a priest."

I stared at Father Buttinelli, who merely looked away. He knew how false his words sounded to my ears.

The search continued. Early in the afternoon, Dr. D'Abate received a phone call.

"I am a fellow attorney," the man said. "My client, an established businessman here in Salta, in the used-car business, has retained my services to aid a Mr. Parini, who is his friend."

Dr. D'Abate sat upright and listened carefully as soon as he heard Franco's alias.

"I'm sure something can be worked out," he told the man.

When Dr. Errecondo related the call to me, my mind raced back to the psychic I had consulted. Were those long-ago predictions now coming to light?

Dr. Errecondo returned to Buenos Aires, leaving me in the care of Dr. D'Abate. I tried to thank him for the help he had given, but the words could not be verbalized, they hung limply in the air. I had trusted him. He had gambled and I had lost. No doubt, he believed he had done his best and was gravely sorry for the disastrous turn of events. I tried my best to tell him I understood, but the words stuck in my throat, I could not speak.

For three days, Dr. D'Abate and the man representing Franco negotiated. I offered a reward to anyone who could supply verifiable information leading to Franco's capture.

On the third day, Franco's lawyer's secretary called. "I have information that Franco and the little girl are planning to attempt to leave Salta tonight. Do I get the reward?" he asked eagerly.

"Only if we can verify what you are saying is true. Do you know where he is? And what time is he supposed to make his escape?" Dr. D'Abate pressed the greedy, unprincipled man.

"I don't know exactly, but I will try to find out and call you back," he whispered.

"If we don't catch him, there is no reward! Do you understand?" Dr. D'Abate said sternly.

My hopes rose as the judge ordered the police to tighten the roadblock around the entire town. Unable to sit still in the hotel room, I accepted an invitation to stay with a local American family to whom Dr D'Abate had introduced me.

I spent the lonely night pacing and praying. At three forty-five a.m., I heard noise outside and sprang to the door, to find Dr. D'Abate, and the Chief of Police.

"I'm so sorry," Dr. D'Abate said sadly. "I'm afraid that Franco somehow got through the police lines and escaped. There is no telling where he is."

I sank in a chair, too weary and exhausted to move. Hot, painful tears rolled down my cheeks.

Dr. D'Abate and a translator came to my hotel the next morning. He informed me that the police had lost all trace of Franco and could no longer help me. Franco was now out of their jurisdiction.

A felling of loss, betrayal and of being totally alone overwhelmed my entire body. There was no choice but for me to return home, without my child.

I saw Carmen for the last time and I gave her the clothing that I had purchased for Triana to wear home. "Please give her these clothes, Nona, and please tell her that I love her very, very much." I gave Carmen a hug and kiss, and pressed a small amount of money into her hand to tide her over.

"My dear, I am working for the church. They pay me fifty cents a day to make spaghetti for them and they will see to my needs. Please do not worry for me."

"Nona, you can't live on fifty cents a day. Let me give you some more money," I insisted.

"My needs are very small. You have given me enough. I will write to my sister and go back to Rome." Carmen kissed me and walked me to the door of the small, ugly house that she now occupied alone.

That afternoon the American friend, Barbara, drove me to the airport. "Chin up," she tried to comfort me. "He can't run forever. Eventually you'll get her back." I appreciated her encouragement, but I was not convinced.

At the airport, Barbara bought me three bottles of Argentine wine. "If your husband is a wine expert, he will love this. It is the best in all Argentina. Here, it's a going-away present to cheer you up!"

I had not cared much for the wine I had tasted so far. Like the steak, it needed a lot of getting used to. But I hugged and thanked my friend and boarded the plane for the long trip home.

The flight to Los Angeles exhausted me. Listlessly, I checked into customs, but some sixth sense roused me from my lethargy. I was being watched. The officer who searched my bags opened the box of wine and stepped back.

"You're only allowed to bring in one bottle, ma'am."

I shrugged. "I'm sorry, it was a gift. Just take it, I don't really care."

A woman customs officer approached the counter. "Will you please follow me, ma'am?"

"Where are we going?" I asked.

As they led me into a small booth, a female officer ordered me to read the sign on the wall. It listed my rights.

"What is going on here?" I demanded.

"We have information that a woman traveling alone is attempting to smuggle drugs into the country. You are one of several who have been chosen to be searched. Please read the sign. We will return shortly."

"Damn it," I yelled, "I have no intention of reading that sign or any other rights your might have for me! Do what you have to do and let me out of this damn place. In the last few days I've had enough problems to last three lifetimes! I don't need this added to the list!"

The two women stood petrified as I proceeded to pour out the details of the last week.

"What kind of nightmare is this? I just lost my child in South America. Haven't I gone through enough? Now you think I'm bringing drugs into the country and you want to search me! How much more can I take?" My emotions were getting the better of me. "I haven't seen my baby in over two years. I was a mile away from her and I lost her again. I didn't even get to see her." I was completely out of control. I didn't know if I was crying or shouting.

When my tirade subsided, the sympathetic officers proceeded with their task of frisking me as gently as possible. After I was released, one of the women handed me a card. "Here, take this," the young woman said. "If there is anything I can do to help you find your child, please call me."

"Thank you," I said, touched by the woman's kindness.

I was allowed to leave, but it was well over an hour before my well-scrutinized makeup bag was sent to the claims area. Stan had already taken his sons to a ranch in Montana and had sent his parents to meet me.

"My goodness," said Stan's mother, "what took you so long?"

"Don't ask," I said. "Everything's all right now. They were looking for drugs. They had a tip that a woman traveling alone was bringing drugs into the country."

"Well, what are they searching you for?" Stan's father replied angrily. "Why don't they pick on the real criminal and leave the decent people alone."

"Dad, sometimes it's difficult to tell the good guys from the bad."

June, 1973
Salta, Argentina

Back in Salta, the winter sun was just beginning to descend behind the hills. Carmen sat in the small parish rectory, placing an overseas call to her sister in Rome.

"Of course, operator, I'll accept the charges!" Lina's voice crossed thousands of miles of telephone cable.

"Carmen? Are you all right? What has happened?"

"Oh, it's so good to hear your voice, Lina. I need your help. I want to come home, but I don't have any money."

"Of course, I'll send you the money immediately. Oh, I'm so glad! But what of Franco and your granddaughter?"

"Well, it's not such good news. I'll tell you everything--in Rome." Just saying the word Rome made Carmen feel better again. She went back to the house and offered a prayer for her son and her granddaughter.

When she rose from her knees, she packed everything worth taking.

June, 1973
South American Wilderness

After they had been hiding out for three days in various locations in Salta, a friend of Father Butinelli's snuck Franco and Triana out of town by shaving Triana's head and dressing her in boy's clothes.

At Father Butinelli's suggestion, and with Carmen's knowledge, the two escapees were taken to his previous church in Jujuy. They would stay at this location until they could cross the Argentine border into Bolivia. The priest in charge of the Jujuy church was to supply them with meals and a place to sleep for two days.

On the third day, the priest waited until after dark to drive the two fugitives north as far as he dared. He pointed out a path through the jungle that would eventually take them across the border into Bolivia. The priest instructed them to stay on the path until they came to a well-traveled road where a car should be waiting for them.

In the pitch-black darkness, penetrated by the cries of nocturnal wildlife, Franco and nine-year-old Triana walked for more than three hours through the thick, tropical underbrush. Triana cried part of the way. She was confused and tired and had been forced to leave her favorite doll in Salta. Finally, she sat down in tears.

Franco picked up the exhausted child and kept walking.

Eventually they reached the road, and waited for over an hour for the prearranged car. The car pulled slowly up to the exhausted man holding a sleeping girl in his arms.

"Been waiting long?" The driver opened the back car door for Franco to deposit the sleeping child on the battered seat.

"It seemed long; I was told you would be waiting for us. Where do we go from here?" Franco examined the driver to make sure he could trust this stranger.

"Tito suggested that you stay out of sight for a few days until things die down. He and Father Buttinelli arranged for you to stay with some priests at a school in *Tarija*. It's about seventy kilometers from here, and should be a safe place." With considerable curiosity, the stranger looked at this man he had been instructed to pick up in the middle of the night. "Ran into some trouble in Salta, did you?"

Franco looked over at him. He was bone-weary, and the last thing he wanted to do was reenact the nerve-wracking escape from Salta.

"No, it was just a case of mistaken identity, but I didn't want to go through the problems of straightening it out. Mind if I take a snooze while you drive?"

The driver nodded, and turned his thoughts to the road.

The school was operated by the Franciscan order, the same as the convent in Salta. It was a clean, modern, spacious facility for boys. The campus included a swimming pool, which delighted Triana. A priest was waiting for them, and showed them to a room with two small beds, and a single window that looked out into the courtyard. Franco was to do the gardening as payment for food and lodging until he could find better accommodations. The arrangement was a courtesy to Father Buttinelli. Franco was plainly informed that it would not be permanent.

After a month at the school, Franco was called into the office of Father Domenico.

"Mr. Parini, I am sorry to tell you this," said Father Domenico, "but you will have to seek other accommodations. We have had a complaint about your little girl. This is a boys' school and people find it unsuitable for a young girl to be present."

"Father, I'm sorry. It's just that we have been so happy here. My child has been happier than I have seen her since her mother died and I was hoping it could last for her sake." Franco lowered his head. "But I will look for a new job; we will be out of here as soon as we can."

With drooping shoulders, Franco rose and left the room. Father Domenico reflected that though Mr. Parini had been a very good worker and seemed sincere, there was something disturbing about the man.

Father Domenico kept Franco on as a gardener and assisted him in finding lodging in a small home outside of town. Franco became restless after a few months and decided it was time for him to take Triana and move on. He headed back toward the Argentine border and then north to *Atocha,* a small town in the southwestern portion of Bolivia.

By the time Franco and Triana had been in Atocha for three

months, Franco was desperate for new documents. The papers from Salta were too well known by the authorities.

Franco and Triana frequently made trips into town on Franco's day off. He would take Triana to a restaurant, and on one occasion they met an official whose name was Enardo. Franco and Enardo became friends, and they began to meet regularly.

One night, Franco and Triana stayed in town late. Franco hadn't arranged a ride back to his cottage, and Enardo offered a solution.

"Why don't you and Lia come spend the night at my place," he said, "and I will drive you back to your house in the morning? My wife is with her sister, who is expecting a baby, so there will be plenty of room."

"That would be great. You're sure it won't put you out?" Franco asked.

To Triana the conversation sounded false, and she felt suspicious.

Franco and Triana ate dinner with Enardo. While Triana prepared for bed, Franco and Enardo sat at the table and talked in low voices for over an hour. Occasionally Triana heard angry outbursts.

"Where do I sleep, Daddy?" Triana, who was tired, mumbled.

"Why don't we all get some sleep? I am also tired," Enardo said. "It has been a long hot day."

As Triana stood waiting for directions, the two men got up from the table and both proceeded to prepare for the night.

"Well, I think that the big bed would be more comfortable for you, so I will sleep here on this couch." Franco walked toward the couch.

"But, Daddy, the couch is barely large enough to fit me. Why don't I sleep there and you have the large bed?" Triana protested, as she looked toward the large bed that was partially hidden by a room divider.

"I said I would sleep here. You sleep in the large bed with Enardo," ordered Franco.

Triana obeyed and crawled into the large bed and quickly fell asleep. Sometime during the night, she awoke to a large hand moving down her body. She turned over away from it and pretended to be asleep, hoping the man would stop. The hand persisted and before she knew what was happening, another hand was over her mouth and Enardo's large body was on top of hers.

Eight feet away, her father lay on the couch while his nine-year-old-daughter was raped.

Enardo's sex drive satisfied, he rolled over and fell into a deep sleep. A stunned Triana, blood dripping down her legs, got out of bed and went over to her father.

"Daddy, I don't feel good, please let me sleep with you. Don't send me back there, please," Triana said. She did not know what else to say.

Franco got up and let his daughter sleep on the couch. He said nothing as he slumped down in a nearby chair.

The next morning as Franco and Triana were washing up at the outside water pump, Triana summoned up enough courage to speak to her father.

"Daddy, that man did some bad things to me last night. I don't want to stay here any longer. Can we leave? I don't want to be around him."

Franco stood up from the wooden trough and frowned at his child, a look that Triana took for shock and anger. At this point, Franco had truly crossed the line from self-indulgent and out of control behavior, to that which was not only bizarre but also depraved. Unfortunately, Triana was to be the victim of Franco's depravity many times.

From Enardo, he now had new papers with new names. He could now travel safely in Bolivia. Two days after Triana was raped, they departed.

On the bus going to Uyuni, Franco sat silently. Triana sat beside him, shocked, feeling betrayed and miserable. She had lived in South America long enough to know that sometimes children were used. She wondered why her father had placed her in such painful harm if he truly loved her. Why had he sold her to Enardo?

It was the first, but not the last time Franco would sell his daughter. Whenever he was penniless or needed new documents with new names, he had a ready financial resource: his daughter.

The next few days Franco and Triana practiced their new names,

Ricardo and Cara Mantilla, as they looked for new quarters and a new job. He heard of a job with an important family a few miles outside of town. He and Triana headed out on foot.

"These people don't know that we have ever been in America and they don't like Americans here. Be careful that you don't say anything that would give us away. This is an important job, and we need it."

"Okay, Daddy, I'll be careful. How much farther is it? My feet are tired."

Triana walked as fast as she could; but she wore old shoes that were a size too small for her feet, with holes in the soles.

They hiked up the steep hill to the house where Franco spoke with charm and poise. Triana was playing with the children of the family and Franco was conversing with the owner. Just as the deal was set and Franco was to be hired, the children's voices could be overheard.

"I can count in English. One, two three," one of the children said.

"Three, four, five," Triana responded.

"Oh, you speak English? I was under the impression you were natives of South America. How do you know English?" the wife asked.

Triana froze. Franco's stern instruction came back to her and she looked over at her dad who had gone white with anger.

Franco interjected coolly, "You must pardon my daughter. I have warned her time and again not to repeat the few English words she learned at the last place I worked, but she is young; she forgets." He tried to recover, but no matter what he said, he could not convince the owner. The job was lost.

The people smiled politely enough, but suspicion appeared in their eyes.

"Well," the owner of the house said flatly, "Mr. Mantilla, we will let you know about the job."

All the way down the hill, Franco wrung his hands. "How could you do that to me? What have I done to deserve it?" His voice rose in pitch with each word until he was screaming at his child. Franco came to a dead stop. He knelt on the ground, crying and screaming at Triana as he waved his arms toward the heavens for emphasis. "You should be ashamed of yourself, Cara. You must hate me, what have I done to deserve such disloyalty from you?" He waved his finger in her face. She looked at the ground, crying softly, unsure of what she had done and wracked with guilt and shame that she did not understand.

Suddenly there was a loud ripping sound. Franco stopped ranting and inspected his trousers.

"Oh, no!" He screamed. "Now see what you have made me do!"

Triana looked at him in confusion.

"My pants are ripped! They are the only ones I have! What am I supposed to wear when I look for a job, now that you have ruined my chances at getting this one?"

"Daddy, please don't be mad at me." She was still not sure what she had done, but clearly, the ripping of her father's pants was somehow her fault. "Please, Daddy, I'm sorry for what I did. Don't be mad at me. Please Daddy, I'm sorry."

Franco remained angry about the incident, and the gnawing guilty feeling grew in Triana's mind. Triana's self-esteem was destroyed with each rape as the nagging guilt escalated. Daily she was blamed for the smallest event gone wrong.

Franco ultimately found a job in Valle Grande cleaning the presses for a small newspaper. He and Triana moved into a room in a small local hotel near the center of town. He made friends quickly with the hotel owner and his family, who watched Triana in the daytime.

Franco soon took up with the local women. He often brought them home. They shared the bed with Triana. Sometimes she slept through her father's sexual exploits, but sometimes the violence of the vigorous activity awakened her. At such times, the child lay there stiffly, unable to sleep. The sex movie she and Amber had seen and her own abuse was nothing in comparison to the activity that went on in the bed she occupied with the women and her father. Triana could only sleep once her father and his friend finally finished and fell asleep from exhaustion.

As months passed and Christmas approached, the town blazed with merriment as everyone prepared for the traditional holiday parade. The owner of the newspaper, Flamenio, had taken a liking to Franco. One day he approached Franco and told him that the parade organizers needed a child performer.

"Ricardo, how about Cara?" he asked Franco. "We are in need of a majorette. Would your little girl be interested?"

"I think so. It would be a lot of fun for her."

Triana played her role as a majorette with skill. The event proved to be one of the happiest times she had known since they left Salta.

The Valle Grande government, however, was in the middle of a fierce political struggle. There were constant riots and arrests of local dissidents. One night Franco and Triana were awakened by sirens screaming, cries from men, women and children in the street. A smoke bomb missed its target and landed in their room. The smoke was so thick that Franco barely managed to find the door and carry Triana from the hotel. Chaos filled the streets. Men hurled rocks at the police, who responded with riot and teargas guns. Franco ducked in and out of doorways, shielding himself and his child, as he headed for his boss' house. After Flamenio put Triana to bed with his children, he and Franco sat up talking.

"Ricardo, how would you like to make a little extra money?" Flamenio asked.

"I sure could use it," Franco answered.

"I have some friends that need some deliveries made. If you are interested, I will ask if you can do the job."

"I'd like to meet them, if it means making more money," Franco agreed.

"I'm not sure they will accept you, but if they do, you will have to be very careful about what you say to them. You must not mention to a soul that you know them."

"Listen, I can keep a secret, believe me. I am willing to take risks if the stakes are high enough."

"Okay, after this situation calms down, I will talk to them and let you know. I can arrange a meeting at the paper. Now get some sleep. This thing could go on all night. You can sleep on the couch over there. It's small, but it is better than the floor," Flamenio said.

Two weeks later, Franco was asked to come into Flamenio's office. "We are having a meeting here tomorrow afternoon after everyone clears out. Can you make it?"

"I'll be here," Franco said, enthusiastically.

The next day Franco picked Triana up from the hotel and started back to the newspaper office. "Daddy has to go to a meeting. You can wait in the courtyard for me while I am in there. It shouldn't last too long," he told her.

Through the large glass windows, Triana could see the men talking to her father. She wondered why she was confined to the courtyard. Her dad had always taken her everywhere before. Maybe it was what she had said when they had traveled by foot up the steep road. She felt puzzled and confused.

Each of the men at the meeting questioned Franco about his background. After he satisfied their questions, they agreed that he would do. Franco would be delivering large sums of money and cocaine to various people. He was not to ask where the drugs and money came from, or where they were going. He would get only specific pick-up and delivery instructions. They would meet in two days, at two-thirty in the afternoon to arrange the first pickup.

The next meeting took place as promised. Once again, Triana was confined to the courtyard, where she could see the furtive meeting from the park bench.

"But why can't I come in with you, Daddy? I don't like sitting out here all by myself. You always took me with you before. Why not now, Daddy?" Triana persisted.

"You are not to enter that room no matter what, you hear? I'll not be long. And stay out of sight of any airplane. If one comes over, hide under that tree over there. It could be bad people looking for us. Do you hear?" Franco was frustrated and angry. He didn't want to leave his child alone either, but it would be worse for her to understand what was going on.

Franco emerged from the building carrying a large bag. He fetched Triana and they departed for the hotel.

In their room, when Franco emptied the bag onto the hotel bed, Triana gasped. "Daddy, I have never seen so much money in my life. How much is there?" Triana stared at it, mesmerized by the large rolls of pesos.

"Never say anything about this to your friends, okay? I have to go on an overnight trip. I'll leave you downstairs. You won't say anything about this, will you?" Franco looked at Triana sideways as she stood over the money.

"No, Daddy, but can we have some of the money for our own?" Triana asked, fascinated by the wads of pesos.

"No, *Penguina*, there is no way that we can have any. I don't want to be on the wrong side of the boss." Franco knew that he would never be able to run fast enough if he touched one peso. These people were very much like the Italian men he had run from in the United States.

Franco deposited Triana with the hotel manager and departed to make his first delivery. As time passed, Franco became less cautious and took Triana on the cocaine deliveries, but for the most part, he left her in the hotel. Soon he began to feel that they had lingered in this town too long. As he prepared to make his last delivery, the old, familiar temptations rose within him. He decided to take the risk. Carefully, he reserved some of the cocaine for himself. And he had started skimming the payoff money. It was time for new names; it was time to move on.

CHAPTER FIFTEEN

June and August 1973
California and Montana

As I tossed and turned in my sleep, I was tormented with nightmares of Triana. She was a rag doll being torn in half by two monkeys hanging by their tails in a tall tree. The two monkeys fought over the spiritless doll, tugging and pulling until all that was left was stuffing from two halves of her limp and lifeless torso.

I had been through a devastating ordeal in South America, and my pregnancy became more important to me than ever before. I wanted this baby more than anything except Triana's return. Perhaps this new child would help ease my loss. No child could ever replace Triana, but a new life to care for would fill my days and lighten the pain.

After I rested a few days, I flew on to Montana to join Stan and his two younger sons, Scott, 13, and Todd, 9. They were spending the summer on our cattle ranch in Victor, located in the southwestern section of the state. Mark, Stan's oldest, was staying in Stockton at the University of Pacific, taking summer classes. The boys had welcomed the trip because their mother had remarried and they disliked their new stepfather, Ken.

Montana is rugged and stupendous. Most of the state is still wild, beautiful and free: truly the Big Sky Country. Victor lies in the Bitterroot Valley of the Great Rocky Mountains. On the east side of the valley, sits the picturesque Sapphire Range, and on the west the splendid Bitterroot Mountains.

A hundred years ago, an ambitious General George Custer had led his cavalry troops through south-central Montana in an intense pursuit of Indians. Unfortunately, he was ambushed and annihilated at the Little Big Horn River by the combined forces of Sioux and Cheyenne, led by Crazy Horse and Sitting Bull.

I'm having quite a battle of my own here, I thought, as I read the inscription explaining the Custer Battlefield National Monument at Crow Agency, Montana.

Stan, his two sons and I had taken a short side trip to the Little Big Horn. The journey had turned out to be too long for all of us. The boys and I were definitely not getting along. Stan had failed to tell them that he intended to remarry until a few days before our wedding. It had come as a great shock to them both since they had harbored hopes that their parents would reunite. After seven months, they still blamed me, rather than their father, for the end of their dreams, and kept me at a distance I found impossible to bridge.

When we arrived back from our trip, I found myself alone much of the time. The boys sulked or took off about the ranch, staying away from the confinement of the house as much as possible. When they were inside, they often locked themselves in their rooms with comic books or buried themselves in some television show. Stan worked around the property, taking care of the cattle, the irrigation and, at the end of the summer, the job of cutting the hay.

These days Stan was often disgruntled and upset. More often than not, he was drinking. My depression at losing Triana and feeling saddled with two unfamiliar and unhappy boys did not help. We were all trapped by our own demons.

"Stan, what's wrong?" I asked lamely.

"Nothing, there's nothing you can do now."

My temper flared. "Haven't I gone through enough in godforsaken South America? Tell me what's bothering you!"

"All right!" he said. "I feel like I've been betrayed and I can't get out, that's what's wrong."

I was shocked. "What do you mean, betrayed?"

"Look, Rosalie, I told you from the beginning that I wasn't prepared for any more family responsibilities. You went ahead, without even talking to me, and got pregnant."

I thought when I returned from Rome that Stan had accepted my pregnancy. I had been sure he was happy about our child, happy that I had not lost the baby in Rome. But now, after a few drinks, all of his frustrations surfaced and his anger raged. I was a dreamer, a romanticist, and unrealistic about my husband. For a moment, I sat stunned and hurt.

Finally, I said, "Stan, you know I discussed this with you before I left for Italy. If you didn't want another child, why didn't you say so then?"

"Rosalie! You told me after you were pregnant.. not before. You know very well I would never want you to have an abortion! With you pregnant, and you and the boys not getting along, it's open warfare all the time. It's just more than I can stand. Doesn't anyone have regard for me? Or am I just the magic moneyman? Never have any one of you given even the slightest thought to my peace of mind. You all seem to think that I'll just keep rolling along.. good old Stan, good old Dad he'll handle it. Well, Rosalie, I've been handling it all my fucking life and I'm just about at the end of my emotional rope." Stan caught his breath and gulped down his fourth drink.

"Stan, if you'd stop drinking and try to cooperate with me, we'd be able to deal with the kids and the new baby. Why don't we have a family meeting and discuss this problem together? If you would just treat the boys like boys and stop this 'poor children' routine, they'd recover. Life goes on, but you cater to the past, and encourage them to stay stuck."

"Cooperate with you. Bullshit! You mean side with you even when you're wrong," Stan muttered and headed for the kitchen in search of the solace of more scotch. "Oh, never mind, what's the use?"

We argued again the following evening while Stan continued to drink. "Stan, this is our child, not just mine," I tried to convince him. "Children are our future, our mark, our gift. This child will be ours, we can manage this responsibility, you'll see."

"Listen, Rosalie," he snapped back, "I've always had to handle everything that comes along. Don't lecture me on responsibility. I was supporting a family while you were still living like a high school girl. I can love the whole fucking world of children as long as I'm not responsible for taking care of them."

"You'll love this child as much as I already do, Stan."

"It damn well better be the last kid you have, if you want this marriage to continue." Stan glared at me.

I had come to Montana expecting peace and healing, a chance to recuperate and relax during the summer, get acquainted with the boys, spend time with Stan. Now I faced hostile rejection and Stan's constant drinking. His drinking had never seemed to be a problem to me before, but now it seemed that liquor had replaced me as his evening companion. I fell asleep with memories of our happier days and I hoped they would return.

A few days later, Stan's ex-wife, Lucy, called to ask him to have the boys home early as she and her new husband were moving with the boys to Oklahoma.

Stan calmly told her he had no intention of allowing his boys to move to Oklahoma and he informed Lucy that he intended to seek permanent custody. He would return them at the end of the summer as originally planned, and they would discuss the issue of the boys' future at that time. I stood stunned and numb as I listened to the conversation on our end of the phone.

The summer wore on. Stan took the boys on outings to rodeos and on camping trips. I stayed by myself, or took long drives through the rugged Montana territory, sightseeing, photographing interesting sights and shopping in out-of-the-way places. It was a long summer.

August, 1973
Irvine, California
When we returned home to California, Lucy agreed that the children could stay with us when she and her husband moved. My relationship with Stan was filled with tension as I constantly fought

self-pity. I resolved that I would take charge of the situation and not let it get me down.

Two weeks after we returned home from Montana, Scott, Todd and one unkempt sheepdog named Snoopy moved into our four-bedroom rented home in the Turtlerock area of Irvine.

"You're-not-our-mother!" became the boys' daily battle cry whenever I spoke to them. The youngsters loved and missed their own mother. They missed their old neighborhood, their friends and their previous unfettered life style. I was a constant reminder that overnight their life had changed, and would never be the same. I didn't have a clue how to reach out to them to make friends with these angry children. Nothing I tried worked to gain the boys' trust.

Eventually I gave up on my pursuit to gain their friendship. Talking to Stan became as much of a battle as communicating with the boys. We existed in a house where the boys watched TV after school until their father came home. They ignored me as I went about the chores of homemaking. They always thanked their father for the meals I prepared. In their eyes, I did not exist.

I was thankful when they were at school. It was the one time I could work on my quest to find Triana, prepare for the baby's arrival and find true solace.

Once in a while, Stan's oldest son, eighteen-year-old Mark, stayed with us when he returned home from school. Of the three boys, he was the most congenial; his maturity and understanding gave me comfort at a time when our house always seemed to be in turmoil.

Three weeks after the boys had settled in, I renewed my attempts at rapport with Stan's sons.

I read a list of chores for which I needed their help: "Trash has to be taken out, weeds need to be pulled in the yard, the dog waste needs to be picked up, the front yard needs mowing and the driveway needs to be washed down and cleaned. I would like each of you to keep your room clean and your bed made. If I can be of any help to you, just let me know. If we cooperate we can get all of these chores accomplished together, and everything will work smoothly. Do either of you have any suggestions?"

After several minutes of silence, the boys gave me a blank look, got up and walked out of the room, leaving me standing alone with my list.

That evening, I attempted to discuss the problem with Stan.

"Why don't you leave them alone?" he yelled at me. "They haven't had to report to anyone since I left their mother. Just leave them alone, and don't ask them to do anything. That's your job."

"Listen, Stan, you didn't consult with me when you made the decision to have the boys live with us. We need to work together as a family for all of us to be happy. I am their stepmother; together we are now their parents. I don't think I'm asking too much."

"Oh, stop moralizing!" Stan raised his voice. "How would you like it if someone presented you with a list and wanted to order you around?"

"Order them around? I tried to talk to them and ask them to pick the chores that best fit them. They need to have some responsibilities as part of our family. I'm not a babysitter. You can't leave them in my care and then tell me to leave them alone, not to bother them."

"Don't you understand they don't want you to be any sort of a mother to them? I know you loved your stepmother, but these boys don't love you and I doubt that they ever will. Their mother chose a life without them and they are mad at the world."

His words hurt me deeply. I tried to respond as best I could. "When I was a child we all had things that we were responsible for doing, and I don't think that's asking too much of your sons."

Stan spoke with quiet sarcasm. "Yes, you've told me all about your glorious childhood. Is that the kind of nightmare you want to make for my sons?"

"Not all of my childhood was a nightmare, just the part that involved my real mother. Jewell was the best mother you could want. And I loved her for that." Without another word, I left Stan sitting alone in the living room, sipping his scotch and water, as I fled into the bedroom. The bitter memories of my early life sprang up out of the dark, inner recesses of my mind.

"It's over," I cried, "that terrible part of my life is over. Why must it keep coming back to haunt me?" At last, I fell into a miserable sleep.

When marriages split up, it is inevitably painful for the children involved and equally painful for decent parents who want the best for their kids. I knew Stan was such a father. He loved his children and wanted them to be with him, yet he knew they missed their mother. The conflicting pressures allowed him no peace. He knew I was right, but he wanted his boys to know he was on their side.

January, 1974 to April 1974
Irvine, California

Life moved inexorably on for us. On January 9, 1974, I gave birth to a healthy baby girl. We named her Tisha. As I had hoped, Stan was excited about his baby girl. She was the apple of his eye. I hoped that she would captivate the boys, that they would love her. Her arrival did bring the boys closer on occasion, but most of the time, I found the wall so thick and impenetrable that it was better to leave them alone. I longed to be their friend, their second mother, but I was left to play the waiting game. I kept telling myself that in time things would change.

Months passed and Tisha became the highlight of my days. I relished caring for her, watching her grow, enjoying a baby's weekly development. I thought constantly of Triana, and wondered where and how my firstborn was. At one point, I feared that the love I felt for Tisha was a surrogate for my feelings for Triana, but I struggled against these emotions. I knew it would be unfair for everyone involved, especially Tisha. *I'll never know for sure*, I reasoned, *until I have Triana back.*

In our home, I kept a bedroom for Triana. I retrieved her treasures from storage and decorated her room with her favorite toys and furniture. *If only her presence was here to fill the emptiness of the room and grief of my loss.*

My determination to find Triana strengthened as I continued my letters to Rome and South America. Through Lea, Kitty's sister, I located Kitty in Texas and began to correspond with her. Kitty could shed no light on Franco's whereabouts. Her best guess was that he had probably changed his name again and moved, possibly to Bolivia, Peru or Brazil. More letters were written to government officials, newspapers, Kitty and a host of attorneys. I received a package from Kitty that contained all that she had managed to get out of Argentina. Franco had watched every move she had made the day she packed to leave Salta. The package did contain a list of assumed names that they had considered using, and it gave the names of friends they had in Salta.

But no news arrived from Argentina, or Franco's aunt in Rome, or from the Wackenhut detective agency. I did receive a long letter from Kitty:

"Triana occupies my thoughts constantly and I would love nothing more than to see her back home with you. She is a wonderful girl, and we miss her terribly. Rosalie, if there is anything else I can do to help you get her back, please, please don't hesitate to let me know. I will do all in my power to help you, and I mean this sincerely, from the bottom of my heart."

I folded the letter and placed it with the other correspondence concerning Triana. The thick stack held over 350 letters, plus hundreds of carbon copies of those I had written. I wrote to Kitty, thanking her for the offer and assuring her that she would be contacted immediately if I thought she could help.

Little Tisha cooed in my arms. "You have a sister, you know," I told her. "She's a big girl and her name is Triana. Right now, she's far away in South America. But we're going to find her and bring her back home where she belongs. And we'll never, never give up." As if to register a vote of confidence, the baby gleefully kicked her legs as she cooed contentedly and tugged at my hair.

January, 1974
Chile

The pig let out one final shriek before it collapsed on its side. Blood oozed from the bullet hole in its head. One of its legs twitched convulsively, as if to hold onto life's final moment. Cheers came from the men in the back of the truck loaded with large metal drums laid on their sides. The V-shaped cracks between the drums served as sleeping places for four people, including Franco and Triana.

As the smell of gunpowder permeated the warm air, the men began to pile out of the truck to retrieve their kill. "The mate got away, let's go get him," called Paco, the driver, as he headed for the thick underbrush.

An hour later, the men returned. The male pig had escaped, but they returned with a large armadillo that had happened across their path. They loaded their kills onto the back of the truck and continued their trip along the dusty dirt road toward Chile, where Franco hoped to find work. It was late and they would clean the game when they arrived.

As the truck rolled along, Franco and Triana switched places with the men in the cab. They both slept. Franco leaned against the door and held his sleeping daughter. Two hours later, the truck came to a screeching halt, jolting Franco from a sound sleep. In the headlights walked the largest spider Franco had ever seen.

Paco's eyes widened as he called out to the crew in the back, "Amigos, want to kill and gut this one?" He laughed.

"*Penguina*, wake up, Daddy has something to show you." Franco shook Triana; as she woke up and saw the large spider, her eyes opened wide. She thought the creature could make a meal out of her in no time at all.

"Daddy, what is it? It looks like a monster spider. Can it get us?" She looked up at him fearfully, then back at the large insect crawling methodically across the road, oblivious to the headlights.

"It's a bird-spider, baby, part of the tarantula family. I've read about them, but this is the first time I have ever seen one. This guy is larger than any I ever read about," Franco told Triana as they stared at the monstrous creature. The spider had a leg span of more then twelve inches. Mesmerized by the enormity of the insect, the group watched in silence until the spider reached the opposite side of the road and disappeared from sight into the thick, tropical jungle. Paco started the truck without another word.

Late the next morning they arrived at the home of Paco's cousin. The party of seven hungry, weary travelers climbed out of the truck and unloaded the pig and armadillo. "Let's get this thing cleaned," Paco called out to the others.

Triana scratched at one of the many mosquito bites on her body, then scratched her head, which itched perpetually. Her dirty clothes hung on her frail body. She stared silently at the predatory scene, then quietly climbed out of the truck and walked slowly toward her father, who was helping the other two men drag the lifeless animals to the side of the drive.

One of the men, laughing heartily, pulled out a six-inch hunting knife. "We will eat well today, eh, amigos?"

"*Penguina*, go back inside," Franco advised. "It's not a sight for a little girl to watch."

"I want to watch, Dad," Triana said simply.

In an instant, the pig was slit open and the air was rendered difficult to breathe by the vile, intestinal stench. Triana covered her face with her hands. As the man proceeded to clean the slaughtered animal, she felt a wave of nausea and rushed to the other side of the dirt driveway to vomit.

Two hours later, as the sun rose high in the tropical sky; the pungent aroma of roast pork filled the house. Everyone waited hungrily for Paco to carve the pig.

"The saints must be watching over us today," a tall skinny man said happily.

"Yes, it is a feast! What wonderful luck!" agreed Paco.

Triana sat quietly, eating the food that had been given to her. "Good luck for us," she thought, "but not such good luck for the pig."

When the meal was consumed, the other travelers departed.

"This child needs a bath," Paco's wife, Yma, noted. "Would you mind if I care for her?"

"No, go right ahead," Franco said to Yma. "We have been traveling so far I am afraid she has gone too long without a bath."

Twenty minutes later Yma returned, her face revealing anxiety. "This child has a head of lice like I have never seen before. I am not sure it can be cured. We may have to shave her head."

Franco's mouth dropped open. "How can this be?" he asked. "What about her beautiful long hair?"

"We will treat it, but you must check it regularly. If it can't be cured, there is no other way to rid her of the lice." Yma left to do the best she could.

The next day Franco set out to look for work, leaving Triana with Yma. Triana ate another portion of the pig. The meat did not smell good to her, nor did it taste as good as it had the day before, but she was hungry and ate it anyway. By the time Franco returned late that evening, Triana was in severe pain. Huddled in a corner of a cot, she moaned as she slept. She moved her head from side to side, and her body shivered.

"Wake up, baby." Franco shook her gently. Triana's eyes opened, and Franco saw that they were glazed. "What is it? Are you all right?" he asked nervously.

The child wrapped her arms around her stomach. "Daddy, I don't feel very good," she mumbled.

"Yma," Franco called out, "do you know a doctor I can take my child to right now?"

Yma entered the room. "I didn't know she was that ill. She just asked if she could lie down for a while. What is it?"

"The child is sick. She has a fever. Oh, my God, what could it be?" Franco said nervously as Triana began to shiver more violently.

"My stomach," Triana cried. "It hurts so much, Daddy."

"I will get my husband," Yma said. "There is a doctor seven blocks from here. We will drive you to him right away."

Shortly the doctor, a short *mestizo* with a dark complexion, examined her.

"Señor," the doctor said, "she is very ill with some kind of bacterial infection of the intestines. She will have to stay here, at least overnight."

"Will she get well?" Franco asked nervously.

"I believe so. However, I want to do some tests on her in the morning. We will know more then. You are her father?"

Franco nodded. "Can I stay with her tonight?"

"We don't like to have extra people staying, but I guess you can sleep on the bench in the other room.

"Fine," Franco agreed. "Just make my little girl well again."

Franco slept fitfully, and in the morning, awakened to a strong hand shaking his shoulder. He sat up quickly to find the doctor looking down at him.

"The child seems to be recovering," the doctor informed him. "Her fever broke a few hours ago, and she is now sleeping peacefully. I think it was some kind of food poisoning."

"Thank God," Franco said softly,

"But it appears she also has worms, for which she will need treatment."

"Worms?" Franco grimaced. "How can this be?"

"From uncooked food, no doubt. It appears she has had them for some time. We can treat her here and then give you some medicine for her to take. She should be checked by another doctor later, just to make sure."

"Doctor, I can't thank you enough. You've saved my baby's life. You know, I'll bet it was the day-old pork that made her sick. Yet we all ate it. The rest of us are fine."

"That happens sometimes. You see, when food is not stored at a cold enough temperature, bacteria begins to grow. Some people resist the bacteria, but others don't do so well."

While Franco drank a strong cup of coffee provided by the doctor's wife and chain-smoked several cigarettes, the doctor added, frowning, "I must inform you that your daughter is not in very good health. Her resistance is quite low. After this attack, she will have to build up her health and resistance to disease, especially malaria, which is running rampant."

The situation was grim. No matter where he looked, Franco could not find a job. There wasn't enough work for the locals, much less for him. Paco was heading back to Bolivia, and since they had no other place to go, Franco and his very sick child headed back to Bolivia, too.

CHAPTER SIXTEEN

February, 1974
Bolivia

The hot, musty jungle hung over the car like a giant smothering umbrella. The driver, Cantez, had picked them up in Uncia, Bolivia. The drive along the dusty road in the broken down Citroen never seem to end. The air was humid and difficult to breath and rendered the occupants lethargic and indifferent to their destination of Sucre, Bolivia. To Franco, one place was as good as any other; Sucre suited him fine. A town, a job and, possibly, a new place to hide. After two hours of driving on a road that paralleled a river, the car pulled off to the side of the road.

"That water looks too inviting to pass up in this heat," said Cantez. Sweat poured down his face.

"You want to take a swim too?" Franco shook Triana awake; she lay curled up in the back seat of the car.

"I'll see you in the water," the man called as he opened the car door and walked toward the river.

Suddenly, a low flying aircraft could be heard. Franco rushed Triana over to a large tree for cover. Across the river they spotted a group of gypsies. The men sat in a circle, conversing, as the women were busy about the campsite. Some of the women cooked and others washed clothes on the shallow, rocky edge of the river. Children played near the water with three large dogs that stood on the riverbank, barking at splashing water.

As Franco and Triana hid under the large tree, they watched as Cantez plunged into the water and swam out a few feet. After the aircraft passed, Franco and Triana hastened to join Cantez in the cool, slow-moving river. As they reached the water's edge, they heard Cantez scream.

Desperately he turned toward shore, screeching in pain. Franco and Triana could see the splashing of small fish. Cantez crawled onto the shore, his body bleeding from the bites of the piranha. Franco and Triana helped Cantez to the car and placed him on the back seat. Blood poured profusely from his wounds and dripped onto the torn car cushions. Franco quickly drove to a nearby farmhouse, shouting for help as he drove up. Cantez, in shock, lay quietly in the back seat of the car, amazed to be alive. Able to strip large animals to bare bones in seconds, the piranha could have consumed him.

Upon arriving in Sucre, as Cantez was being given medical attention, Franco and Triana drifted off unnoticed. Like other Bolivian towns, Sucre consisted of either dirt roads or cobblestone streets. Everywhere whitewashed adobe buildings were next to decrepit shacks built long before their current inhabitants had been born.

After two frustrating days of sleeping in alleys and stealing enough food to stay alive, Franco abandoned all hope of finding work. He and Triana boarded a bus headed for the deep interior of Bolivia, where Franco hoped he would began to feel safer from his enemies from the States, Rosalie and the drug lords in Valle Grande.

Once again, they had new names and new documents. Once again, Triana had paid the price with her body. Franco and Triana--dazed and quiet--sat and practiced calling each other by their new names for hours, until they felt sufficiently confident to risk using them in public. Antonio and Tina had replaced Recardo and Cara in their vocabularies.

Triana's complaints to a priest about the abuse she was suffering fell on deaf ears. When she told the priest that her father had sold her, he did not believe her and scolded her for accusing her father of such a sinful thing. The priest thought Franco to be a good father and a trustworthy man. Triana believed help was hopeless; no one would save her.

By the time they arrived in the town of Oruro, a town large enough to hide in and perhaps find work, Franco was desperate to find a job. He had spent the money gained from selling a stolen watch on two packs of cigarettes, a small piece of candy for Triana and two bus tickets. That left a paltry two pesos in his pocket. Night had fallen and he would have to wait until the next day to look for work.

Franco and Triana were famished as they walked to the marketplace. Triana knew her role well. While Franco distracted the proprietors, Triana stole food, hid it in her dress, and walked rapidly away.

This time their prize was some fruit and a small box of dried bread. They sat in the alley voraciously consuming their take, filling the aching cavities of their stomachs, which constantly reminded them of their poverty.

Franco lit his customary cigarette and pondered where they would sleep. An alley had often provided sleeping accommodations, but tonight he decided to search out a park where Triana could play for a bit and perhaps meet a friend. Sudden friendships had come in handy so many times that Franco used the "park" strategy whenever he could find a suitable green spot.

As they walked down the street past houses surrounded by waist-high grass, Franco scolded Triana for walking on the outside of the walkway. "You are too conspicuous," he chided; he had warned her many times. Triana immediately moved to the inside where a large dog with glazed eyes behind a chain link fence captured her attention. She didn't back away since, seconds before, her father had scolded her about standing near the street. A man in the yard pointed a rifle at the savage animal, which growled and foamed at the mouth, ready to charge his owner. As Franco and Triana approached, the large animal swung around and in seconds jumped the fence and charged Triana, grabbing her left leg in his strong jaws. She screamed and the man rushed out of the yard, pointed the gun at the dog and pulled the trigger, nearly hitting Triana, the mad dog dropped to the ground. Dead.

Triana moaned in pain as blood gushed from her leg. Frantically, Franco grabbed Triana and pressed on the bleeding leg.

The owner tried to apologize. "I am so sorry. I was going to shoot him and I was afraid I would hit you. Is your child all right?"

"That damn dog bit my child. We will have to take her to the hospital. And I expect you to pay, do you hear?" Franco screamed.

"I am sure the dog had rabies, that was why I was going to shoot him," said the agitated dog owner. "Come, I will take you to the doctor, *Señor*. Please, come with me. My car is in the back."

Like many hospitals in South America, the building was old and rundown. The doctor examined Triana's wound, washed it thoroughly with soapy water, and applied what looked like an iodine solution.

"I have ordered the dog picked up for examination," the doctor said. "We can tell more at that time."

"Will she get rabies and die? Will she?" Franco searched the doctor's face.

The doctor smiled reassuringly. "Sit down, *Señor*. I will explain to you what we are dealing with here."

Franco allowed the doctor to lead him to a wooden bench.

"Would you like a cup of coffee, *Señor*?" The doctor bent over a dented coffeepot on a small warmer and poured two cups of strong, black coffee. "Now, about your little girl.."He smiled at Triana, who sat patiently on a cot about ten feet away. "Such a good little patient. When has she had her last tetanus shot?"

"I don't know, doctor. You see, since her mother died.."Franco spoke in a low voice to keep Triana from hearing.

The doctor ignored him. He wasn't interested in life stories. "In a few minutes, I will give her a shot that will protect her against tetanus. This is standard procedure in all deep puncture wounds. Tetanus is lockjaw, you know, incurable.."

"But if you give her the shot, she can't get it?"

"No, she won't get tetanus."

"How about the dog bite, is she going to be okay?"

"First of all," the doctor said slowly, "you should know what rabies is. It is a one hundred-percent fatal viral disease, affecting the brain and nervous system. It is carried in the saliva of all rabid animals, not just dogs."

Franco listened nervously, shifting his position on the bench.

"Since the virus travels along the body's nerves to the brain, the closer the bite is to the head, the more quickly a person must receive treatment. If the wound is on the face or neck, for instance, the treatment must begin immediately, because the virus can reach the brain very quickly. In your daughter's case, since the bite was on the leg, we have a little time."

"Time for what?" Franco stood up. "Why wait?"

"Just a moment, *Señor*. The shots are painful and can have harmful side effects. We are ninety-nine percent sure, due to the circumstances, but we need to run tests on the blood of the dead animal to be sure."

"Well, why don't they find out?" Franco was becoming more and more upset and impatient. "Then why the hell don't they start the procedure and find out?"

"We'll start right away, *Señor*. The animal's brain will be examined. If the test proves positive, your daughter's treatment will begin at once. By the way," the doctor continued impassively, "it's fortunate the owner didn't shoot the animal in the head. A vicious animal suspected of rabies should never be shot in the head. A damaged brain yields little information in the laboratory."

But Franco had long since tuned the doctor out. All he could think of was Triana, sitting there on the cot while chewing a piece of candy the doctor had given her.

"Why don't you leave your little girl here? Then if we need to immediately begin treatment, she will be here. *Señor*? What do you say to that?"

"What? Oh, yes, of course, doctor," Franco agreed. "But I'll stay around until you find out, if you don't mind." He had no other place to go and even if he had, he was too paranoid and frightened to leave Triana. She might say something or someone might recognize her from a flier. If he had to run he needed to be able to grab her.

Franco sat in the hospital lobby for the rest of the night.

Late that evening, the laboratory report confirmed the diagnosis of rabies. Triana's anti-rabies treatment began immediately. Triana screamed in agony as each shot was administrated. She did not suffer any serious side effects from the shots, but the bite left a large sore that took several weeks to heal.

Soon she was well enough to travel.

March, 1974
Viacha, Bolivia

In the pitch-black darkness, filled with the pervasive cries of nocturnal wildlife, the vintage bus wheezed slowly up the hill, bumping and jostling along the unpaved road. Triana pushed the poncho over her baldhead. Her scalp had been shaved so many times she had lost count. She was constantly plagued by head lice. She could not remember the last time she had had a bath and had hair long enough to wash. Every time it grew a few inches, someone promptly shaved it. "To thicken the hair," they said. In South America, shaving heads was a common practice to cure lice infestation and everyone used the same euphemism. For some reason Franco never seem to have head-lice. Triana wondered if his short hair and the fact that he always washed at every faucet he could find made a difference. Franco had told her to wash, but the water was too cold and he didn't insist.

In the last week, her clothes seemed even larger than before, but the hunger pangs were gone. As he had so often done, Franco had given her a cocoa leaf. She had become quite used to its effect. The sensation it produced made her feel good, and the empty spaces in her stomach were suddenly gone.

It had been ten months since they had left Salta, and she still wondered who the bad people were. Why were they after her and her dad? What did they want? She had stopped asking her father those questions. They only made him angry and there were never any answers.

By the time the sky outside had gradually begun to lighten, Franco and Triana found themselves nearing the outskirts of a sleepy, mid-sized town. Watching the bus as it drove away, continuing its slow, arduous journey without them. They stood holding their small bag of belongings on the outskirts of Viacha. Franco hoped it might do for a couple of days, perhaps even a week.

"Come on, *Penguina,*" Franco said, "let's start walking. I saw a big park about a half-mile back."

That was fine with Triana; she liked parks. They were soon sitting in the tall grass under a large tree, lush with deep green foliage.

Soon, they both dozed off, and slept well into the morning.

Franco was the first to stand up, stretch and look around. He relieved himself at a convenient bush. The warm sun shone overhead. He shaded his eyes with his hand and several yards away, on the other side of a clump of trees, he spotted a small, chubby girl around Triana's age playing in the grass. Nearby sat a heavy-set, white-haired man who was fairly well-dressed. He looked old enough to be the child's grandfather.

Franco woke up his daughter. "See that kid over there?"

Triana squinted in the sunlight and nodded.

"I want you to go over and make friends with her."

Triana obediently waded through the tall grass toward the child. After a while, Franco strolled over to the bench where the gentleman was sitting. By now, the two youngsters were busily engaged in a contest to see who could braid grass more quickly.

"Warm day," Franco said, chewing on a blade of grass.

"Yes, it is," the older man answered, smiling. "But my granddaughter likes to come to the park to play, despite the weather."

"Ah, kids, they want to play no matter what else is going on in this world," Franco said pleasantly, sitting down and stretching his legs. "I am looking for work and my child wants to play."

They continued to talk, and before the hour was over, Franco and Triana were accompanying *Señor* Alfonso and his granddaughter, Ana to their home. The medium-sized stucco house was clean and orderly, and sat on a little more than an acre of land about half a mile from the park. It was more than comfortable by the town's standards: it had a bathroom with a sparkling tub, something Triana and Franco had rarely seen.

Franco soon learned that *Señor* Alfonso and his wife, Concheta, were raising their granddaughter because the child's parents had been killed in a street riot during recent political unrest.

"We are getting a little old to be caring for an energetic young child, but we love Ana so much, and that makes everything easier," Señor Alfonso explained as they sat at the neatly set table drinking strong coffee and eating chocolate rolls. The children's large ceramic cups were filled to the brim with cool, fresh milk.

"I know what you mean. I've been raising my little one alone," Franco said soberly with downcast eyes. "Since her mother passed away two-and-a-half years ago."

Triana looked up sharply, but Franco gave her the usual quick side-glance to be quiet.

"I couldn't bear to stay in La Paz after the tragedy. Such pain to stay in the home, around her things, and around our friends. So I took my baby and went on the road.."

"I'm sorry, *Señor,*" Alfonso said sincerely.

"Thank you," Franco replied, "but one must learn to accept whatever the Lord sends us. We will survive."

Alfonso had an idea. "What type of work do you do, *Señor?* I have a friend who may need a gardener. She has a very large estate a few miles outside of town. She is the widow of an assassinated political figure. I will arrange for an interview with the caretaker, and he will take it from there. Are you interested?"

The trip took over an hour, but as they turned the car into the long driveway, Franco and Triana were dazzled. It was by far the most elegant home they had ever seen. There was nothing in Beverly Hills that could match this, Franco was certain. The estate seemed to go on forever, with a huge, rolling lawn that covered several acres, and lush landscaping.

As the car pulled around the circular driveway, Franco could see two tennis courts and a large Olympic size swimming pool. Equal care had been given to the rear gardens. The mansion seemed out of place in this poor country.

Alfonso walked around the house, out of Franco's view, to the caretaker's cottage. Twenty minutes later he returned to the car.

"Come on, he wants to talk to you."

Franco got the job and was given a cottage of his own. The rooms were smaller than the caretaker's, but the place was a palace compared to anything they had stayed in since their arrival in South America. The woman turned out to be the ex-president's widow and she had a child a year younger than Triana. The children made friends quickly and soon became inseparable. They played around the grounds while Franco worked with the other gardener.

Franco felt safe enough to once again contact his mother. This place would make a fine spot for them to settle down. He wrote to his mother and asked her to stand by until he could make the final arrangements.

However, after three months on the job, Franco once again was let go. Items had vanished from the estate and Franco was the likely suspect. Carmen would have to wait for a better time.

CHAPTER SEVENTEEN

April, 1974
Irvine, California

I picked up a human-interest article from the Long Beach newspaper to read over coffee. A friend had found the article in her newspaper and sent to me. As I read it for the third time, I stared at the picture of a smiling woman about my age, her arms around two grinning children. The happy reunion had taken place only recently. Like me, she had suffered many years of not knowing where her son and daughter were. Now they were back together again.

All day long I could think of nothing else but that woman and those children. Would I ever experience their joy?

The next morning I called the newspaper and spoke with the reporter who had written the story. "If you could put me in touch with this woman," I explained, "perhaps I could find out exactly how she got her children back. Maybe she can give me the name of the detective she used."

"Well," the reporter answered reluctantly, "we are forbidden to give you her phone number. But if you will give me your number, I will try to call her and have her call you."

"Please," I begged, "if you could, I would appreciate it. Tell her to call me collect. I'm sure she'll understand how much this means to me."

"I'm sorry I couldn't be of more help to you," the reporter replied.

A couple of days later the woman called. She was friendly enough, but understandably reserved. "I was told that you have a situation similar to mine."

"My child is also in South America and has been gone almost three years. Her father was going to take her on a fishing trip and that was the last I saw of her." I paused. The next words were difficult to speak. "I found them last year, but he escaped." I gave the woman a brief account of my ordeal.

"I know what you are going through," she sympathized. "My children were gone for over two years, and I thought I would lose my mind. Is there something I can do to help you?"

"Can you tell me how you went about getting them back?" I asked.

"Well, my husband stayed in contact with his family and I was able to trace him through them. I hired a detective who accompanied me to South America. It was because of him that I was able to pull it off," the woman told me.

"Was he very expensive?" I asked.

"Yes, he was. However, without him I don't think I would have gotten anywhere. He charged me ten thousand dollars plus expenses. I should also warn you that if you use him you must agree to do whatever he asks, without question. I know that sounds a little scary. It did to me anyway, but it definitely worked. The man is very good at his business."

I had no idea where I could put my hands on ten thousand dollars. But I was curious and ready to grasp at any straw.

"Just what did he ask you to do that seemed unreasonable?" I inquired.

"This may sound strange, but he told me bluntly before we left that he would expect me at his side at all times. It was in case we had to make a quick change in plans," the woman replied.

"You mean all the time? Even at night?" I was taken aback.

"I not only mean that but in the same bed, if that was all there was," she responded.

I was too embarrassed to ask any further questions. There was a long silence when neither of us spoke.

"By the way," she finally said, "he was perfectly safe. A little rough-looking and all, but you know, he never."

"He's got a heart of gold, is that it?" I asked and smiled to myself.

"I don't know about that," the woman said seriously. "I think he's just, you know, hard as nails. Of course, in his profession, he has to be."

"Could you give me his phone number?" I felt uncertain, yet he had restored her children to her.

"I would be glad to," she said.

I wrote down the number the woman gave me and thanked her for her help.

At the present, Stan and I were getting along more amicably. The children created friction at times, but the bond that baby Tisha created had succeeded in achieving a certain amount of peace. At least Stan and I were talking and we were both making an effort. That evening when I told him the encouraging news, he was interested.

"Maybe he can help you," Stan said. "It's worth a try."

"We'll soon find out. I have an appointment with him day after tomorrow in Long Beach. I don't know how we could ever get that much money together for him to help us, but I'll meet with him and see what he has to say."

"Do you want me to go with you?"

"No, I'll be fine. Thanks anyway."

"You be careful, Rosalie. From what this women told you he sounds like a rough guy. Where are you meeting him?"

"Denny's in Long Beach. Don't worry. He's not going to do anything to me. He's a professional, and from what I hear, he's very good at what he does. He sounded like Humphrey Bogart with a Spanish accent. Sort of blunt."

"Well, if he can help you," Stan said, "I would disregard his manner. After all, we don't have to make friends with the guy."

"Somehow, I don't think he has too many friends," I agreed. "And I'll bet he'd be the first to admit it." I lowered my voice and mimicked the detective. "In my business, lady, you can't have too many friends--you're on your own. But that's the way I like-- Play it again, Sam."

We both laughed. That night I slept soundly, cuddled in Stan's arms, with Triana dashing in and out of my dreams.

I arrived at the restaurant first and took a seat in the waiting area. I had no idea what the detective looked like. From the window, I saw a short, stocky, overweight Mexican man with a mustache slowly get out of his car. He looked around carefully, closed his car door and walked toward the restaurant. He noticed everything that moved around him as he approached the door to Denny's. I knew at once that this was the man I was to meet.

As soon as he entered, I approached him slowly and introduced myself. As he shook my hand, he looked me over very carefully. We were shown to a booth where he ordered breakfast while I had black coffee. I told him my story as briefly as I could. Halfway through, his order came, and I paused to allow the waitress to leave before I continued. He watched me intently as I spoke. I began to feel that despite his appearance, he was sharp, cunning, and competent. By the time I had finished my story he had devoured his breakfast and was sipping his third cup of coffee.

"Do you know what I charge?" the man asked.

"Yes, but can you explain more about your fee?"

"The fee's paid in advance. As we go, you pay all expenses; that means airfare and anything that might come up: Payments to certain people, officials, under the table, hotel rooms and general traveling expenses. I keep my fee whether I get your child back or not. But let me tell you, my percentage of recoveries is very high. There have been very few cases where I haven't produced, and those were beyond my control.

"One thing more. If I take this job, there are certain things that I will ask of you, and you must do what I say without question. That means that if I ask you to sleep in the same bed with me, you must agree to do so. It will be for a good reason." Seeing the look on my face, he added, "Don't worry, I can get all the screwing I need elsewhere. It's not for that. There are times when we must move quickly, and you must be ready to jump and run. I want you right there beside me so that there is no chance of delay. I'm good but it's only because I am always alert. You give me no arguments and I will get you your child back."

"I will need to talk to my husband about this. Can I get back to you?"

My spirits had plummeted at the thought of the accumulated costs. We had a little extra saved, but nowhere near ten thousand, and the likely five to ten thousand more in expenses. There was no way I could think of to raise that amount. It was taking everything Stan brought home just to make ends meet.

"Listen, no problem," he said. "Call me in a few days to let me know one way or the other. If I am not there, leave the message with my wife. I am on a case right now anyway." He left the restaurant in the same manner as he had entered, wary and watchful, as though expecting trouble any second.

I drove home in a mood of deep depression. Though I realized he might be my only chance to recover my daughter, I could see no possible way to raise that much money

I tried to borrow the money from a close friend, but she was unable to comply with my request.

My heart sank as I struggled with the knowledge that fifteen thousand dollars was the only thing that separated me from my child.

September, 1974
Santa Cruz, Bolivia

When Franco arrived in Santa Cruz, he immediately contacted the relative of a friend he had made when he lived in Cochabamba. For a few weeks, Franco and Triana stayed with the family. Franco did some side jobs and when he had enough money, he rented a small apartment and set about broadcasting the fact that he was an English teacher. Largely through the church, he managed to make enough money to support the two of them. He taught lessons in their small front room while Triana sat patiently coloring and listening to the lessons her father gave.

Triana was growing up rapidly. Franco realized that soon she would be a young lady and that her menstrual periods might start any day. He wanted her to be able to take care of herself and he set about looking for a suitable school where Triana might have some womanly guidance, which he knew he could not provide. *Hermanas Sagradas Corazon*, a convent just outside of Santa Cruz, seemed the perfect place.

Franco and the Mother Superior first met in the visitors' room of the school.

"My son, what can I do for you?" she asked.

"Mother, I have a daughter who needs some guidance and education from you," Franco explained as he rose to greet this imposing woman.

"I see. How old is the child?"

"Ten, Mother. Since her mother died, I have been caring for her. She knows nothing of what to do for herself," he hesitated, "when her time comes, if you understand me, Mother. Could you explain some of these womanly things and give her an education?"

"Mr. Valaverte, I see that you are an intelligent man, but I am puzzled. Why hasn't your child been sent to school before this?" The Mother Superior looked intently at Franco.

"Oh, Mother, you are right, so right." Franco returned her gaze. "I should have had her in school long before this, but I was so upset when her dear mother died. I just could not stay in La Paz. I have been traveling ever since. I guess I have just now come to my senses. I am giving English lessons here in town and I would like to make this our home. I have written to my mother in Italy to come and take care of Tina. My mother is like a nun herself, Mother, and since we lost my father, she has taken a solemn oath to serve God."

Mother Superior hesitated no longer. She believed Franco and wanted to help him. "Can you bring your daughter here this afternoon? I would like to meet her."

"Oh, thank you, Mother." Franco paused and smiled at the Mother Superior. "May I impose on you for one other favor? May I use this address to receive mail from my mother? We are in the process of moving and I need to write to her immediately."

"That will be fine. We have a post office box. I will write the number down for you."

That afternoon a puzzled Triana solemnly looked at her father.

"Why do I have to go to school? Why can't I stay here and have you teach me?"

Franco was conflicted. He was afraid to have her out of his sight. However, he knew he needed to buy some time, time to pursue the well-off widow he had just met. "You will do as I say. You must go to school. It is time and there are things that you must learn that I cannot teach you. Not another word now, you hear?"

"Daddy," Triana said softly, "what about those bad people? Will they come and take me? You have always told me that we would not be separated. I don't understand."

"If I thought those people were anywhere near here, *Penguina*, I would kill both of us before I let them take you." Franco got down on his knees beside the bed and searched his daughter's face.

"But, Daddy, who are these bad people? Why do they want me?" It was the one question to which Triana wanted an answer.

"*Penguina*, one of them is your mother. She wants to take you from me."

"You said she was dead. I heard you, Daddy!"

"Well, she's not. If she ever comes here and tries to take you, you must promise me, *Penguina*, that you will kill yourself before you ever go with her. She is an evil person and would do you great harm."

"Daddy, I promise. I will. No one will ever part us, will they?" Triana flew into her father's arms and sobbed on his shoulder.

"No, no, my *bambina*, no one will ever come between us again," he comforted her. "I will see to that. Now, come along, get ready to meet the Mother Superior. And, *Penguina*, not a word of our little talk to the nuns, remember? And don't speak of anything that might cause them to question you about our past, okay?"

From the moment she set foot on the grounds, Triana disliked the convent. She disliked the Mother Superior even more. In their opening interview, there were questions, questions and more questions. There were always questions about things she was not supposed to discuss.

"And her mother died when?" Mother Superior asked as she busily filled out the required forms. She looked up and peered through her bifocals.

Franco wrung his hands. "In nineteen, uh, nineteen…oh, what does it matter? I don't like to talk about such painful things. Surely you can understand."

Triana looked up in surprise. How could this be? Only a few hours ago Franco had warned her about her mother's possible attempt to take her away. Only a few hours ago he had told her that her mother was alive. The child's look of surprise had not escaped Mother Teresa.

"For the record, *Señor*, just for the record. Sometimes it may be best to talk about matters, no matter how painful."

Franco ignored her comment. "Mother Teresa, what I want you to understand is that it is very difficult for me to leave little Tina, even in your capable hands. For a long time now, I have been both mother and father to her."

"But perhaps it is time to change all that, for both of you. Tina will be fine with us."

The nun rose. The interview was over.

The parting was difficult. Triana screamed and cried and clung to her father.

"Daddy! When will you be back?"

"Saturday morning, my *bambina*. Saturday morning. I promise."

Triana clung to him desperately. Mother Teresa approached her and Triana could hear the loud clanking of her keys that swung from her waist as she walked.

"Come along, Tina," the nun said firmly. "I will show you to your room and introduce you to the five other girls with whom you will share it. Then Sister Suzanne, our nurse, will examine you."

"Why? What for?"

"My dear, to make sure you are in good health. Come along, Tina."

Franco stayed and watched his daughter walk down the long hall with the Mother Superior. Triana was the one person who was his, the one person over whom he had total control. Walking away from her was difficult. What if he needed her in the next few days? Depressed and dispirited, he left the convent and waited outside for his ride to take him back to town.

The nuns took Triana in hand, bathed her, and washed her hair only to discover the inevitable crop of lice. Once again, Triana's head was shaved.

"I will never, never have my long beautiful dark hair back," Triana moaned. A week later, they shaved her head again, just to be on the safe side. The nuns disposed of all her clothing and dressed her from their store of donations.

October in the small sleepy town of Trinidad proved to be extremely humid for the time of year. Trinidad sits on the Monroe River in northern Bolivia and is accessible only by boat or plane. Franco had opted for the trip by air. He wanted to be able to return to Santa Cruz and Triana quickly. He unpacked his few belongings in the hotel room and began to sort out his plans.

One day in Santa Cruz, in early September, one of his students had brought along an older woman to the tutoring session. The student had introduced the woman to Franco as his cousin.

"Who is this lovely young lady, Antonio?" Franco had flattered the older woman. She blushed and laughed the embarrassed laugh of a woman unaccustomed to flattery from men. "*Señor,* you are too kind," she managed to say.

"Are you married, my dear?"

"I am a widow. Why do you ask?"

Franco smiled. "Would you think me forward if I invited you to join me for dinner tonight?"

Delia Mendez was startled. "Dinner? Oh, no. Quite impossible. When I leave here, I will go directly to the airport for the trip to Trinidad. I don't usually take the day off. This is quite unusual for me." She did not know what to say to this man.

Franco stared into her eyes. "I understand," he said softly.

"Tomorrow, then? I would be honored if you would dine with me tomorrow."

Delia caught her breath. Something about this man made her feel young again. She found courage to accept his invitation.

"Thank you. I would be delighted to join you for dinner tomorrow night."

The arrangements were made. Franco walked with her to the car and waved as she pulled away. He returned to the apartment and checked his limited finances. Whew! He had just enough to show her a good time.

The following night as he walked to her house in Trinidad, he considered the woman he was about to see for the second time. Dark-haired, middle-aged, and stocky, she was hardly a Bolivian beauty, but she was good-hearted and kind, and, more important, she was more well-off than most. She owned the only pharmacy in Trinidad. He had already decided to marry her--he figured it would take him about three days.

Delia Mendez was proud of her home. It was considered one of the better homes in Trinidad. All her life she had been accustomed to respect and she was used to being surrounded by fine things, at least by Bolivian standards. Her grandfather had emigrated from Argentina and had played a prominent role in founding Trinidad. He and his family had earned the town's respect, and Delia had achieved considerable stature in her own right. She was a sound businesswoman and a solid citizen. She had married well and fulfilled her role as faithful wife and capable mother. She had grieved over her husband's death, but she was naturally resilient and had resumed her community life after a decent mourning period. Not until she met Franco did she realize that something was missing from her life. Delia thought she had fallen in love.

Franco had assessed the situation perfectly. After three days, he proposed and she accepted. They decided to marry in Brazil. They agreed that Triana was to stay with Delia's daughter and granddaughter.

October, 1974
Santa Cruz, Bolivia

When Franco returned from courting Delia, the panic returned. He muttered to himself and worried constantly. His imagination worked overtime. He pictured the Mother Superior telephoning the Argentinean police. Or even the Americans. The embassy. The consulate. She had been far too interested in Triana's mother. Maybe she already knew something. Maybe Triana had told her something that made her suspicious. What if Triana was playing on the convent grounds and Rosalie found her, pulled up in a black car, and grabbed her?

Franco rushed to the street and hailed a cab.

"Mother, I have come to take Tina out of the school."

Mother Teresa eyed him warily. "Mr. Valaverte, you are making a terrible mistake. Tina is bright and capable. She learns quickly. She needs schooling. She is doing well."

"Mother, get her ready to leave. My mind is made up. It will not change."

The Mother Superior stood beneath the archway and watched the strange pair drive away. She suspected there was more to the picture than this emotional man had revealed. Once she had overheard the child say that if she were ever separated from her father, she would kill herself. Mother Teresa would never forget those words. Try as she might, Mother Teresa had not succeeded in getting "Tina" to discuss the situation further.

Franco returned to the convent one more time. There was one more footprint he needed to erase from his immediate past.

"Mother, I will no longer need to use your post office box for my mail. I will soon be married to a woman from Trinidad and will be receiving my mail there. My mother will join us in a short time. I thank you for your help." Franco spoke formally and finished his words with a slight bow.

"And Tina, Mr. Valaverte, how is Tina?"

"She awaits me in Trinidad. Now she will have a proper home and a good education."

"I hope all will go well for you." But there was doubt in Mother Teresa's heart as she watched Franco walk away from the convent for the last time.

CHAPTER EIGHTEEN

October, 1974
Irvine, California

In addition to caring for Tisha and the boys, I enrolled in a photography class. Triana's passport, which I had kept in my safety deposit box for years, had expired. She would need a current passport when I found her. I was able to take Triana's last school picture, photograph it in black and white, and print it on the required paper. I sent the whole thing in for a renewal. Three weeks later, I received a notice to come down to Los Angeles for identification purposes, and pick up the passport.

As I was returning from grocery shopping near the end of October my neighbor, Julie, stopped to visit.

"Want a cup of coffee?" I asked, as I placed Tisha in the playpen and started putting away the groceries.

"Sure. How is your class going?" Julie inquired as she leaned over the pen and played with Tisha.

"I got Triana's passport four weeks ago. They accepted the picture. I think I'll drop the class now that I have accomplished my purpose. I sure enjoyed it though," I said.

"What do you hear about Triana? Anything new?" Julie had picked Tisha up and was bouncing the child on her knee.

"I got a letter from Lina three days ago. Evidently, Franco's mother, Carmen, heard from him. Lina saw the letter from Franco-- it was from Cochabamba, Bolivia. When Lina asked Carmen about Franco and Triana, Carmen said they were fine and that they would like her to come to live with them. The letter didn't have a return address. All Lina could tell me was that the information was three months old at the time she saw the letter. I doubt that Franco is still there, three months later, because he doesn't tend to stay in any town very long."

"Bolivia?" A strange look came over her face.

"Yes, that's what Lina said. She's going to try to get me additional information and an address. There's no way I want to repeat what happened last time," I replied.

Julie thought for a moment. "Look, I've got to go now. I'll talk to you later!" She left rather hurriedly.

What was that all about? I wondered. Julie didn't even wait for her coffee.

The next afternoon, Julie knocked on the front door.

"Listen," Julie said excitedly, "I have to talk with you. I didn't want to say anything until I spoke with Joseph, but I have a friend who was raised in Cochabamba by his uncle. I met him when I was separated. I don't want you to think badly of me, but I love him, I have been seeing him, and eventually we will be together."

"Julie, you are my friend, that's all that is important. Don't worry about what others think. Now, come in and tell me about this Joseph and Cochabamba."

"I want you to meet him," Julie continued. "He's planning on going to South America soon. He has family in several towns there. Maybe he could do some investigating for you."

"Sounds wonderful," I said. "I'd love to meet him."

Julie was delighted. "Oh, maybe he can help you. Maybe this will be it, and you'll get Triana back!"

"First things first. You go ahead and make the arrangements, and we'll take it from there. When is he going to make the trip?"

"I think within the next four or five weeks. I will try to get him down from Los Angeles next week so you can meet him."

That evening, I told Stan about the new development.

"I guess it certainly can't hurt to meet the guy," he said with some skepticism.

Julie, Joseph, and I met at a restaurant in Tustin. I told Joseph my story.

Joseph pondered for a few minutes before speaking.

"It is hard for me to imagine a man like that," he said finally. "I'm planning to go down to Bolivia in a month. Believe me, I'll be glad to do all I can to help you find your daughter."

"Where will you travel in Bolivia?" I asked.

"My uncle still lives in Cochabamba. I will spend some time there, and then I will visit my brother who lives in Santa Cruz. I plan on staying about a month. If I find out anything while I'm there, I'll contact Julie."

"Perhaps we can get together before you leave," I said. "I would like you to meet my husband and we can go over any details that might help. I don't know what name Franco's using now, but I'm sure he changes names like we change clothing. I can give you pictures of him and information about what I think he might be doing. And I might get another letter from his aunt before you leave."

"Anything specific would help me," Joseph told me. "Bolivia is a big country. People have been hiding out in our country for centuries."

December, 1974
Rome, Italy

In her sister's apartment in Rome, Carmen slowly re-packed her suitcase. Since she received the most recent word from Franco, she had wanted to be ready to leave for Bolivia. Carmen picked up Franco's latest letter, the one with the partly torn envelope; she had given the portion with the stamp to her neighbor's boy. *Maybe I shouldn't have given it to him*, she thought. She worried about things like that. *Oh, well, nothing will come of it. Let him have his stamp. A collection is a nice thing for a boy to do. And it was such a pretty stamp. He was so happy to get it.*

There was a knock at the bedroom door.

"Just a minute!" she called out nervously. She closed the suitcase and pushed it under the bed. She knew there was no sense advertising her departure.

The knocking continued. "Carmen, it's me, Lina!"

"Yes, come in, my dear." Carmen opened the door to her sister.

"I hope I haven't caught you at a bad time, but I thought you might like to take a little walk this afternoon." Lina noticed the open closet door; she saw most of the hangers were empty, but she made no comment.

The soft sunshine of a lovely Roman afternoon caressed Lina and Carmen as they strolled past the *Piazza Fontanella de Borghese*, filled with small open-air shops.

"Do you want to have some coffee and a bite to eat?" Lina asked her sister as they neared a small outdoor café.

"Lina, my dear sister, I am without funds today. I'm afraid I cannot join you," Carmen replied.

"Come along, Carmen. It's my treat today."

The sisters had exchanged these words many times. Carmen was always broke and Lina rightly suspected that she sent Franco almost every penny of her pension checks as soon as they arrived. It was not a subject that the sisters discussed. But today, Lina was determined to speak forthrightly. Even so, she chose her words carefully.

"What do you hear from Franco? Will you be leaving for South America soon?" Lina busied herself with her coffee.

"Nothing escapes you, my dear sister," Carmen said. "So yes, I'm going. I got another letter from Franco. But I don't know when, or where. You know how secretive Franco has to be."

"I also know how secretive you can be," Lina replied.

"Look, my dear Lina." Carmen touched her sister's arm. "You have been so kind to let me stay with you, your generosity has been more than I deserve, but please don't pass judgment on me. I believe I am doing the right thing, and only God is my judge. To me, life's burdens are just another step in the long stairway to heaven."

Lina smiled. "Yes, I understand the way you think. As for me, I hope he sends an elevator!" The sisters laughed in the soft Roman sunshine.

"Carmen," Lina spoke clearly, "when you get there, will you call

Rosalie or get in touch with her somehow? Will you call me and let me know where you are and that you are well?" Lina reached over and took her sister's hand.

"Lina, I must do as Franco says. Please, please, no more questions. But yes, I will let you know that I am well, when I can."

Lina pressed her further. "What about your promises to Rosalie to see that Triana is returned to her? What can you be thinking? Is it right that this little girl should live in a jungle?" Lina was weary of the charades her sister played with her worthless son.

"Lina, please. I know you mean well. But what I do is between me and Franco, and between me and God."

The sisters spoke no more of Franco; it was too painful for Carmen. Lina paid the bill and they parted. Carmen boarded the bus for church. Nothing ever prevented her daily attendance at mass.

Lina watched Carmen's bus until it was out of sight. Hurriedly she returned to her apartment. In Carmen's room she walked straight to her dresser and opened the top drawer. She lifted a pile of neatly folded clothing; but, finding nothing hidden, replaced the clothes. Several drawers later, she found what she was looking for, an envelope; unfortunately, it was torn through the postal stamp and the return address was missing. She was disappointed but she could make out a portion of the last line of the postmark. Santa C. something.

Lina could not remember a time when she had violated another person's privacy. She was surprised at herself, spying in this way. And on her own sister, too. But this business of dragging an innocent child all over a primitive continent had to end.

She pulled the thin tissue sheet from the torn envelope and read it. In an angular Italian hand that she recognized at once, Lina read Franco's pleas for his mother to bring money and come to Santa Cruz. There was more about some woman he had met and a few optimistic sentences about the future. Lina sighed. Another woman. Always another woman. She replaced the letter where she had found it, and left the room.

From the tone of the letter, Lina realized she must act quickly and she knew that the neighbor's stamp-collecting boy, Geno, might provide the necessary clue. "Between you and God," she muttered, thinking of her sister's words. "Perhaps, Carmen, but my decision is between me and my conscience."

She found Geno playing with two other little boys.

"Geno, come here, please," Lina called the boy. "I want to talk with you."

"Hello, Señora," the boy greeted her.

"You know my sister, the Signora Allatere, who always gives you fancy stamps?"

He nodded.

"Has she given you any stamps recently?"

"Oh, yes," the boy smiled, "and a beautiful one it is, too. Do you want to see it?"

"I'd like to very much. I didn't get a chance to look at it before she gave it to you. I'll bet it is a beauty."

The boy grinned widely and ran inside. He emerged immediately with a small book from which he expertly pulled a stamp that was still attached to a torn portion of an envelope.

"This is it," he said. "It is the latest one she gave me." He handed the scrap of envelope to Lina.

Lina pieced together the postmark and read: Santa Cruz, Bolivia. To the left she could barely make out part of a number. "Could I have a little piece of this envelope?" She pointed to the side of the torn envelope that contained part of the return address. "I need something to write on and I didn't bring any paper with me."

Geno accepted her explanation easily. "Sure, as long as it's not too close to the stamp. I will tear it for you," he offered. She held her breath and watched him. In a minute he handed her the small scrap of paper. Lina had what she wanted; half of a postmark and part of an address.

"Thank you, Geno. That was kind of you," Lina smiled at the boy. "Your stamp is truly beautiful. Perhaps some day you will show me your other stamps."

Lina returned home and once again retrieved the letter in Carmen's dresser. Putting the two portions together, she read Santa Cruz, Bolivia, and more importantly, the information she needed. Lina replaced the letter after copying down the return address.

The very next day Lina rose early. She headed for her friend Bianca's house. She needed a letter written in English; Bianca had performed this task for her many times in the past.

Lina spent a full hour at Bianca's. When they were finished, Lina marched directly to the post office and mailed the letter she had had Bianca write. It was addressed to Rosalie Hollingsworth, Irvine, CA, USA.

December, 1974
Irvine, California

"Julie, you won't believe the letter I just received. I have just heard from Lina!" I shouted into the phone. "Triana and Franco are in Joseph's brother's home town. Santa Cruz, Bolivia!"

"Rosalie, that's perfect!" Julie shared my happiness. "Joseph is planning to leave the first of the year."

"Maybe by the time he is ready, I'll even know exactly where he's living. If we get much more information, I may just head down there myself."

"You know," Julie said slowly, "I have a funny feeling I'll be meeting Triana very soon."

I hung up the phone, more optimistic than I had been in many months.

Stan and I sat in our living room, waiting for Joseph. The boys had long since gone to their room and Tisha was tucked soundly in her crib.

"I am so happy," I told him. "I cannot believe that Lina was able to find the address and muster the courage to send it to me. I'm too excited for words. It's such unbelievable luck."

I realized that I was babbling.

"Stan, you do understand, don't you, that I am going to South America?"

"Rosalie, please. Let's not start that again. What if you do go? What will you find? Have you thought that after all this time that Triana might not want to come back? Have you considered what shape she may be in?"

"Not come back!" The words shot from my mouth. What was he saying? In all my crazy, desperate moments I had never considered that Triana would not want to come home with me.

"Rosalie, what about your responsibilities here? What about Tisha? What about the boys?"

He was serious. He did not want me to go. He was thinking of every argument he could muster to keep me from taking a second trip to South America. I tried to speak evenly.

"Wouldn't your mother come and stay with Tisha and the boys? I don't expect to be gone that long."

"Of course she would. But that's not the point. I think you are making a serious mistake. Triana will be eleven soon. She has lived with Franco for nearly four years. Rosalie, have you ever thought that perhaps it is best for her if she stays with her father? Maybe she is happy there."

I stood up. "Stop it, would you ever give up if it were one of the boys, Stan. No, you wouldn't. And I will never give up my search. It's no use. No matter what you say, I am going to go to South America. You're acting as though I could stop loving my child. How can I stop, Stan? I love both my children and I will never stop looking for Triana. You knew that when we got married. I cannot stop loving Triana just because I have Tisha now. Love doesn't work that way. I love Triana, I miss her and I am never going to stop looking for her, and I will get her back." I sobbed and continued, "Franco had no right to rip her out of my life. I would have never done that to him, and he had no right to tear my life apart."

On this subject, Stan knew it was useless to argue with me. He backed away from the lioness, ready to devour anyone who threatened the recovery of her cub.

The doorbell rang. Joseph stood there smiling.

The three of us sat in the living room, but Joseph and I did most of the talking. As Stan listened to us, he thought we sounded like two children planning an exciting scavenger hunt. He said very little until Joseph was ready to leave. The two men shook hands.

"Joseph, I hope the two of you don't land in some filthy jail down there. I don't approve of this, you know."

"Stan, stop worrying. I won't allow any harm to come to Rosalie. She won't be out of my sight for a moment. We will leave in a few days, as soon as I have made the final arrangements. We'll be back before you know it."

Stan's last words were brief. "Be careful, Joseph. Just be careful."

As I listened to Joseph's car pull away from the house, I realized that the next few days would be like those I had spent in Salta: tedious, long, endless hours of suspense. Now I was a nervous wreck, wondering what would happen this time. Would I finally succeed? I know that each coming hour would drag on like centuries, until we boarded the plane for Santa Cruz.

November, 1974
Trinidad, Bolivia

While Franco and Delia went off to Brazil to be married, Triana stayed with Delia's daughter and granddaughter, Tita, who was Triana's age.

When the wedded couple arrived home, a quiet, dignified party was held at Delia's home above the pharmacy. Franco and Triana were duly presented to Delia's relatives and friends, many of them prominent officials. With his customary composure, Franco handled himself beautifully. In spite of the recent head shaving Triana looked delicate and pretty in the new dress Delia had bought her. She sat on a brocade chair off to one side and tried to take it all in.

Delia's nephew, Salvadore, a young boy of thirteen, dressed in a gray suit and a dark tie, approached her. "Tina, it's so hot in here. Let's go outside. I'll ask Tita if she wants to come with us. All this talk is so boring." Once outside, the children took off their shoes and ran through the grass. Salvadore discarded his coat and the three of them sat on the lawn.

"I guess we are cousins, Tina," Salvadore observed.

"I guess we are," Triana agreed. She hadn't really thought about that. Everything had happened so fast. Her father had told her that Delia was a good woman, that they would have a fine place to live, that they would no longer have to run from alley to alley, or to scrounge or steal food.

"You will have me, *Penguina*," he had said, "and a new mother. Now you can go to school."

A new mother? Triana was not so sure. Her memory of her own mother had dimmed through the years, but it had not disappeared. She often wondered about her mother and whether the horrid things her father had told her were true. She was grateful that they would no longer have to run from town to town. She was less pleased with the prospect of going to school.

"If you two are cousins, what does that make me?" Tita piped up. Triana looked up from her thoughts. "I think I am your aunt."

The children giggled.

"Look, Tina, look!" Salvadore shouted. "There's Wolfe. Isn't he great?" He whistled. "Here, boy, come here. I want you to meet Tina."

Triana had never seen a dog of this size. "Is it okay to pet him?" she asked Salvadore. The huge, husky animal gamboled over and Salvadore affectionately stroked his thick fur.

"I've never seen a dog like this," Triana told him.

Salvadore laughed. "But he's not a dog, Tina. Not at all."

"He's not?" Triana was surprised and looked more closely at the animal she was petting.

"Well, what is he then?"

"He's a woo-oo-lf!"

Triana drew her hand back. A wolf! "But, he's so tame."

"Oh, grandmother likes animals," Tita explained. "She really loves them. She found Wolfe and his sister when they were only a few days old. Their mother had either died or abandoned them. Their eyes weren't even open."

Tita squeezed her eyes tightly shut in imitation of the wolf cubs. Triana understood. She knew that almost all animal babies are born with closed eyes.

"Grandmother just took them right in," Salvatore went on, "fed them from a baby's bottle. Wolfe's sister died. But Wolfe, well, he turned into the family's favorite pet. Isn't he terrific?"

The wolf nuzzled Triana's arm. "He sure is. He even thinks he's a dog."

"Oh, no," Salvatore laughed," he doesn't think he's a dog, he thinks he's a person. Don't you, Wolfe?" Salvatore gave the huge wolf an affectionate hug. "That's not the only unusual animal we have. Tina, Delia also saved the life of a baby fox. He's around here some place. We call him Foxy."

Something in Triana's long ago memory flashed through her mind. "I had a friend once who always named her pets like that. She always called her cats Kitties; her mother cat was Mother Kitty, and her dog was Poochie." Triana stared into space. She could clearly see Kathy's face, but the name was vague.

"Is your friend in Santa Cruz?" Tita inquired.

"Oh, no. My friend is a long, long way from here. I don't think I will ever see her again." Soon the mood passed and the sadness vanished from Triana's face. She wanted to see the fox. "Will Foxy come out to play, too?" she asked her new relatives.

"I think he will. I'm so glad you are here, Tina," the friendly smiling boy told her. "Now the house will be even more fun. We'll be great friends! Come on; let's see if we can find old Foxy."

Salvatore was a delightful boy, blessed with a warm and generous spirit. He and Tita ran off loudly calling "Foxy!" Triana followed at a slower pace.

Inside the house, the adults celebrated the wedding and the two new additions to their family.

CHAPTER NINETEEN

January 25, 1975
Los Angeles, California

In the crush of travelers at the busy Los Angeles International Airport, Joseph and I boarded our plane for Santa Cruz, Bolivia. Julie had given me an emotional embrace and wished me good luck.

"Now, Rosalie, I don't want you to let Joseph get into any trouble!" She smiled good-naturedly as she kissed the man she loved goodbye. Stan had wished me good luck, too, as we kissed goodbye. As we walked down the long boarding ramp, Joseph and I waved until Stan and Julie disappeared from our view.

The flight to La Paz was uneventful. From La Paz we took a small plane to Santa Cruz. The sun was setting as we arrived. There was no one waiting to meet us. The old fears and doubts swept over me.

"Joseph, I am so frightened."

"Stop worrying, Rosalie. Just hang on for a minute. I'll call my brother."

I was stunned. "Doesn't your brother know we are coming?"

"I thought I'd surprise him. Actually, I haven't been in touch with him for a couple of months."

"What? What is your brother going to think? You can't just pop in on him with a strange woman in tow. Why didn't you write them and tell them we were coming? What if they aren't here? What if they are on vacation?"

The questions tumbled from my lips as I frantically considered what a bad start the trip had taken. Had I put my trust into another person who would fail me?

"Rosalie, listen. I thought it over carefully and decided it was much better for us not to involve my brother in this business. I am just going to tell him that I am helping you with some legal matters down here, that you are a close friend of Julie's. He'll believe me. He won't ask any questions. Trust me. It will be fine."

No one answered the phone. Joseph's brother was not at home. Joseph was not at all perturbed, but I was uneasy. I wasn't sure I accepted Joseph's explanation that his brother was just off on his plantation for the weekend. He suggested that we find a hotel for the night and visit the post office in the morning to find out to whom the box was rented. As we waited for the desk clerk to check us in, I heard the sounds of lively music from a street carnival passing the hotel.

"You see, this town is pretty energetic." Joseph smiled at me.

The desk clerk handed Joseph a single key and we started up the stairs. I stopped.

"Joseph, why is there just one key? You aren't planning on us sleeping in the same room, are you?" We had reached the top of the stairs before he answered me.

"You'll see. I'll explain to you later."

As we rounded the corner of the second floor, I could see the hotel's central courtyard. Tables and chairs circled a lovely pool and a bar was set up at the far end. Joseph opened the door to the room he had engaged. When I looked in, I could see two twin beds in the large room, and a door on the far side of the room.

"Joseph, this is not going to happen," I said irritably. "Why didn't you get two rooms?"

"Look, I promised Stan I would see that you were safe. I am not going to let you out of my sight. There are twin beds. Take your pick. What are you worried about?"

"Stan did not mean sleeping in the same room," I replied testily. "This is going too far. You go downstairs right now and get another room this minute."

Joseph just smiled at me. "No, Rosalie, absolutely not. Look out the window. There are people down there who would just as soon slit your throat as buy you a drink. We will both sleep in this room. I don't need to worry about you. I need to know you are safe and in sight. Listen, Rosalie, you will be less conspicuous if others think we are together. A woman alone here is more at risk. So be quiet and choose your bed."

I felt absolutely out of control but I gave in.

"Okay, okay, I'll take the bed next to the bathroom." I said. "It just seems like I've been through all this before. Julie said I could trust you and I hope that is true. Let's not carry this too far. I am allowed to use the bathroom alone, am I not?"

The night passed peacefully enough and Joseph was the perfect gentleman.

In the morning, I woke up early, showered and dressed, and decided to go down for breakfast by myself, no matter what Joseph had said. Joseph was still asleep and I did not think I was in any danger. After all, who knew I was there? As I drank my coffee, I recognized the sounds of English speech from several of the surrounding tables. Two of the couples had looked at me curiously when I descended the stairs. When Joseph finally appeared, I told him how conspicuous and out of place I felt. The way these people looked at me made me very nervous.

"Take it easy, Rosalie. They probably think we are married." He grinned.

We finished breakfast and I paid the check. I tried to shake off my fears of a second failure as we walked to the post office. The lobby looked much like an old-fashioned U. S. post office. There were rows and rows of different sized mailboxes. We found the one we were looking for and stood there staring at it as though it could speak.

"What do we do now, Joseph?" I felt as though Triana was locked inside that box and there wasn't a key. "Joseph, for God's sake, do something!"

"Walk away from me, Rosalie. Just amuse yourself over there for a minute. I am going to rent us a box. We'll go from there."

Joseph stood in line and finally spoke to the clerk in Spanish. I saw the clerk motion toward the stairs. Joseph beckoned to me.

"We need to sign up officially. There are forms to fill out. The office is up the stairs," Joseph explained.

We quickly reached the second floor. At first, we could see no one. Finally, behind the fogged glass of a partitioned office, we could barely make out a dim figure. Joseph knocked on the door and an old man, possibly as old as eighty, lumbered over slowly. He and Joseph conversed in Spanish then the man retreated and closed the door. Five minutes seem to turn into hours. The clerk finally reappeared. He was carrying a large book in his hands. The elderly postal clerk fumbled through the pages slowly. I could see that the box renters were listed in the order of their number.

Joseph smiled at the old man. "Could you please bring me the application to open my box? I'll be filling out the form for you if you'll just give it to me. As the old man vanished, Joseph quickly thumbed through the pages, located the box we were looking for, and wrote down the address. Quickly, he flipped back to the original page just as the old fellow returned with the forms.

"*Señor*," Joseph said in Spanish. "I have changed my mind. I won't be needing a box after all."

The man threw up his hands. "*Señor*, why do you bother me when you are not sure what you are doing?"

We left the building hurriedly. As soon as we reached the sidewalk, I demanded to know who the registered owner of the box was.

"Rosalie," Joseph said. "It's a convent on the outskirts of town with a Mother Superior. Mother Teresa!"

Surprised as I was, I couldn't help feeling a little bit stupid. I should have guessed. That was Franco, all right, use the church for every possible purpose except its true mission.

After Joseph made another unsuccessful attempt to reach his brother by phone, he suggested that we drive out to the convent. That didn't suit me at all. I had no intention of coming to South America a second time to risk repeating the debacle the priests had made of my initial trip.

"Joseph," I said, "why don't we just watch the convent for a few days. Let's find out what is going on out there. We really need to think this through. I don't want to make the same mistakes that were made before."

But Joseph either didn't hear me clearly, or decided not to pay attention.

"We will see," he merely answered. "I will make up something. You just leave it in my hands."

"No decisions will be made without my permission, Joseph," I stated. "You have to accept that. Please, let's take it slowly and make absolutely sure we know where Franco is before he is alerted again."

Back at the hotel, Joseph left me in the courtyard having coffee while he went to use the phone again. At the next table sat an American woman. We smiled at each other. The woman spoke first.

"Are you and your husband here on vacation?" She inquired.

"Well, not exactly." I didn't know quite what to say. "That isn't my husband. We're here on business."

It was good to hear the voice of another American. I felt alienated in this strange situation.

"Oh, business," she said. "Are you in oil? That's what my husband does."

I paused. All my life I had lived openly and trustingly. I had no talent for clandestine games, so, I blurted out the truth.

"I'm down here looking for my daughter, who was taken from me by her father," I confided. "It's been four years now. The gentleman I'm with is helping me find her."

"Oh, my dear, how dreadful. Is the child in Santa Cruz?"

"I think so. At least I know they were here two months ago."

After I introduced myself, she told me her name. "I am Estella Henry. My husband works for Gulf Oil."

We sat chatting until Joseph returned. When I introduced them, I saw the questioning look in Joseph's eyes. I reassured him and turned the conversation to his brother.

"It was just as I told you. They were out on their plantation. They are expecting us later this afternoon."

We said goodbye to Estella and I promised to call her when I found Triana.

Joseph watched the woman leave and confronted me angrily.

"Rosalie, you need to keep your mouth shut!"

"Joseph, she was so nice. I hardly told her anything. She's not going to interfere. I'm a good judge of character. I felt perfectly safe in confiding in her."

"A good judge of character? Does that apply to Franco?"

Joseph had me there. I had no answer for him.

January 27, 1975
Trinidad, Bolivia

Triana could not decide whether to go out and play with the animals or stay in and listen to the radio. She enjoyed the new house. She had much more freedom to do things she wanted to do. She decided to curl up on the couch and listen to the radio. When Delia came in, she found a contented child listening to some music.

"Finally, I have a free half-hour! Tina, your father does such a fine job at the pharmacy. I have a chance to breathe. It's wonderful."

Triana looked up at her and smiled.

"What are you doing in here? Why aren't you outside playing?"

Triana shrugged. "I felt like listening to the radio. But pretty soon I'm going out to find Wolfe and Foxy. They are so much fun."

"You really love animals, don't you, Tina?"

"Yes," Triana answered enthusiastically. "I do."

"I love animals very much, too. That's one thing we have in common, my dear."

"One time a monkey bit me on my finger." Triana lifted her hand to show which finger." And, another time a rabid dog bit me, and I had to have shots."

Delia smiled down at Triana. "When I was a child, I was bitten more times that I can remember. My mother always used to tell me that people who love animals are very special people."

"Really? My dad always tells me to be more careful."

"I suppose he's right, too," Delia agreed. "Although I have to admit that's one lesson I have never learned."

They both laughed and suddenly Delia felt very close to this lovely child.

"Tina, can you keep a secret? If I tell you one, will you promise not to tell?" Delia knelt down by the chair Triana was sitting in.

"Oh, yes, I am very good at keeping secrets. I have had to keep lots of secrets."

"Tina, I am going to have a baby. You are going to have a new brother or sister. But you must not tell anyone. Promise?"

Triana looked at her stepmother solemnly. "I promise, Delia. I promise."

Delia returned to her work in the pharmacy and Triana sat very still on the couch. She wasn't sure just how she felt about her father having another child.

Triana frowned at her image in the gold-framed mirror. Her half-inch of stubble hair stood straight up. She doubted that her hair would ever grow long again.

She realized it was nearly lunchtime. Maybe Tita was in the dining room. Triana found her father gobbling down the meat and rice, which the maid had just served.

"Ah, there you are, my *bambina*," he greeted her, giving her a big hug.

"Hello, Daddy." Triana returned the hug.

"What are you and Tita and Salvadore going to do today?"

"We were talking about going to a movie. Do you think you could take us, Daddy?"

"Oh, *bambina*, not today. I am working in the pharmacy. Delia has some errands to run and appointments to keep. Maybe Thursday. Could we manage that, Delia?"

Delia smiled. "You really enjoy your work in the pharmacy, don't you, Alberto?" It pleased her to see her new husband taking so much interest and responsibility in her business.

"I do, indeed, my dear. It reminds me of my father's place. I spent so much time in his pharmacy as a child that it is all second nature to me. But, if it's all right with you, I will take the children to the movie on Thursday."

"Can you get all three of them on the motor bike?"

"Of course," Franco assured her. "I'll take Salvadore and Tita first and then come back for Triana. We'll manage just fine."

January 26, 1975
Santa Cruz, Bolivia

Later that same day, as the scorching afternoon sun beat down on the dusty streets of Santa Cruz, Joseph and I took a taxi to his family home, where Joseph was greeted warmly. His family was excited to have him in town.

Joseph had told me that his family was considered wealthy by local standards. The house was a small adobe tucked away on a dirt road. Nevertheless, it proved to be very comfortable, and it reminded me of the house my mother and stepfather rented in Stockton, California. This house, unlike the Stockton house, radiated an energy: an abundance of love and laughter. Joseph's brother's little home was a mansion of peace and joy.

I never knew how Joseph explained my presence, but they seemed pleased to meet me. I didn't understand a word they said, but I could read their smiles and gestures.

Joseph played translator as his sister-in-law, Charito, welcomed me.

"Thank you, Charito, for your hospitality. You are gracious to have me in your home," I told her.

"And this," Joseph said proudly, "is my big brother, Antonio, who never stops laughing."

Antonio was a fine, substantial man of good humor. His eyes laughed good-naturedly most of the time. His wife mirrored his love and tranquility and shared his happy disposition.

"And these three little mites are my nephews." Joseph called them by name as each one stepped forward and shook my hand.

The three boys were hustled into one bedroom and I was given the oldest boy's room, a curtained, glassed-in porch. Joseph was given the run of the living room and slept on a huge, comfortable couch.

Joseph had explained the family circumstances to me earlier. His brother ran a small business in town and his wife taught in a private school. On the weekends, the whole family visited their sugar plantation, which Antonio managed. He had conscientiously seen to the clearing of the acreage and the cutting of the sugar cane. Joseph explained that the government sponsored a program that allowed Bolivians who cleared jungle-growth to work the land. After a specified period of years, the land became theirs as long as they paid the required taxes.

After the family retired for the night, Joseph and I conferred on our strategy for the following day.

"Joseph, you must understand what happened the last time I found Franco and Triana," I said as we sat on the front porch. "No one would listen to me about what Franco would do if he knew I was there. Consequently, I lost Triana due to their stubbornness and refusal to heed my warning. I did not come down here to go through that a second time."

"Rosalie, I believe you. However, you don't know how things work down here. You need to trust me. I will see that you get your daughter back."

I had a sense of *déja-vu*. Why were men so stubborn? I asked myself. "Look, Joseph, I know you mean well, you're honest, trustworthy and reliable. Franco has none of those qualities. He lies, swindles and is a thief. He has no honor. He uses people and then discards them. He has regard for no one but himself. The law means nothing to him, and he thinks he can outsmart anyone." I was feeling frightened and desperate as I tried to make Joseph understand the man we were dealing with.

"Triana could be next door, on the next street and with just one mistake I could lose her again. Joseph, I am so close, please let's do this very carefully and be aware that every one we talk to could be under his spell or be his new best friend," I pressed on.

"Look, you were talking to that American lady, why weren't you more careful then?" Joseph asked.

"The last person Franco would talk to is an American. He would be too suspicious, and too paranoid," I pointed out. "Joseph it's getting late. I'm going in, though I don't think I can sleep; I am so close I can feel Triana in my arms."

In bed, I gazed at the ceiling of the small room for hours. I wondered what Triana would look like, how much she had grown, if she would recognize me. She could be with me within hours, home in Irvine in less than two days. I didn't know how I would get through the night. I could hardly breathe from anticipation and fright. Triana, Mommy is here to take you back home. I love you, darling. We will soon be together as a family. This time I will do it right; I'll get you back. Tomorrow, Triana, possibly tomorrow.

I hoped that this time, the task would be simple.

CHAPTER TWENTY

January 27, 1975
Santa Cruz, Bolivia

The taxi drove past the convent once, did a complete U-turn, and slowly drove past the dirt driveway again. Joseph told the driver to pull over and stop.

"Joseph, please promise me you won't tell them who you are. What if they suspect that I'm here and warn Franco of my presence?" Dear God, I am so nervous. This could be Salta all over again. "Please, please, don't mention what you are here for."

Joseph tried to be patient. "Look, I will not give you away," he insisted. "Trust me and try to stay calm. Wait here while I speak to the Mother Superior. I will be back soon. Try to hang onto your nerves."

"When you tell me where Triana is and that the nuns haven't warned Franco, my nerves will be just fine."

The minutes ticked on mercilessly slowly. What is he saying? What are they talking about? Will they tell him where Franco is? Oh, my God, maybe Triana is in the building this very minute. I suppressed a mad desire to rush in and look for her, and tried to sit in the shadows of the rear of the cab so that no one would notice me. What if Franco should appear?

Inside the convent, Joseph faced Mother Teresa. She eyed him with suspicion. Whether he was a friend or a foe of Sr. Valaverte's, she was not sure that she should trust him.

232

As Joseph studied the suspicious, wary nun, he decided that the only chance he had was to tell her the truth.

"Mother," Joseph began tentatively, "the truth is that I am not looking for this man at all. I am looking for the little girl."

"Oh, really? And why is that? What do you have to do with this man's child?"

"Mother, the child is his daughter. That is true. But he kidnapped this girl from her mother, who has legal custody. The mother has been searching for her for four long years. Please, we need your help."

"Just where is the child's mother?" Mother Teresa asked.

"She is right outside, Mother, in the taxi that brought us here. We have come all the way from the United States."

"Here! Bring her in at once. I must speak to her."

Joseph rushed out to the taxi and told me what he had done.

"Oh Joseph, you didn't?" I exploded in tears. "How could you, you promised?"

The figure of the nun was standing halfway down the driveway, leaning forward and peering at me.

"Rosalie, I told her because I had to. I think she wants to help you. Please come in and talk to her."

"How do you know she wants to help? Maybe she will tell Franco. I can't believe you did that."

I emerged from the cab and faced the Mother Superior. If Joseph had spilled the beans, in spite of all my warnings, I would have to cope with the consequences myself. Joseph introduced us, and we walked into the convent.

"So," Mother Teresa said, "you are Tina's mother. Yes, yes, I can see the resemblance."

"Mother, her name is Triana, not Tina. I have been looking for her for such a long time."

"This is all very confusing. Nothing you are saying matches what *Señor* Valaverte told us. Nothing at all."

"Sister," I choked back tears, "he kidnapped my little girl almost four years ago. I traveled all the way to Argentina two years ago and almost got her back, but at the last minute he ran away. Please help me; I need to find my child."

Mother Teresa instructed one of the nuns to bring tea. She wanted time to think. She leaned back in her chair, seeming to attempt to make some sense of the disordered and conflicting facts.

"My dear, I believe you," she said finally. "I could see that there was something terribly wrong with this man the first time I saw him."

As the Mother Superior and I exchanged information, Joseph translated rapidly. She told me that Franco had brought Triana to the convent to go to school, but that she had stayed only a few weeks before he removed her.

"I did not like their relationship," she said. "Not one little bit. It all seemed so unnatural. But that was not what disturbed me the most."

I sat patiently awaiting the next words from this perceptive woman. "The little girl said that she was terribly confused, that her father had told her you were dead. But just before she arrived here, he changed his story. Tina herself told me that her father had instructed her that if you ever tried to take her away, she was to run away instantly and that if she were ever parted from her father, she must promise to kill herself. When I asked her why this was to be so, she simply wouldn't talk to me any further."

"Oh, God, no. What has Franco done to her mind? Joseph, what should I do?"

I had never imagined such a risk. Would finding Triana be the very thing that would bring her harm?

"He must be losing his mind," Joseph muttered.

"My friends, this man is very sick," Mother Teresa said. "It is not right for this child to be with him. You must find her and get her back. She's such a lovely, intelligent child. I am sure that she will recover with the proper care and attention. You must make her understand that suicide is a crime against one's self as well as against God."

I listened to her and I understood, but the thought of Triana harming herself devastated me. And the thought of her doing it because of me made me limp with fear. Dimly I felt Joseph touching my arm.

"Rosalie, you can't give up now. What will become of Triana if she stays here? No child is going to harm herself unless there is something seriously wrong, and I don't think Triana will think of it again if we can get her away from Franco. Once you take her home, she will begin to feel safe and happy once again."

"Joseph, ask Mother Teresa if she knows where Franco is. Can she tell us the last time she saw him?"

"He picked up the child about two months ago," the nun stated. "He said he would no longer need to use our address because he was marrying a woman who lives north of Santa Cruz, and that his mother was coming from Italy to live with them."

"Enter Carmen," I said, half to myself. "Again Franco plays his mother like a violin."

"He was nervous, but he did seem happy and relieved. Perhaps delirious is a better word." Mother Teresa shook her head. "I do not believe this man is well."

Joseph leaned toward her. "Can you give us the name of the town and the name of the woman he married?"

Mother Teresa did not hesitate any longer. "I can do better than that," she said opening her desk drawer. "The woman lives in Trinidad. She operates a pharmacy. Here is the name and address."

After she handed the paper to Joseph, she took both of my hands. "I do hope you find her and take her home with you. I know that this is right and best for the child. God be with you."

Tears of gratitude rolled down my cheeks as I gave the nun a hug and thanked her profusely.

On the way back to Joseph's family's home, we scrutinized the name and address.

"My instincts were correct," Joseph reminded me. "Mother Teresa did not like Franco."

"I thank God. But you took a great risk. Franco has easily fooled many people. The world is littered with them. I'm sorry I distrusted you and screamed at you, Joseph. I just had visions of my going home alone...again."

"It's all right, Rosalie. I understand. It's all right. Mother Teresa is undoubtedly praying for us."

"Joseph, I hope so. We need all the help we can get." I closed my eyes and offered up a prayer of my own.

By the time we returned to Joseph's brother's house, Joseph had decided that our next move must be a legal one.

"Rosalie," he kept saying. "This is not a spy movie! What do you suggest? Throwing a blanket over her head and grabbing her off the street?"

"That sounds perfectly fine to me. Experience has taught me that the only chance we have is complete surprise." I'd been burned badly once and I didn't intend to feel the pain of disappointment again. "This may sound like something out of a novel, but believe me, it is the only way to succeed. All the legal papers in the world will not matter to Franco. I have her passport. That is all I need."

Joseph was adamant. "No. We must do this legally. I don't intend to get thrown into some Bolivian jail because of your melodramatic sense of intrigue. In Bolivia, they throw the key away. And I don't want to call Stan, either, to tell him you are in jail. Absolutely not. We will do it my way."

"Joseph, you are wasting time: Yours and mine. I have been through this before and by the time I finished the legal papers the last time, it was too late. I had mountains of legal paper, but I didn't have Triana."

"Rosalie at least let us get the proper Bolivian papers. Then if we run into trouble, we have something to show the police."

Exhausted and with no ally to support me, I finally gave in. "All right, Joseph. I think I'll go to bed. I didn't sleep a wink last night; I can't hold my eyes open any longer."

"Good idea," Joseph agreed. "We have a big day tomorrow."

Joseph probably slept well, but I did not. Nightmares of Salta disturbed my rest as my recurring dream haunted my sleep. Franco continually tormented my dreams. He was dashing through a forest of churches, his face filled with terror, as he ran faster and faster. As he sped from door to door, he dragged behind him a battered, broken doll, its arms hung limply, its bruised legs scraping along jagged rocks cutting and tearing at her flesh. The doll's face was always Triana's.

The rest I needed to prepare for the coming day was denied me. I awoke exhausted.

The next morning brought the beginning of the tiresome, interminable trek through dirty, disorganized cubicles that housed lazy, inefficient, pompous, second-class officials in a country whose national pastime was expressed in two words: *dinero* and *mañana*. I had seen it all before in my Salta days, but for Joseph it was a painful eye-opener.

Joseph's brother referred us to a local government flunky. Dispiritedly I agreed to go, but even Joseph grew impatient after a two-hour wait resulted in a cursory examination of the papers that had been issued in Argentina and an admonition to "Come back after lunch, *Señor*, after lunch." The word "lunch" means three hours of dead time. There was little we could do but return to the house and wait it out. When we went back, we entered the same dingy office with its broken chairs and piles of unfilled official papers, only to be referred to a *Señor* Valdez in yet another office in yet another building.

"Come back tomorrow, *Señor*. With a little assistance, I may be able to help you."

Joseph made his first indignant statement: "What do you mean assistance?" he demanded, scowling.

"*Señor*," the clerk answered slowly, eyeing Joseph, "I don't know exactly. At least I don't know just now. But if you come back tomorrow to see *Señor* Valdez, perhaps." His voice trailed off. "If you come back tomorrow, I could possibly, er, uh, put in a word for you?"

He stared at Joseph, clearly wanting to be sure his message had been received. "Well, in any event, *Señor*, it is too late today to do anything."

"That man wanted a bribe, that's what he wanted!" he told me furiously outside. "I was tempted to accuse him of it. If I had, he probably would have had us arrested for slander. No way. They are supposed to do their job, no way will I give anyone a single *centavo*."

Joseph and I had reached yet another impasse. If it meant securing papers to get Triana back, I would gladly have slipped the devil some money. Clearly, we saw dealing with lower-level South American officials in two different lights.

Joseph rushed down the street and I tried to keep up. "Where are you going?" I shouted.

"To one more office, before business closes," he called back over his shoulder.

Joseph went through his speech again and presented the papers. This time it was "out of my jurisdiction. You want the Juvenile Department, *Señor."* And of course, the conversation closed with the customary, "Perhaps, I could, let's say, put in a good word for you if you are willing."

The next morning, still another Bolivian official pointed out pedantically that the stamp on page six of my papers did not match the stamp on page ten. But perhaps they could overlook that minor detail, if.. Joseph exploded. "No, *Señor*, we will manage!"

Outside on the street his wrath fell on my deaf ears. "They are nothing but a bunch of crooks. Crooks," he fumed. "Every last one of them. This country will collapse in their hands. It's disgusting."

Our roles reversed. "Calm down, Joseph," I soothed. "You've been away from Bolivian justice far too long. It's just the way they do things down here."

"But, Rosalie, how did you get these papers in Argentina?"

"I hired an attorney. And I paid him the money. How he spread it around I never knew. As a matter of fact, I didn't even care."

"Well, I'm not going to let these flunkies get away with it. I'm going to talk to my brother."

"I thought you didn't want him involved."

"I've changed my mind," he said curtly.

That night after the children had been tucked in for the night, Joseph confided in Antonio and Charito. I sat at the table with them, straining to understand a word or two. Antonio kept shaking his head and Charito finally got up and came around to my side of the table to hug me.

"Charito says she is very, very sorry and she will do everything she can to help," Joseph told me gently. "Antonio, too. They know a woman who works for Juvenile. They will call her in the morning."

Antonio smiled at me as large tears rolled down my face.

The next day wore on as we wearily trudged from office to office, disillusioned, bewildered, frustrated, and discouraged by the ineffective labyrinth in which we found ourselves. As we returned home in the taxi, I could feel Joseph's disillusionment and fatigue. I was sure he felt that he was in for more than he had bargained for. I sat back in the seat, lost in my own thoughts, trying desperately to find my way through this nightmare. I began to think I might never see Triana again.

By the time dinner was over, Joseph had surrendered. Quietly he told me that Antonio knew of a man who worked for an international agency and had very heavy connections. This man carried a gun and had carte blanche to do as he pleased. Antonio had offered to contact him. But Antonio had said he would want money.

"Fine," I said. "I'll give it to him."

The man's name was Jose Garcia. He traveled with a companion who remained nameless. Their guns were clearly evident as the revolvers bulged through their tight-fitting coats. Once they had agreed to do the job, the negotiations over money began.

"Offer them a thousand dollars," I said, "including his expenses."

"But what if they want more?"

"Well, begin with three hundred and work your way up if you have to."

A long bargaining session ensued until finally Mr. Garcia's face relaxed and he smiled. He jumped up and shook Joseph's hand and nodded to me.

"They've settled for the five hundred and asked if we needed Franco killed," Joseph whispered.

"No," I said adamantly. "I just want Triana back."

Later I discovered that both of these men spoke perfect English.

Joseph filled me in on the plans for tomorrow. "They will hire a small plane and pilot. You will supply the photographs and we will fly to Trinidad, find Franco and his bride, and bring Triana back to you."

"You mean, just like that?"

"I mean just like that."

"I'm going with you!"

"No! It's too dangerous. Absolutely not."

"Did you hear me? I'm going."

"Did you hear me? No, you are not. You would be too conspicuous. You will stay here and wait for us. That's it."

The next morning I watched Antonio drive Joseph off in the pickup truck to meet Mr. Garcia. The house was empty. Charito had left for work and the boys were outside with their friends.

I paced for an hour, downed several cups of black coffee, and attempted to read. Nothing worked. The suspense suffocated me no matter what I did. I picked up the phone and dialed the hotel.

"Could you connect me with Mrs. Henry?"

The phone rang promptly.

"Hello, Estella? This is Rosalie. Do you remember me? We chatted at the hotel restaurant several days ago."

"Yes, of course, I remember you. How are you? Rosalie, my dear, have you found your little girl?"

"Estella, I'm fine. No, that's not true. I'm not fine. I desperately need someone to talk to." I stopped. What was I doing? What was I saying? Would this perfect stranger think I was absolutely mad?

"Could I come over and visit you for a while?"

This lovely lady did not hesitate.

"Where are you? I would be happy to see you. I'll have a taxi sent round right away."

Sitting in the rear of the cab on the way over to the hotel, I wondered if I was doing the right thing. What if something went wrong and Joseph called the house for me? At least I had had the presence of mind enough to leave the hotel phone number beside Antonio's telephone.

I walked through the hotel to the back patio, where I found Estella talking to a fellow resident.

"Come, have a seat," Estella called out as soon as she saw me approach.

"Estella, thanks for seeing me. I needed to talk to someone. I need to keep myself occupied for a while."

Estella stared at my shaking hands. "What is the news of your child?"

"We've found her in Trinidad. Joseph and some men have flown up to Trinidad this morning to pick her up. I'm so afraid that something will go wrong and I'll lose her again. The waiting. It's so damn difficult. I feel like I'm going to go crazy."

"Of course, I understand." Estella spoke kindly and patted my arm. "May I get you something, drink or some coffee? Or would you like something to calm your nerves?"

"No thank you, Estella, I just had to get out of the house, the walls were closing in on me. I felt if I had someone I could talk to, I would calm down."

"I'm a good listener, Rosalie."

"They should be returning any time now, the wait is killing me. My heart is in my throat and every nerve in my body is going to explode. I could have my child back in the matter of hours or I could lose her forever."

CHAPTER TWENTY-ONE

January 30, 1975
Trinidad, Bolivia

Jose Garcia lit his last cigarette, crumpled the empty package, and threw it on the ground of the small outdoor café. "Amateurs are all alike," he said to his companion, watching Joseph nervously eye the house. "He doesn't take his eyes off the house for a moment. Well, he'll have something to tell his grandchildren thirty years from now. Big fucking deal."

The stakeout had begun two hours earlier. José and his partner, Pedro, were bored. "I hope the kid comes out soon," José muttered, looking at his watch. Moonlighting brought him extra money, but he could certainly think of more exciting ways to spend his time.

"Let's run through it one more time," Joseph whispered anxiously, wiping his face with a handkerchief as the late January sun beat down and the stifling heat and humidity increased. José and Pedro exchanged contemptuous glances. Few people ever questioned their moves; they were the experts.

Joseph rehearsed the situation again anyway.

"As soon as she gets close enough, we grab her, carry her to the car and we take off." He drummed his fingers on the table. "I hope nothing goes wrong, like the car not starting. He's a good man, the driver, right?"

"Fine. Perfecto," José answered irritably. "How good does he have to be to drive a getaway car?"

"Right, right," Joseph nodded his head. "But what happens if she doesn't come out today?"

Pedro shook his head and smiled.

"Look, let's just play it by ear, all right?" José snapped.

"Oh, sure, sure," Joseph hastily agreed. "I was just asking; that's all. I'm not used to this kind of thing, you know."

"No shit," Jose said sarcastically to Pedro. "Couldn't prove it by me. Should've left him behind with the woman. Oh, what the hell, it'll all be over soon."

But Joseph could not overcome the anxiety that swept over him. "José, have you talked to the local police, to make sure they'll not interfere?"

The two men gave Joseph a contemptuous side glance. "If you're so concerned, buddy, maybe you should go talk to them."

Joseph took the suggestion. He headed for the nearest police station. When he found it, the place was almost entirely empty. Only a single police officer sat at the front desk. Joseph approached him cautiously, trying to size him up. He felt insecure about broaching the subject of Franco's abduction.

"Looks like you're here all by yourself," Joseph began tentatively.

"Yeah," the officer replied. "We don't have much trouble in this little town. The rest of the men are at lunch." He glanced at the clock. "Been gone a couple of hours."

Joseph plunged ahead. "I want to talk to you about something important. You see, I'm here to take a fugitive back to Santa Cruz. It's all legal, you understand. I just thought I should let you know. We don't want to cause you any trouble." Joseph dug into his pocket and took out some large bills that the officer eyed greedily. Joseph held the bills in his hand.

"You see," said Joseph, more forcefully, "we don't want any help, any interference. I want to be certain that if you receive a call from the pharmacy down the street, that you will ignore it. We won't be long, just long enough to pick up the criminal and return to the airport." Joseph put the bills on the desk. The policeman hesitated, but only for a moment. He put his hand on the money and fingered the bills: One hundred dollars. Quickly he pocketed the money.

"Fine. Just fine. You better get at it. The rest of the boys will be back pretty soon."

Joseph didn't answer. He turned and walked quickly down the block, knowing that he had just done one more thing that would help them to get Triana back safely. As he passed the pharmacy, he decided to go in. He wanted to be certain he would recognize Franco when he saw him.

Franco was behind the counter, talking animatedly to a woman about the children and taking them to a movie. Joseph assumed that the woman was Franco's wife. As soon as Joseph reached the counter, Franco turned and disappeared into the back of the store. Politely, Joseph asked for some medicine for an upset stomach, and tried to answer Delia's questions casually. Obviously, she thought he was from out of town. He passed it off by saying that he was visiting some friends. Then he paid for the remedy that Delia suggested, and left.

Within a few minutes, he was back in the café with José and Pedro.

Inside the house, Triana picked at her lunch.

"What's the matter, baby? Don't you feel well?" Franco asked.

"I feel fine, Dad," Triana replied softly.

"Then why aren't you eating?" Franco took another helping from the bowl. "The food's delicious. See? Tita is eating her food, too."

Triana shrugged. "It's just too hot today to be hungry."

"The theater will be cool and the movie will take your mind off the heat," Franco said enthusiastically. Triana nodded. She wasn't sure she wanted to go to the movie after all, but Tita was counting on it and Triana hesitated to argue.

"You really like it here, don't you, *Penguina*?" her father asked.

Triana smiled weakly. "Yes, Dad. It's a nice place. And I never thought I'd have my own wolf and my very own fox."

"Good," Franco said, finishing his lunch. "Now hurry up and get ready, Tina. Salvadore is meeting us here in a few minutes. I will take him to the movie house and then come back for the two of you."

"Can't we all three go together?" Tita asked, "It would be so much fun."

"The motorbike will only hold two. You know that. I'll take Salvadore and then the two of you can ride together." Franco gave Triana a hug. "I'll be back for you two in a little while, *Penguina*."

The motorbike sped around the corner from behind the house and surprised the three men waiting at the small café across the street.

"Here we go! Who's that boy with the man?" Jose asked Joseph.

Joseph shrugged. "That's not the kid we want, but that's definitely the man. I heard him talking about the children and a movie; he probably needs to take them in shifts."

José took charge. "He'll be back. Pedro, you go to the corner. Joseph, you go the opposite direction. As soon as you know it's the right child, start walking toward them and come at them from that end."

José pointed down the street. "Remember," he said to Joseph, "you're the one who knows what she looks like. Your job is to finger her. I'll come at them from here."

José looked at his watch while Pedro and Joseph walked to their posts. Joseph was nervous, unsure of himself, but he obeyed Jose's instructions. Within ten minutes Franco returned. He parked the motorbike and entered the pharmacy. The door opened and Franco emerged with the two little girls.

"Oh, boy!" Joseph said to himself. "That's her! This is it!" His stomach felt queasy and his body was sweating. He nodded to Jose and walked toward Franco.

"You grab the child; I'll take care of the man." Jose's instructions kept ringing in Joseph's head. What if he grabbed the wrong child? What if this wasn't really Triana? The child looked different from the picture that he had in his pocket.

Franco was too busy placing the children on the motorcycle behind him. He never noticed the three men approach. Suddenly, there was a gun at his head. He froze.

Triana felt strong arms surrounding her. She struggled but the arms held her tight.

"Daddy! Daddy!"

"Don't be afraid, honey, nobody's going to hurt you," a strange voice said into her ear. "You are Triana, aren't you? And he is your father, Franco, and you are from the United States?" Joseph spoke rapidly to her in Spanish.

"Yes, he is my father." Suddenly she stopped. The months of running, the weeks of lies, the life she had been forced to live surfaced and she changed her story.

"No, no, *Señor*, I'm not Triana. My name is Tina. You... You have the wrong people." Triana spoke in Spanish as she tried to break loose from his hold and run to her father, who struggled with Jose and Pedro.

Joseph held her firmly. "Do you know these people?" Joseph asked in English as he held out a picture of friends of the family Triana had known since birth. Everything came to a sudden stop. Forgotten memories flooded the child's mind.

"They are my friends Kathy, Barbie and Sherrie. Daddy... Daddy, look!"

In her confusion, Triana forgot her promise to her father. Somewhere from deep in her memory, the faces evoked another life, a life where she had spoken English. She stopped quickly and looked at Joseph. She had been tricked. Her father would be enraged at her mistake.

"Thank God, I've got the right one!"

Joseph picked Triana up and quickly carried her to the car. Triana heard Franco's voice, shouting and swearing. She was acutely aware of the sounds of fighting behind her as they reached the car. Triana was too frightened to make a sound.

"Let me go!" Franco shouted. "Baby! Where's my child?"

"My daddy!" she whispered, "Don't hurt my daddy!"

Her voice sounded weak and faint in her own ears. Nothing in the darkness of the car seemed real. She could hear Tita's cry from somewhere, but she could not tell where it came from. The strange man who had placed her in the car was holding her close to him. She thought the other men had forced her father into the back seat but she couldn't see him. When the car took off, the force of the careening vehicle threw her even closer to the stranger who held her. She was petrified. Who were these men and what did they want?

"Daddy," she whimpered, "I'm scared. Daddy, where are you?"

Joseph held her and spoke quietly. "Don't be afraid, Triana... nobody's going to hurt you."

"Okay, what do we do with the other child?" Pedro's loud voice blared out. "We don't want her, too, do we?"

"Stop the car down the street; we'll put her out there. She'll find her way home."

José's voice came from the back seat where he was forcing Franco down, holding the gun to his head.

The car stopped. A bewildered Tita was put out on the sidewalk. The car sped away in the dust.

The small airport was crowded. They pulled right onto the airfield and quickly walked to the chartered plane.

"The pilot should be ready to take off," José said as he and Pedro half pulled, half carried Franco toward the waiting aircraft. Joseph tugged along a reluctant Triana, trying his best to comfort her.

"Oh, he'll be there," smiled Jose, "that prick wants to get paid."

Pedro agreed. "He knows I'd cut his balls off and make him eat them if he screws us up."

As they walked quickly across the field, Franco grabbed his one opportunity.

"Help me! For God's sake, help! They're going to kill me!" he shouted at the top of his lungs.

Several men and women in the crowd turned. They stood still, trying to decide what to do, trying to read the situation. No one moved or came forward to challenge the menacing glares of the three men.

"Please!" Franco screamed. "I am very wealthy... I'm being kidnapped... help me... I'll give you anything!"

Franco grabbed the chance to shove José, but Pedro hit Franco with such force that he crumpled to the ground. José recovered quickly, picked Franco up and moved him sharply forward to the plane, while Pedro shoved his gun into Franco's kidney so hard that Franco gasped.

"Now you listen to me, you cock-sucking wop," José said softly. "I don't like your kind in my country and it would give me great pleasure to spend about a week cutting off your dick in little pieces until you bled to death. Right now, I'm taking you and that kid back to Santa Cruz. But all you have to do, asshole, is make me have to waste a couple of those people you've been yelling to over there and I won't care how much money it costs me… your ass will be mine! You understand?"

In all his life, even when he had lived on the fringes of the criminal world, Franco had never heard the voice of an angry professional killer. He shut up.

As soon as the party boarded the plane, the pilot taxied down the runway.

When they were airborne, a desperate, cringing Franco pleaded with José. "Please, when you kill me, don't do it in front of my child. That's the only thing I ask of you! Please, I beg of you." Tears rolled down his face. Franco thought he knew who had sent these men. He was sure his time had run out.

Pedro, sitting in the front with the pilot turned and looked at José. "What a way to earn a living," Pedro said, "Picking up this bag of shit!"

"Stop it!" Joseph interrupted and for the first time, he spoke directly to Franco. "We are here to pick up Triana and have no intentions of killing you."

"What?" Franco said incredulously. "But I thought you were from... you mean Rosalie sent you?"

"Who else would be looking for Triana, you idiot?" Joseph felt nothing but hostility toward this man.

"Oh God, oh God," Franco moaned. Rosalie? He had never even thought of Rosalie. Only of men in Salta, in Valle Grande, and in many, many other parts of the world who had reason to want to find him. They had reasons far more life threatening than Rosalie.

Franco felt a few brief moments of relief, but he realized that the conspiracy and the adventure were over. What is to become of me without Triana? he thought. How can I live? They might as well kill me.

Joseph, his back to the pilot, relaxed his hold on Triana as the jungle below quickly passed. Triana, facing her dad, sat dazed and scared. José, giving the pilot instructions, sat next to Franco facing Joseph. Franco reached for his daughter's hand, giving her a knowing smile as he gave her a tiny squeeze. Franco crept inch by inch toward the airplane door, slowly, ever so slowly. Deep inside of him a desperation he had never felt before became overwhelming. Inch by inch, closer and closer to the door. Franco lunged for the door and eternal freedom with his one true possession.

CHAPTER TWENTY-TWO

January 30, 1975
Santa Cruz, Bolivia

On the hotel veranda, the late afternoon sun cast a blanket of sunlight over the surrounding trees, which filtered down through the thick branches like a golden shimmering shadow. The leaves silently danced their patterns on the people sitting quietly on the comfortably cushioned wicker chairs below.

The wait was the most exhausting experience I had ever endured. "I guess I'm all talked out," I said at last to Estella.

The hours had stretched on interminably, like all the hours, all the days, all the weeks, all the years I had been without my daughter. Since I had left Los Angeles, everything I held dear was riding on these few hours. And once more, I sat alone, helplessly dependent upon someone else. Kind as Estella had been to me, she could not possibly understand.

I had deliberately placed myself where I could face the lobby and see through to the street.

I leaped from my chair. "Oh, God! There he is! There's Joseph!" I jumped up and ran toward him. "What happened? Did you find her? Where is she? Is she here? Did you have any trouble?" The words tumbled over each other.

"Rosalie, calm down." Joseph's stern voice irritated me.

"What do you mean calm down? Are you telling me that she isn't here?" I grabbed his arm roughly.

"Rosalie! Stop it! Triana's been through a great shock," he tried to explain.

I didn't even listen.

"She's here... she's here... but where is she? Where's my baby?"

I ran through the hotel lobby with Joseph tearing after me, trying to catch me and hold me back.

"Wait a minute. Don't go out there like this. You don't understand what that child has gone through. Franco tried to jump out of the plane with her. Thank God we stopped him before he managed to kill them both."

"Joseph, I've got to see her right now. I'm not going to upset her," I pleaded.

"You must be calm. Stop right now and think." Joseph took hold of my arm.

I shook him off. "Joseph! If she's here, I want to see her now. I want to hold her in my arms, touch her. Oh, Joseph don't you understand, I've waited so long for this day and you want to hold me back. Where is she? Please?"

I ran through the lobby, with an exhausted Joseph following close behind, trailed by Estella who was also caught up in the drama of the moment. When I reached the street, I looked frantically up one side and down the other. Finally, I spotted the pickup truck parked half a block up the street. "That truck! It's that truck... my baby's in that truck!" I cried. Without waiting for an answer, I ran toward the truck as fast as my shaky legs would carry me.

Five feet from the truck I stopped and then cautiously approached. I opened the passenger door.

Sitting on the large seat was a small, frail child. Half-inch stubs of hair covered her head. The big hazel eyes stared at me. We looked at each other. She was so fragile, so undernourished, so terribly thin. For a moment I thought I was looking at a picture of a ravaged, starving, bewildered orphan. Could this little girl be Triana? The child bore very little resemblance to Triana. And yet...

"Oh God, oh, my God. Triana? Are you my Triana?"

The years of disappointments, the nights of fear, the days of longing, the misery that had so long been my companion, faded.

Tears ran down my face as I cried out the name of my child. "Triana!"

The little girl stared at me blankly.

"Triana," I called again, reaching into the truck as Jose began to help Triana down from the seat.

I took this child, my child, into my arms, and held her in the late afternoon South American sunset and I cried and cried.

"My baby... My Triana... I can't believe it's you, I've waited so long to hold you," I sobbed, hugging her. The child stood limply and passively, in a state of shock. Only later, much later, did I learn that Triana did not know who I was.

A shadowy movement from the back of the truck aroused my attention. Franco! "What's he doing here?" I turned to Joseph.

"Rosalie," Joseph said quietly, "You've got Triana. It's for the authorities to deal with Franco. Surely you want him charged."

Joseph gently herded Triana and me into the front seat. He joined Pedro in the back of the truck with Franco. José drove us away, leaving Estella standing on the sidewalk, tears of compassion and happiness streaming down her face.

As we arrived at the jailhouse, Franco spoke for the first time. The sound of his voice jarred me.

"Well, Roe, I guess you've finally won," he said quietly. "I guess the best person finally won."

I couldn't look at him, tears rolled down my face; it was all a game to him. The games he had played with my life and with Triana's. I couldn't answer, as my tears turned to fury, it was so strong I wanted to kill him myself and for a moment I wished I had taken the offer from José and Pedro. All the rage, all the pain, all the sleepless nights this man had caused me boiled up in one instant. I wanted to attack Franco for all the misery he had inflicted on me these last four years. I truly had never hated anyone as I hated this man, this minute. Well, Franco had played his last game with me.

Joseph's quiet, soothing voice calmed me, and for the balance of the ordeal Franco said nothing. Jose sat down at an empty desk in an adjoining room and processed his report for the authorities. Franco's incarceration was handled swiftly and with few questions.

José's connections and influence with the authorities were obvious, as advertised. For his part, Franco was shaken by the knowledge of how close he had come to death, not only at the hands of these men but by his own hands as well. He held onto Triana's hand, a beaten man. He knew this was the last chance to see his child. He broke down and cried.

"Why don't you act like a man in front of your child? Do you want her to remember you like this?" Joseph asked angrily.

But it wasn't only that. For a fleeting moment, Joseph wondered if he had done the right thing in taking this child away from her father. Joseph was angry not only with Franco, but at himself. Joseph knew what many others had known. This man would have been able to fool him in an instant. At times during this long day he had almost succeeded. Franco had behaved the way Franco always did: charming, desperate. He was believable and Joseph realized how close he had come to adding his own name to the long list of Franco's victims.

Franco straightened up and looked at Joseph. "You are right. It's just that I love her so." He said as if it was justification and rationalization of all the harm he had inflicted on so many people.

"If you had really loved this child," Joseph retorted, "she would not be here in this place, looking as she does. How can you call what you've done to her love? You believe your own lies."

"Roe," Franco turned to me. "Please, take good care of Triana and ask Stan to be kind to her."

Joseph grabbed me as I stood to attack this arrogant man who had nearly destroyed my life.

"Triana, don't forget that I love you," Franco called to his daughter as the officers took him into custody. Triana cried as her father disappeared.

Antonio arrived to take us home. Our goodbyes to José were abbreviated. I handed him the money, and we left.

As happy as I was to have Triana back in my arms, the evening proved to be an awkward one. The maid fixed dinner and the boys chatted with Triana in Spanish as we ate.

Triana managed to smile occasionally. But her big hazel eyes constantly searched our faces: mine in particular. Here she sat among strangers, trying to sort out all that had happened to her in a few hours. And of all the strangers in that room, perhaps I was the strangest of all.

I took Triana to our room, showed her the bathroom and the shower. I borrowed some pajamas for her and I tucked her into our bed, I held her in my arms for a moment.

"Triana, I'm your mother. I am truly your mother. And I am so happy to have you back."

She stiffened, laid her head on the pillow, and turned her back. The sobs began. Huge, wracking, sobs. It was the first of many nights that Triana would sob herself to sleep.

In the living room, I sat quietly lost in my own thoughts. How long would it take for my daughter to accept me again as her mother? The sobbing continued, forcing me to confront something that my fantasy and anticipation had not included. My search had been a relentless crusade. But now that I had her back, I knew that it would take months, perhaps years, to bridge the yawning abyss that her father had created between us.

Joseph came in from the porch, his face serious and darkened.

"What's wrong, Joseph?"

"It's the jail. The jail that Franco is in," he replied.

"Why are your worried about that? It's the best place in the world for him, as far as I'm concerned," I said vehemently.

"You don't know the jails down here, Rosalie. They're the worst in the world. They won't even give him a blanket. If you want a blanket, you have to beat up another prisoner to get it. I'm going back down to the jail and make sure he is kept in a separate cell until after you leave. I'll take him some bedding."

Somewhat reluctantly, I agreed. "I just wish you had left him on the streets in Trinidad. Go if you think it is best; take him a blanket, just be careful." What I didn't tell Joseph was better left unsaid. Even though I had hated Franco for years, even though he had brought me enormous pain, even though he had distorted Triana's childhood, I found myself almost feeling sorry for him. At one time we had been married. For a short time I had loved him and for a short time, we had been happy.

By the time Joseph returned, I had retired to the small glassed-in room and was dozing with my arms wrapped around my child.

Antonio met Joseph at the door. "How's the good Samaritan?" Antonio said jovially, slapping his brother on the shoulder.

Joseph sighed. "You're not going to believe this, but his wife came down from Trinidad and bailed him out."

"Well, there's nothing he can do. After all, Rosalie's papers are in order. All he can do is defend himself later in court," Antonio reasoned.

"What if he gets hold of some money... maybe even finds Jose and Pedro?' Joseph said in a hoarse whisper. "Do you think for a minute that those two would be above taking the child back? Even turning Rosalie over to Franco in the bargain?"

"I guess you're right. However, as rough as José and Pedro are, they took Rosalie's money. But to be on the safe side, Triana and Rosalie should leave right away," Antonio agreed.

"You're forgetting something. This is Thursday. There are no more flights until Monday morning. We've got to get Rosalie and Triana away from here before the weekend," Joseph said.

The next morning, Joseph's entire family, Triana and I piled into a pickup truck and made our way out of town to the family plantation for a long weekend.

"I've never seen anything like it. It's beautiful," I said to Antonio. "What are those houses made of that we passed? Who lives in them?"

"They are made of clay and straw," Antonio explained, "and the people who live there with their families are Indians. They work for me here on the plantation. Tomorrow, I will show you around. First, though, let us get you and Triana settled."

There were two small rooms partly screened-in on the sides that were not connected to the house. One storage room was in the front, on the left side of the long narrow porch, and the other room was on the right side of the house in the back. The rooms were quickly cleaned and furnished with cots. One of these primitive rooms was readied for Joseph and the other for Triana and me.

It's like a small storage room, I thought. "I hope that there are no spiders, or snakes," I said to Joseph.

"Don't worry about it. You're just used to a different way of life. You'll be comfortable, think of it as camping. Just get some rest," he told me.

It took me some time and considerable ingenuity to dress for bed in that room, exposed as it was to the wilds of the night, with absolutely no privacy. Triana quickly lay down on her cot and turned her back. I could hear her crying softly, as I prepared for bed, slipping on my gown before removing my clothing.

I lay awake worrying. Had Stan been right? Was I doing the right thing for Triana by bringing her back to a lifestyle she had long forgotten? Would Triana ever love me as she had once? After many hours, exhaustion claimed me, and I fell into a deep sleep.

At three in the morning, a shrill scream awakened me.

"Oh my heavens, Triana," I went to her. "It's only a bad dream," I said softly, holding her close, "only a dream."

But throughout the night, Triana cried constantly, and in the morning, she was no better.

"Come on," said Antonio the next morning, hoping to bolster Triana's spirits, "I'll show you around the plantation. Joseph, come on, let's go."

As we toured the spacious farm, I carefully watched Triana for some reaction. The child followed woodenly, distancing herself from all of us. Repeatedly, I tried to start a conversation.

"I guess you're used to all this, Triana?"

Triana looked at me, but did not answer.

We started back only as the sun began to set.

That night at supper, Triana's appetite improved. She ate well and joked a little with the other children. However, that night, I still didn't sleep. Triana tossed and turned on her cot, moaning and crying all night long.

By Sunday, Triana seemed to perk up. The events of the past few days seemed to be fading. Her instant friendship with Antonio's wife and her three boys helped immensely to bring her out of her shell.

"Do you like to ride horses?" one of the boys asked in Spanish.

Triana smiled. "Oh, yes!"

"Come on then! Let's go out in the field and get the horses and go for a ride."

"Oh, what a good idea. I haven't seen Triana look this happy since we got her back," I commented.

Triana and Alfonso ran into the field, but before they could catch any of the horses, a heavy rain started.

"Oh, wow! I guess this is the tropics," I laughed, rushing to grab an umbrella.

"Here, could you take this out to Triana so she won't get wet?" I offered the umbrella to the smaller boy, who had remained behind.

Although he spoke no English, the combination of the rain, the umbrella and my finger pointing towards Triana proved sufficient. He snatched the umbrella from my hand and went running off toward his brother and Triana.

"Don't forget to open it!" I said, laughing, as I mimed the way to open an umbrella. Already soaking wet, he looked back and did as he was told with such force that the umbrella turned inside out. The young boy stood there in the downpour, looking perplexed.

Joseph laughingly called to him in Spanish. "Never mind, just go ahead."

The boy galloped along holding the useless inside-out umbrella high over his head. Soon all three children returned, soaked, but laughing. They even had one horse in tow. At last, Triana seemed to be enjoying herself and I was cautiously relieved.

As the rain subsided, the children ran out of the house. "Come on!" said one of the boys. "Let's get some fresh milk."

"Okay," Triana agreed.

Joseph and I trailed along to watch, while Triana and the boys drank the milk freshly drawn from a patient cow that watched the hubbub with a bovine lack of concern.

"Ever taste really fresh milk, Rosalie?" asked Joseph.

"Maybe once, but it was so many years ago that I have forgotten. Let me try some." I sipped the milk that the children seemed to be enjoying so much.

"Good heavens!" I sputtered. "That's just horrible. How can you drink that stuff?"

Chuckling, Joseph admitted, "It does take some getting used to."

"It's good!" Triana said, taking another deep swallow from the battered cup the children were sharing.

How different our worlds had been in the last four years.

After dinner on Sunday, Antonio suggested that we return to Santa Cruz. "You'll be safe enough. Then you can catch the early flight to La Paz."

"It's all right with me," I replied. "Visiting your plantation has been such a treat. Thank you so very much. Both Triana and I enjoyed it tremendously. It has clearly helped Triana to adjust before we return to the States."

We piled into the pickup for the return trip. I held Triana on my lap and felt the stiffness in her thin little body.

"Look, Triana, up there! What is it? We saw the same thing on the way out here yesterday."

As we neared the house, a grove of trees shone in the darkness.

"Look at the trees!" I urged. "They're all lit up. Isn't it beautiful?"

"Fireflies," commented Triana softly.

That night Triana lay on our bed and cried herself to sleep. It was another sleepless night for me. Another set of hours spent wondering if I had done the right thing. Another night of listening to the child I wanted to make happy sob her little soul out.

"Joseph," I confided, "Triana is so unhappy. I just hope that Stan wasn't right and that I haven't made a terrible mistake."

"She'll be all right," Joseph said softly. "She's been through a terrible experience. Just give her time. She'll be okay, you'll see."

In the morning, we said our goodbyes. I thanked Joseph's family for their kind hospitality and help.

Antonio drove us to the Santa Cruz airport. Joseph had agreed to come with us. I was relieved that I did not have to cope without an interpreter. My fear that Franco would find me before I reached the States constantly plagued me. I continued to be nervous and anxious. Joseph seemed even more nervous and cautious than I did. He was aware that Franco had been bailed out of jail and could be anywhere.

Five hours later, we checked into a decent hotel in La Paz. The flight back to the United States did not leave until the next day.

The first thing I did was to call Stan. I had tried to reach him repeatedly from Santa Cruz but could never get through.

When I heard Stan's voice on the other end of the line, I began to cry.

"Did you hear me, Stan, she's here with me, Stan, I have her back."

"Oh, I'm so glad!" Stan said in a relieved voice. "How is she?"

I held the phone tightly. "She's very upset. But, I think she'll be fine."

"Well, that's great, honey. Everything's fine here. Tisha keeps asking where mommy is."

I smiled. "Give her a big kiss for me and tell her that mommy is coming home tomorrow with her big sister."

"Will do," Stan replied.

"Oh, I almost forgot. Could you go and get Triana a coat? It's very hot here and I'm afraid the sudden change in climate may be hard on her. She has nothing but what she's got on," I explained.

"No problem. Consider it done," Stan assured me. "Can't wait to have you back," Stan finished gently.

"I can't wait either. Goodbye, darling."

Stan hung up the phone and turned to look at Tisha. She was sleeping soundly on the couch, where she had dozed off while he was reading her a story.

"Well, little girl, you've got some competition now. I hope that you and Triana will get along. I hope you won't resent each other or compete for your mother's attention. We'll just have to take it a step at a time." Stan's thoughts were less than easy as he gently picked up the baby and carried her to the bedroom to tuck her into her crib for the night.

As I hung up the phone, I looked fondly at Triana. One of my girls was home and the other would be soon. Joseph interrupted my thoughts, "Come on," he urged, "let's not hang around here all day. Let's go sightseeing. La Paz is a beautiful city."

"Great," I agreed. "Won't that be nice, Triana? Would you like to go see the city?"

Triana nodded unenthusiastically.

"Daddy," she whispered, "I want my daddy." The tears I had heard for so many days began anew. I took her in my arms and tried to comfort her, but I felt her body resist immediately. She stiffened and said nothing more.

We took a taxi and rode past the Plaza Marila in the center of the city, past Palace Legislación and the stores and shops on the Calle Comercio. Soon, we passed a big marketplace. I asked Joseph to have the driver stop. The central market with its picturesque blend of native Indian vendors hawking their wares was lively and cheerful. The women were dressed in brightly colored shawls, their thick, black braids topped by flat, wide-brimmed hats. Triana walked along, holding my hand. A little puppy stuck its head out from under one of the stalls, and Triana instantly bent down to pet it.

"Hey," said Joseph, noticing her interest in the animal, "the zoo is right down the way. Want to see all the animals, Triana?"

Triana's face brightened. We took another taxi a short way along Avenida Camacho to a small zoo in the Parque Infantil. Triana walked briskly, noting each animal with interest. I was delighted to see her responses.

"Too bad they have to be in cages," Triana commented in Spanish. "But, I guess they have to be there," she finished in English.

We smiled at each other and spent our most pleasant time together sharing observations of the animals. It encouraged me to find some common ground at last.

Joseph skillfully played his role as guide, interpreter and bodyguard. As we left the zoo, I noticed that he became especially vigilant, looking over his shoulder frequently and staying close to both of us. I appreciated his caution but knew that Franco was finally out of my life and I knew the first peace I had felt for many years.

At the airport the next morning, it startled me to hear my name being called.

"Rosalie! Wait!"

My apprehension vanished as I recognized the couple that I had met with Estella on my first day in Santa Cruz.

"Oh, my," the woman exulted, "you got her. This must be your daughter. How wonderful!"

I beamed and put my arm around Triana, but she cringed and looked down at her shoes.

"Triana, say hello to mommy's friends. They're so happy to see you," I encouraged her. Triana glanced up momentarily, but immediately lowered her eyes and uttered not a word.

"Oh, we're so happy for you both," said the woman.

"Yes, it's just great," agreed her husband.

An anxious Joseph fidgeted over the interruption. His mind was concentrating on getting us safely on the plane.

That bastard, or someone he's hired, could be here right now, anywhere, Joseph thought to himself.

As our flight number was called, Joseph hurried us toward the gate and when we reached it, he put his arm firmly around my shoulders.

"Well, the adventure is over. Take care of yourself, and the little one," he said encircling Triana's narrow shoulders with his other arm. "Tell Stan that I will see all of you in a few weeks."

"Oh, Joseph." My eyes filled with tears and my voice choked with emotion. "How can I ever thank you for what you've done for us? You are truly a dear friend. No one else would have gone through what you have in the name of sheer friendship. Someday maybe I can do something for you and Julie."

Joseph bowed low. "At your service any time, my ladies."

Laughing through my tears, I tugged gently on Triana's hand and boarded the plane, waving at Joseph until we entered the airplane. Heaving a sigh of relief, Joseph turned from the terminal window as the jet lifted smoothly into the deep blue morning sky.

Joseph watched the plane disappear. The episode had been more than he had bargained for, but he felt satisfied with the job he had done. *They're together, as they should be, and it'll be fine, just fine.* Joseph smiled to himself and gave himself a little mental pat on the back.

EPILOGUE

June, 2008

What lay ahead were more adjustments for Triana and myself than either of us could have imagined.

Triana entered an unfamiliar household, inhabited by five people she did not know. She became a part of a home already dealing with growing pains and adjustment problems.

I faced the responsibility of renewing our relationship, of helping an eleven-year old who barely spoke English to reenter a country that she had largely been forced to forget. I understood that at the same time I needed to consider the needs of Tisha and Stan and the boys. Triana must somehow become a part of the lives we had already established. *It would take patience,* I told myself. *Skill and patience.*

From the moment Stan met us at the plane, he welcomed Triana into his heart. In that instant, she became his child. All the years of living through my pain, through my endless trips and now through my happiness, had prepared him for this moment. He loved me sincerely and he adored all our children without exception.

My stepsons were another story. They accepted Triana's presence in our house, but she represented another distraction that demanded a piece of their father's life that they felt was rightfully theirs. Gradually, however, our lives assumed a manageable routine.

The greatest and most continual burden, of course, was Triana's. She now had to simultaneously pick up the lost years of her life and discard the brainwashing, abuse and lies she had been forced to endure. This was not easy for her. Her father's magnetic and monstrous personality had left its mark. It would be many years before the threads of truth would unravel the lies and allow her to heal and feel strong.

Returning to school, relearning her native tongue and beginning to resume her place in an American home represented an enormous task. It required constant energy from her, and from me, as she began to take her place with her peers, not one of whom could possibly imagine what she had endured.

The problems we faced were daily ones. Some were merely small moments of relearning: the taste of a baked potato and a hamburger, a shopping trip to choose the fashions she would now begin to wear.

Many were major. The many rapes of her young child's body, those heinous and despicable moments, required the skills of a professional therapist. The separation from her father was more profound than I'd expected. Hardest of all for her was learning to trust again. It would be many years before the deep scars inflicted on her soul would be understood, dealt with and accepted. As Triana and I worked our way along new paths together, both of us thought many times of Joseph and the last words he had spoken to us at the airport.

"Goodbye, my ladies. Everything will be all right."

Today, at the age of forty-four, Triana is a mature and extraordinarily beautiful woman, both in looks and in soul. The distorted, mixed emotions about her years with Franco in South America remain. She has come to realize that Franco gravely endangered her life on many occasions for no legitimate reason other than to gratify his own desires. Her painful acceptance of the facts conflict piercingly with the emotions she felt for him. She cannot understand him, nor forget him and she will never understand why he did some of the horrific thing that stole her childhood, destroyed her innocence and devastated her self-worth. To Triana the word "father" does not pertain to Franco. To Triana, Stan is her father. Today, Triana is in nursing school, and the mother of a seven-year-old son, Julyen.

Triana in her own words: "At first, I refused to remember my life with Franco. Some situations were so painful that I just wanted to blot them out and remember only the good times, the pleasant moments that I spent with Franco, my grandmother, Kitty and her girls. Later, I realized that all experiences make up my life; I am not free to choose only those things that happen to please me. Someday, maybe after I'm married, I'd like to go back to South America, to see the places where we lived, to talk with some of the people who played their roles in my life.

"And if there is a half-brother or sister, I would like to know them.

"Eventually I want to be able to share this part of my life with someone. I know that it is something I will want to tell my own children.

"And Franco. I've talked to him but I never want to see him again. At least not now. Perhaps I will never be ready. Stan says I'm ready for anything, so maybe I am. I don't know. I suppose I'll see Franco sometime, someday, somewhere, but I have no idea how I'll feel when we find ourselves face to face. There's no way to find out except to see what happens. If and when that time comes maybe I can say, 'I forgive you'.

"As for my life, I think I'm pretty well-oriented now. I know where I'm going and I look forward to the next day without fear or remorse. It's sort of "Jungle girl comes home," I suppose.

"I know that my life here is much better than it ever could have been if I had been left in South America. I would have never known the beautiful person my mother truly is.

"Although my mom and I sometime disagree, we love each other very much. I now understand the ordeal she went through to find me and I'm glad she didn't give up the search. She is a very strong woman and I respect her for it." I now have a child of my own and could never imagine being parted from him. I don't know how she survived.

As Triana continues with her reminiscences, I see the dual picture of the little, lost girl, following her daddy sleepily through the jungle, and of the mature, young, cosmopolitan woman making decisions about her own future. The difficult years have left their mark on her-- she had had to deal with feelings of unworthiness and low self-esteem. But she has made remarkable progress. The contrast is marked and difficult to understand, but I am continually grateful that Triana has become more levelheaded and emotionally sound with each passing year. She has demonstrated great strength of character, sturdiness, and tenacity. These are qualities that I like to think she and I have in common.

As for Franco, his wife turned him over to the authorities when she learned of his false papers. Franco went to prison for three years in Bolivia. The last we knew, he was back in the United States, living in Florida with his new wife.

When I look back, I wonder about the deep forces that drove me to go blindly forward. The pain of the loss of my child over powered any thought of danger and failure; but had I known what lay ahead, I would have felt an overwhelming terror. Even so, I know that I would have done just as I did to find my child.

Stan puts it more succinctly: "Of all the people in the world I wouldn't want to cross, Rosalie heads the list. My wife has a will of iron!"

Why did I write this book? Why all this effort?

It was, in large part, cathartic therapy. But the primary reason was I wanted to tell our story because I believed that somehow it may give courage to others, not only in their pursuit of locating their children, but to have the courage to share their stories with others.

Child stealing is pervasive in our society today. No tragedy in life can compare with the endless despair of a parent's enforced separation from his or her child. Such separations increase in horror and intensity when parents do not know where their children are, whether or not they are alive, whether they are cared for and loved, protected and nurtured. It is a state far worse than death. Every day from the moment your child is missing, you live holding your breath. There is no final resolution until you know the truth of your child's whereabouts. The "what-ifs" do not stop. For some it never ends.

I tell Triana's and my story so all mothers and fathers who read about us will understand there can be hope.

Resources for Missing Children

National Center for Missing & Exploited Children
www.missingkids.com

International Center for Missing & Exploited Children
www.icmec.org

National Missing Children's Locate Center
www.nmclc.org

Missing Children – Child Locator Non-Profit Organizations
www.Klaaskids.org

Laura Recovery Center
www.mychildid.org

Delta International
www.abductedchildrecovery.com/

Protect the Children
www.angelfire.com/id2/ourchildren/

LaVergne, TN USA
27 January 2010
171271LV00007B/149/P

9 781440 125027